The Life of Dick Haymes

Hollywood Legends Series
Ronald L. Davis, General Editor

The Life of Dick Haymes

No More Little White Lies

Ruth Prigozy

UNIVERSITY PRESS OF MISSISSIPPI • JACKSON

www.upress.state.ms.us

The University Press of Mississippi is a member of the Association
of American University Presses.

First edition 2006

∞

Library of Congress Cataloging-in-Publication Data
Prigozy, Ruth.
  The life of Dick Haymes : no more little white lies / Ruth Prigozy. —
1st ed.
    p. cm.
  Includes bibliographical references (p.), filmography (p.),
discography (p.), and index.
    ISBN 1-57806-551-8 (cloth : alk. paper) 1. Haymes, Dick.
  2. Singers—United States—Biography. I. Title.
  ML420.H257P74 2006
  782.42164092—dc22   2005028606

British Library Cataloging-in-Publication Data available

For Roger Dooncr, who has been there from the beginning, and for Maurice Dunn, Susan Calter, Clive Fuller, and Denis Brown, with gratitude and admiration

But let anyone born in 1926 try to stay alone at home on a Saturday night in 1998 and listen to Dick Haymes singing "Those Little White Lies." Just have them do that, and then let them tell me afterwards if they have not understood at last the celebrated doctrine of the catharsis effected by tragedy.

—PHILIP ROTH, *The Human Stain*

I was told to imitate musicians rather than singers. If I had imitated singers . . . in my day it probably would have been Dick Haymes, who I liked very much.

—TONY BENNETT, *Off the Record*

CONTENTS

ACKNOWLEDGMENTS

Because so much had been written about Dick Haymes in fan magazines and in newspapers that focused on his troubled marriages and financial problems, it was difficult to trace with accuracy the various stages of his life and career. I could not have written this book without the help of many people who knew and/or worked with him. First, I should like to acknowledge the members of his family who either in person or on the telephone graciously shared their memories: former wives, Fran Jeffries and the late Wendy Haymes Maree, and children, Richard Haymes Jr., Joanna Haymes Campbell (Pidge), Sean Haymes, and Samantha Haymes Maree Shiner. Peter Marshall was gracious and helpful, and I am indebted to him and to his wife, Laurie, who answered my e-mail queries. I appreciate Andy Maree's hospitality during my stay with him and Wendy.

My first interview was with Margaret Whiting. Her warmth, openness, and humor made it seem that the whole project would be simple. It certainly was not, but without that interview I would not have had the inspiration and courage to go forward. Others in the music and film world who helped me were Ian Bernard, who since my first interview has responded quickly to my e-mail questions; Alan Copeland, who traveled what I thought was a great distance for our interview in California; Al Lerner, who gladly shared his memories; Russ Jones, who put aside his own problems to recall his good friend and helped particularly with his memories of the last days of Dick Haymes; Herb Jeffries; Maureen O'Hara; the late Rosemary Clooney; Joy Holden; Steve Blauner; Marion Evans; Rosemary Hutton Starrett; and the late Cy Coleman. In particular, two gentlemen who were instrumental in re-starting Dick Haymes's career helped me enormously: Tee Dooley and the late Loonis McGlohan. Others who helped fit the pieces together and to whom I am grateful are Vern Howard, Ken Barnes (who has become a good friend along with his wife, Anne), the legendary Joe Franklin, Buddy Bregman, Peter Elliott, Pete Moore, and Jean Halliburton. Two outstanding writers on popular music have been generous from the start: Gary Giddins and Will Friedwald—thank you both. I am grateful to Roy Tresadern, of the Sinatra Music Society in England; to Martin McQuade, a Bing Crosby expert who offered his expertise on popular music and Dick Haymes; and to Phlip Furia, biographer of Johnny Mercer.

Personal friends supported my efforts over the years, notably, Milton Stern, Ronald Berman, Jim Meredith, Kirk Curnutt, Susan Shillinglaw (who sent me some heavy packages of Haymes material from California), Horst and Ursula Kruse, Philip McGowan, Dino Caterini, Michelle Jonas, Walter Raubicheck, Jeanne Fuchs, Tom MacCary, and Natalie Datlof, who really started everything when she asked me to present a paper on Dick Haymes at the 1998 Frank Sinatra Conference at Hofstra University. I will always be indebted to Joanne Thier and Susan Prigozy for their help and Ted Prigozy and Maddie Runger for their support. I am grateful to Frances Ring, who offered me her incomparable hospitality on my visits to Los Angeles.

For help with my research, I wish to thank Ned Comstock at the Doheny Library of the University of Southern California and the staffs of the Margaret Herrick Library, the Motion Picture Academy of Arts and Science, and the New York Library of Performing Arts at Lincoln Center.

Very often writers thank people without whom they could not have completed their projects. The five individuals to whom I dedicate this book have been extraordinary: Roger Dooner was available every single day, indeed, often twice a day in Minnesota; he never refused to answer my urgent telephone calls. In England, I was happy to meet Maurice Dunn, Clive Fuller, and Denis Brown, longtime Haymes devotees who have been extremely generous to me. And Susan Calter, who runs the Dick Haymes website, has been an invaluable source of information and has made it possible for me to secure interviews with people who knew Dick Haymes—and whom I would never have been aware of without her help. John Hartnett, a devotee of Haymes, has been generous in his support, as has Harriet Wasser. And I must thank the members of the Dick Haymes Society for keeping his memory alive for so many years. My special thanks go to the remarkable critic and reviewer Laura Wagner, whose meticulous reading and vast knowledge eliminated errors that I might not have discovered. I am grateful for her time and effort.

The staff of the University Press of Mississippi has been unfailingly helpful, in particular Seetha Srinivasan, Walter Biggins, and Anne Stascavage.

And finally, my thanks to Hugh Jackman, "the Boy from Oz," who, at each of the many performances I attended at the Imperial Theater on Broadway, kept my spirits high and showed me the power of unflagging energy and dedication when I feared that I would never complete my work.

The Life of Dick Haymes

Introduction

The death of Dick Haymes on March 28, 1980, was a tragic finale to his heroic efforts to revive a career that had been shattered more than two decades earlier. From the early 1960s, when he sought refuge in England, to 1971, when he returned to the United States, Haymes had become a distant memory in the annals of show business history. If he were remembered at all, it would be either as a good singer from the 1940s who starred in *State Fair* or, disparagingly, as a World War II draft dodger or an abusive husband, notably, of his most famous and beautiful wife, Rita Hayworth. The scandal sheet *Star* even printed a fake posthumous "confession" by Haymes, emphasizing the most lurid details from his past encounters with the media.

Even the obituaries were inaccurate. Many printed the wrong date of his birth, several listed successive wives as Fran Makris and Fran Jeffries (actually the same person, real and stage names) and stated that his most successful film was *One Touch of Venus*—a major error. The *New York Times* erred in the listing of his last recordings, but most painful in all of the obituaries was the remark that he died alone, implying that he no longer had any friends or family. Of course, he did not die "alone." His daughter Nugent and his good friend Russ Jones had just left Cedars Sinai Hospital before he died—and in the preceding days and weeks, his children and three of his former wives and many of his old friends visited him and/or telephoned. There were over 150 persons at his funeral.

Perhaps most hurtful to his reputation in the mass media obituaries was the focus on his successes as a very young man, with virtually no mention of the recordings and personal appearances of the fifteen years preceding his death, with his voice and delivery almost unchanged from the most brilliant of his recordings of the mid-1950s. Nobody quoted some of the critics of the late 1970s who remarked on the quality of Haymes's voice and his incomparable phrasing years after the days when his recordings sold millions of copies. Critic Peter Reilly, reviewing a 1976 album, *For You, For Me, For Evermore*, declared, "He's back in a very big way with his new album, singing—wonderfully well—with meltingly graceful musicianship and that distinctive vocal style that sounds better, richer, and more elegant than ever." In 1979, another critic, Brian Case, reviewing a re-release of an earlier album, said, "Haymes is the best there has ever been on the ballad, Sinatra, Tormé and Bennett notwithstanding," Shortly after Haymes's death, Roy Carr, in a review of the same re-released album on CD, continued the Sinatra comparison (as most critics had done from the very outset of the careers of the two singers), stating that Haymes was arguably Sinatra's "only real rival in the ballad stakes. . . . In terms of warmth, phrasing, intimacy and sheer musicianship, Haymes's interpretations of the two dozen evergreens that bedeck this compilation are beyond criticism. File alongside Sinatra's 'Wee Small Hours' or Lady Day's 'Lady in Satin.' Yes, it's that great!" Doug Ramsey, another music reviewer, commenting on his last album, *As Time Goes By* (1978), said of Haymes's rendition of the standard "But Beautiful": "I thought Crosby's version couldn't be surpassed. Haymes has surpassed it." And in a 1979 review that Haymes treasured, just one year before his death, Peter Reilly again offered unqualified praise:

> What Dick Haymes is doing today needs no nostalgia to excuse its enjoyment, and any kindly patronization is as out of place for this man (who miraculously sounds on his latest records like he's still in his thirties) as it would have been for Leonard Warren or Jan Peerce or Maurice Chevalier in their later careers. . . . Another thought: Sinatra recently scheduled a

recording session and then backed out, leading one to believe that he's finally faced what everyone else has known for some time, that his voice has become a very worn and ragged instrument. Yet his diehard fans are probably not even aware that Dick Haymes *is* recording, and recording superbly, much of the repertoire that Sinatra is no longer able to handle.

Dick Haymes achieved extraordinary success in the 1940s, first as a band singer, then as an independent recording artist who made the *Billboard* top-selling records/jukebox charts with more than fifty song hits in nine years. His own radio show and his contract with Twentieth Century–Fox, which produced several popular film musicals, including the major success, *State Fair*, and two films with Fox's leading screen goddess, Betty Grable, brought him to the pinnacle of Hollywood stardom. In 1946, Fox named Haymes as its top male box-office star, and he was in constant demand at nightclubs and theaters. *Motion Picture*'s poll named Haymes "Hollywood's Crown Prince of Crooners" in 1946. Ten years later, he was all but forgotten as a film star, his recording career had ended, with the notable exception of perhaps his two finest albums cut in 1955 and 1956, and he was bankrupt, owed alimony and child support, and had barely survived one of the worst media onslaughts ever directed against a celebrity in Hollywood history.

Although he was making a comeback in the early 1970s, there was really no second act in his life as there was in Frank Sinatra's. Sinatra was Haymes's predecessor as a band singer, his rival as a popular vocalist with audiences of screaming teenagers, and a 1940s star of several forgettable film musicals, with one uneven but popular release, *Anchors Aweigh* (1945), and one major hit, *On the Town* (1949). Many today forget that Haymes's popularity was as great as Sinatra's in the mid to late 1940s; they played the game of rival baritones, teasingly referring to one another on radio shows and in public appearances. Haymes's singing style evolved throughout his life; he did not, as many assume, learn from Sinatra, but he did graciously acknowledge Bing Crosby's influence on many occasions. He was repeatedly asked about Sinatra some twenty years after they first met, and he always praised his former friend and rival. Sinatra never spoke of Haymes except on one rare occasion, when he told an interviewer that one of his idols was Dick Haymes because of his phrasing.

It is almost impossible to discuss Dick Haymes without mentioning Sinatra, but few of the Sinatra biographies mention Haymes. Yet their lives until the early 1950s had many parallels, not only in their roles as band singers, but in their personal lives as well. By 1953, Sinatra's career had plummeted, and his tumultuous marriage to the beautiful actress Ava Gardner often made headlines in the tabloids. At almost the same period, Dick Haymes married an equally, if not more, beautiful actress, Rita Hayworth, and their marriage would provide similar headlines. But Sinatra had managed to re-make himself, and Haymes—for reasons that I will discuss in ensuing chapters—was unable to rekindle the flame of his early success.

Sinatra's second life began when he won a coveted role in the Academy Award–winning film *From Here to Eternity* (1953), for which he received the Oscar as best supporting actor. He had new management and a new singing style—and he never had to look back wistfully on his early golden years. Although they were not close, Sinatra cast his shadow on Haymes's career, particularly during his tragically aborted comeback in the 1970s. Margo Jefferson best described Sinatra's appeal after the latter's death—his sexual charisma:

> The jaunty manliness was sexy; so was the melancholy introspection; so was the edgy rebelliousness one saw most clearly in his best film perfor-mances. He was a star, and he had what real stars have: the ability to take their gifts, their limitations and their influences and mold them into a uni-fied whole called My Personality. The force of that personality is what makes Sinatra unforgettable. . . . Not only did Sinatra have unparalleled power in the music industry, he got to act out a lavish drama of masculin-ity that thrilled the entire culture.

Haymes was never able to lose the image of the boy next door, which he so effectively conveyed in his early films, especially in *State Fair*. His success with women was legendary—but it was not played out on the public stage that Sinatra so deftly constructed. It is ironic, because Dick Haymes was a sophisticated man who spoke three languages fluently, was well educated and an avid reader, and had associated with the cream of European society when he was just a teenager. And he was decidedly more introspective than Sinatra, both in his singing (with the notable exceptions of Sinatra's "Wee Small Hours" and "Only the Lonely") and in his life. But he was certainly unskilled at remaking his persona to fit the rapid cultural changes of the postwar years. He was also an incurable romantic—and his longing for the love and security missing from his troubled childhood would haunt him until the end of his life.

What happened to this gifted singer/actor? Why was he unable to sustain the momentum of those early years? To what extent did the shift in musical tastes affect his career, and to what extent did his own miscalculations, youthful egocentricity, and persistent inner demons cause his precipitous decline?

Dick Haymes's story is on one level a classic tale of American celebrity culture. He lived high and associated with the most important stars of the era, including Tyrone Power and Errol Flynn. Fan magazines adored him and his wife, Joanne Dru, and countless articles on the two and their growing family appeared in *Motion Picture, Photoplay, Modern Screen*, as well as publications devoted to radio and, later, television. Critics joined the general public in applauding his rich baritone voice and impeccable phrasing and delivery, which never—even in the most difficult years—deserted him.

The story of Dick Haymes's life is complicated. The closer we seem to get to answers, the more elusive they become. Virtually everyone with whom he worked closely—singers, musicians, actors—praised his sense of humor, his friendliness, his courtesy, his warmth, and his ability to work with others. Yet at the same time, he was a reserved, often difficult, and certainly complex man who fought demons all his life and spent years searching for his identity. He found it necessary to reconstruct his career and his personal life again and again. The headiness of his early success, along with the complications that ensued from successive marriages—six in all—and alcohol dependency, not to mention his obligations to six children and the enormous publicity his personal life attracted in the burgeoning scandal sheets, undoubtedly prevented him from finding his own answers to all of his questions. Some of the obituaries tried to explore the reasons for his tragic decline, as Dave Gelly did so acutely in the *London Observer*:

> It is easy to speculate about why he ran out of steam just when his con-temporaries were embarking on second, even more starry careers. Perhaps he was a bit too subtle and light of touch, possibly he was badly managed. The reason may, however, lie in his character. There was some-thing wayward about him, a touch of the Errol Flynns, a lack of ruthless-ness and drive coupled with a fatal love of having a good time.

A friend to whom I'd recently introduced Haymes's recordings touched on an important aspect of his personality that is reflected in his singing: "They [his recordings] suggest a deep wistfulness, which indicates the sensibility that will understand loss and longing." It is that sensibility that makes him an intriguing and ultimately sympathetic figure, and it is undoubtedly one of the qualities that make him such a fascinating subject for a biographer.

Haymes's friend Turnley Walker, who delivered the eulogy at his fune-ral and understood him as well as anyone, commented on his character: Dick was "a lovely man who underwent some terrible wounding and grind-ing. He died bravely and even humorously, nothing trivial in the humor, but a warm, sardonic understanding of the whole human predicament." Perhaps that search for meaning makes Dick Haymes's life so intriguing: he did not flinch from the truth, about himself or his work. Ultimately, he did not blame others for his misfortune, but rather looked inside himself to discover the reasons for his failures. He could be difficult, even arrogant and condescending. He had a temper and could be cutting to those he disliked. But unlike Sinatra, he was self-reflective and never tried to excuse himself when he exhibited poor judgment, anger, or, often, alcohol-induced loss of control.

It has been difficult to piece together his life, particularly those years that he spent abroad in England, Ireland, and Spain. And it is even more difficult to assess the accounts of former associates, for example, the recollection of his manager in England, Peter Elliott, who remembers Haymes writing to Sinatra to ask for money to return to the United States from Spain in 1971—an account disputed by Wendy Haymes, Dick's wife at the time, and by his brother, Bob Haymes, as well as by Russ Jones, a close friend both in England and in California in the 1970s. Because Haymes and Sinatra had had very little contact from the 1950s through the 1970s, it is unlikely that he would approach Sinatra, and Wendy Haymes told me exactly who arranged for their expenses. There are also many reports of involvements with other women—including Betty Grable—(which Haymes forthrightly denied), and I have had to assess each of them against the knowledge I have gained from the many interviews and written accounts by others close to him. I have been fortunate that so many family members and former associates graciously shared their memories, and I trust that this biography of the life of Dick Haymes is accurate in its account both of the events described and of his strengths and weaknesses, his successes and failures. Self-critical to the end, perhaps he never suspected that many of the next generation would treasure his legacy and attempt to restore him to his rightful place among the legends of Hollywood. I hope that this biography will be the first step toward that restoration which he so richly deserves.

CHAPTER 1

The Early Years

Wandering between Worlds

By the early twentieth century, Buenos Aires was the center of trade for Argentina and its gateway to the world. For more than three centuries, it had grown as a commercial port, surviving wars involving Paraguay, Uruguay, and Brazil; and by 1880, a Federal District was created encompassing the city and substantial land to its north to ensure future development. A railroad that could enable companies to ship refrigerated meat to Europe was introduced in the 1870s, and cattle ranchers around the city became wealthy. "By the end of the first decade of the twentieth century, the city had grown from a relatively modest trade and political center of 180,000 inhabitants to a major world port and metropolis with a population of 1,300,000." The city itself had become a sophisticated cultural center, and all of the modern improvements— garbage collection, sewers, modern electricity—signaled its entrance into the world as an exciting place for sports, the arts, and education.

It was here that Richard Benjamin Haymes was born at 10:45 PM on September 13, 1918, in the home of his parents, Benjamin Haymes, forty-three, and Marguerite Lou Wilson, twenty-three, at 1209 Calle Posedas. Benjamin Haymes's family had a distinguished ancestry. His own father, Henry Haymes, was the son of George Haymes, one of the British officers who came to Buenos Aires in the first years of the nineteenth century when England attempted to take Montevideo and Buenos Aires from Spain. During the British invasion of 1806 and 1807, many British were drawn to the Plata River, and both English and Scottish families soon established residence in Uruguay.

Those who came to Argentina and Uruguay from the British Isles were of a different class from the Italian and Spanish immigrants who arrived en masse around the turn of the twentieth century. Most of those were impoverished and many were illiterate. The British were an elite group who came over to manage the construction of Argentina's railways by British companies, to serve as station managers, to drive the trains, and to manage the cattle ranches and the meat-packing houses.

Henry's mother, Benjamina, was the only daughter of one of the most celebrated fighters for the independence of Argentina, Chile, and Peru, the legendary hero General Mariano Necochea. Henry's wife was Maria Stewart, daughter of Duncan Stewart (of the Scottish clan Stewart of Appin), who came to the Rio de la Plata in the early years of the century. Duncan Stewart was the son of Duncan Stewart of Glenbuckie and Margaret Stewart, thus a descendant of the lairds of Acharn, Ardsheal, and Appin, whose ancestry reaches at least as far back as King Robert the Bruce.

During the Buenos Aires occupation of the early nineteenth century, the British and Scottish settlers intermarried with residents. Duncan Stewart arrived in 1818, established himself in Buenos Aires, and soon went to Montevideo, where his twin daughters, Maria (Dick Haymes's grandmother) and Dorotea, were born from his marriage to Dorotea Agel. Maria Stewart Haymes and her sister, Dorotea, were eighty-seven when their birthday was noted in the *La Nacion* newspaper in October 1936. The Stewarts played an important role in the history of their country, and at the time of the newspaper article, one of their descendants was an admiral in the Uruguayan navy. A brother of Maria and Dorotea was a member of the Uruguayan senate and for a short time assumed the presidency of the country, replacing the incumbent, President Idiarte Borda, who died in office. A street in Montevideo was named for Duncan Stewart in the 1930s.

Maria Stewart Haymes and her husband, Henry, returned to Buenos Aires shortly after their marriage and settled in Villanueva, a Buenos Aires province where Haymes started ranching. His two sons, Benjamin and Duncan (a favorite family name), developed the fifteen-thousand-acre cattle ranch where they raised Aberdeen Angus cattle, first introduced to the area in 1879. Benjamin Haymes was born in 1875, just across the Rio de la Plata in Montevideo.

Benjamin met and fell in love with a beautiful young woman, Marguerite Lou Wilson, who was a member of the chorus of a traveling musical show. They were married on August 6, 1917, in a Roman Catholic ceremony at the Church of Nuestra Senora del Socorro in Buenos Aires. Haymes was almost twenty years older than his dynamic and restless young wife. Their home on the fashionable Calle Posadas reflected the wealth and position that Benjamin Haymes had acquired over the years.

Marguerite Haymes was probably the most powerful influence on the lives of her sons, Richard (Dick) and his younger brother, Robert (Bob). She was born in Dublin to working-class parents, John Francis Wilson, who was English, and Catherine Wood, who was Irish. The family settled in Santa Barbara, California, when Marguerite was a child. Very little is known of her early childhood, primarily because of her penchant for embellishing even the most prosaic details of her life and—by extension—the lives of anyone with whom she associated. Dick's comment about his mother is probably the best assessment of her tendency to mythologize her life: "My mother has that unique ability to tell a story the way she wants to believe it and that eventually becomes fact, so my mind isn't totally clear about my earliest beginnings."

The fortunes of the Haymes family were affected by the inflation of the 1920s. There was a great demand in Europe for Argentine primary products, beef, cereal, and grains, thus resulting in an economic boom that lasted until 1921. But for several years there were a great many strikes by workers affected by the mounting inflation. "The boom ended abruptly when the British government ceased stockpiling supplies from Argentina, abolished meat control, and began to liquidate its accumulated holdings." The number of cattle for export fell by more than half, as did the prices. A serious recession ensued and caused financial ruin for many of the wealthier families, the Haymeses included. Benjamin Haymes lost his ranch, was forced into bankruptcy, and the family had to move from their elegant home to a far less expensive residence in a suburb of Buenos Aires, Temperle.

In the early 1990s, researcher Walter Boettger found an aunt of Dick Haymes, Marta Viana, then eighty-four and living on Central Park West in New York City. She and her husband, Jacob, who were radio personalities in Argentina, spoke out courageously against the Peron regime and were forced to leave the country in the mid-1940s to avoid imprisonment, or perhaps death. The couple worked in Spanish-language radio programming in the New York area, appeared on the stage, and eventually dubbed television shows. She remembered that as a girl of ten she attended the wedding of Benjamin and Marguerite in 1917. Of Benjamin, she said, "He was a strange one, a poet, a dreamer, a strange one like me." She also said that she believed that the couple were in love but had many disagreements. She felt that Marguerite was more realistic about their dim prospects than was Benjamin, and that her personality was also a factor in their increasingly difficult marital life. Marta felt that her sister-in-law was wildly extravagant, erratic, strong-willed, and very independent, the kind of woman who would have felt stifled in the stratified Argentinian society. In many ways, Marguerite was a woman ahead of her time, but ultimately her admirable sense of freedom and independence would prove destructive to her two sons, especially to her firstborn.

Marguerite left Argentina in 1922 with her son, Richard. Her younger son would later dispel the mystery of her departure. She maintained that she had planned to return to the stage in New York, claiming that she had been a musical comedy star appearing on Broadway in *Blossom Time* and that she had performed in London in *The Merry Widow*. Her name does not appear in cast records of either of these shows. Indeed, her only recorded appearance is in the musical *Gay Paree* at the Shubert Theater in New York City in October 1925. There is no record of her in London theater files, so it is probable that if she had ever performed there, it was only as a member of the chorus. She would later embellish her London adventures by hinting that her son, Richard, had royal lineage. Both Marguerite and her child were unhappy in Argentina. Richard was blonde, blue eyed, and fair skinned, in contrast to his relatives, who had olive skin and dark eyes and hair. Even as a toddler, he was taunted and ridiculed by his relatives as an outsider, an anomaly who could never be anything but an alien in their culture. Marguerite, too, was unlike any other woman in this society: even her attempt to win their favor by singing Argentinian songs, accompanying herself on a guitar, met with disfavor.

Every effort to ingratiate herself was resisted by a social group that saw her behavior as too aggressive, unwomanly, and even flirtatious. Benjamin did not support his wife, but instead scolded her for her colorful clothing, her outspoken opinions, and what he regarded as the neglect of their son when she went out alone (despite the presence of a governess for the child). Perhaps these were the most crucial years of Dick Haymes's life, as he and his mother clung to one another in an environment that did not mask its hostility to these obvious social outcasts.

But young as she was, Marguerite Haymes was not without resources. Despite her anxiety, she carefully planned her escape from an intolerable situation. She had a part-time maid, Carla, who adored her and her child. Fortunately, the young woman agreed to help facilitate Marguerite's melodramatic exit from Argentina. The three, mother, child, and maid, walked together daily, which soon became a routine pattern. At Carla's family home in a poor section of the city, as her little son napped on the back stoop, Marguerite wrote an imploring letter to a former admirer who had been a high-ranking army officer, indeed, a general, now residing in New York City. She made certain that his reply would be delivered to Carla's house.

A few weeks passed, but one day Carla walked into the nursery and quietly informed Marguerite that a packet had arrived for her from the United States. Marguerite lost no time in packing only the most necessary items in a suitcase and surreptitiously departing the Haymes home, carrying young Richard in her arms. However terrified she was, she kept on walking until she was given a ride into the city by a passing teamster. When the pretty young Irish girl and her young son stood on the deck of the American Sugar Company freighter sailing to New York, they looked to a future filled with hopes that could never have been fulfilled in Buenos Aires.

Perhaps Benjamin suspected that Marguerite's affections had wandered, but he never found out how she had maneuvered her escape and never forgave her. His punishment was to refuse to give her a divorce. Benjamin remained in Argentina. He had ambitions as a writer, but was never published. His sister remembered that he always seemed to have some new invention that he tried to promote and that he later worked as an extra in the Argentine cinema. He kept his vow to never divorce Marguerite and died in 1933.

Neither Benjamin nor his family could have envisioned her life upon her return to the United States. Her second son took the family name, and Robert Haymes was born on March 29, 1923, in Greenburgh, New York, weighing twelve pounds, with a head size that he claimed was seven and three-quarters. For years afterward, Marguerite would describe her difficult childbirth in the pleasant house on a quiet street, particularly the ear-shattering screams in her full-throated soprano. She was attended by a physician and a nurse, but there was another individual present in the room: a tall, mysterious man in the shadows who would make all of the decisions for the family and serve as its benefactor as well.

The former officer had good reason to keep his relationship with Marguerite Haymes a secret. He was married to a chronically ill, bedridden woman; but even more important, he was the president of one of the most important banks in New York City and served on the boards of several prestigious companies. Any implication that he was having an out-of-wedlock affair with a married showgirl who had run away from her husband, not to mention the arrival of an illegitimate son, would have ruined him financially.

Looking back, Bob Haymes realized that his mother was not so frightened that she was unable to make some shrewd decisions regarding her future and those of her sons. She agreed to put Benjamin Haymes's name on her younger son's birth certificate and to conceal the identity of his real father—even from the child himself—if he would generously support her and her two sons, including tuition for their education at the best schools in Europe and ample support for herself, including lavish travel expenses.

The next move in the family's peripatetic existence, after a short stay with Marguerite's father and mother in Santa Barbara, would be to Brazil, a journey hastened by their benefactor's fear of exposure were they to remain in New York. In Rio de Janeiro, Marguerite met another man who would help her develop the poise and sophistication that would enable her to triumph over the many adversities that she would face throughout her life.

Ruy Barbosa was a wealthy Brazilian businessman who fell deeply in love with Marguerite. He recognized that she needed independence and challenge, and so he supported her desire to become a dress designer—she had an innate sense of style—and provided the funds for her to open a dress shop in Rio de Janeiro. Marguerite scored a personal and financial success, and after selling her shop for five times the amount it had cost, she decided to realize her dream of living a wealthy and exciting life abroad.

Whatever Marguerite had seen or heard of exciting Continental life, she had never forgotten and wanted desperately to be part of it. The devoted Ruy helped Marguerite acquire an elegant townhouse, complete with a ballroom on the top floor, located on the Rue de Varenne, adjacent to the famous Rodin Museum. From their bedroom balconies, the boys, now ten and five years old, could look out at the famous sculptures that attracted visitors from all over the world. Marguerite and Ruy had an active social life and spent little time with the boys. Bob would always notice the pain in his brother's eyes when his mother, beautifully gowned, would depart for an evening's festivities. Both Richard and Bob suffered enormously from Marguerite's pattern of neglect and desertion, but Richard was the primary victim, for Bob had his older brother to serve as buffer for their mother's capriciousness.

The boys were cared for in Paris by a "Mademoiselle" whom Bob remembers as "muscular." She would unceremoniously pull them out of their beds at 6 AM and toss them roughly into shower or bath. They would breakfast in the smaller of the two dining rooms and wait in the courtyard for the Cadillac limousine, chauffeured by Edouard, who Bob describes as resembling Douglas Fairbanks. The boys adored Edouard, who at times succumbed to their pleas to skip school in favor of ice skating at the Palais de Glad, where Richard soon showed amazing dexterity, performing tricks on the rink that were remarkable for a ten-year-old who had not benefited from years of training. Richard also had a schoolboy crush on Lulu, an attractive young woman of twenty, whom he managed to seduce into skating with him, despite the disparity in their heights. Even at this age, Richard had a smooth charm that his brother envied. Both boys were astonished on one occasion when Lulu leaned over and kissed Richard on the lips! Bob was warned by his brother not to tell anyone, so that her reputation would not suffer.

Edouard was the beloved facilitator of the boys' extracurricular exploits. He would pick them up at school and either drive them home or, more frequently, take them to a movie theater. They went to the George Washington Theatre for the fourteen days that constituted the run of *The Iron Mask* (1928), an American film (a follow-up to the 1921 Fairbanks hit, *The Three Musketeers*) that the boys could enact perfectly by the time it moved on.

Because of their improvised after-school activities, both boys' school records were distinctly below the expectations of their mother and Ruy. Bob was sent immediately to a school that would focus on spoken English, but, to his dismay, Richard was to be sent away to boarding school at College de Normandie. For Bob, a child who had grown dependent on his older brother, the news was devastating, and he wept inconsolably, begging for Richard's return. Instead, Marguerite decided to send him to join his brother. He remembered vividly the day of his arrival at school as he and his brother watched the Cadillac driven by their beloved Edouard leave with Marguerite inside. He could never forget the look on his brother's tear-stained face, his eyes reflecting the pain of another wrenching separation from his mother. The hurt caused by Marguerite's recurring pattern of abandonment would remain with Dick Haymes throughout his life, and undoubtedly led to a pattern of disintegrating personal relationships in his own life.

The separation was not the worst of the boys' new situation. The school was made up of old, decaying stone buildings, damp and forbidding. But what occurred within its walls could have served as the basis of a kind of Dickensian film about the terrors of childhood. Members of the staff were uniformly cold and harsh. They routinely whipped their young charges, and Bob remembers the time a teacher flung his brother down a flight of steps. When he cried out in protest, he met the same fate.

Among the other students, these two stood out. Like Richard and his mother in Argentina, he and his brother were outsiders, despised by the other boys. Bob, particularly, as the younger, was the victim of a gang mentality among the other students. Shortly after arriving, he was forced to stand naked in one of the dank unused buildings as the other boys whipped him with a towel, until he heard a familiar voice calling out, "Stand off or die!" Richard delivered Fairbanks's line with the grim determination of their screen idol, and when the boys turned to him, his face was coldly staring at them—and he carried a long pole. The gang left as Richard calmly ordered them never to bother his brother again or, "You will taste the steel of my revenge." From that point on, Bob was never tormented by them and the brothers were left alone—but were never to be part of the group.

Richard often spoke aloud of their mother, wondering how she could have left them in such a place. Bob's feelings toward Marguerite began to harden—even at the age of six, but Richard's were far more complicated, remaining ambivalent to the end. Years later he would lash out at her and speak unflatteringly of her to his friends, yet he would lend his support to her business endeavors and, in his last years, despite his own financial difficulties, would write a check for one hundred dollars to the "poor woman."

Despite their unhappiness at the school, the boys did learn: Latin, Greek, literature, mathematics, and history. They even made one or two friends before the year was over, and both found that they were natural athletes.

They looked forward to leaving the school for the summer vacation in 1929, which was to be spent in Biarritz, perhaps the most elegant resort in the south of France. They cheered when Edouard arrived to transport them to Paris, where they would pack and board the train that would transport them to what they came to regard as paradise.

Marguerite and her house staff in Paris were busy packing clothes and household goods, and after a few days, she, Ruy, and the boys boarded a first-class compartment in a wood-paneled train destined for a summer vacation that would prove to be the happiest of their childhood. On the train, the excited boys played their game, as D'Artagnan would intone, "One for all," and Aramis would reply, "And all for one," as they clasped hands and cheered.

The train with its elegant amenities reintroduced the boys to the kind of life that they had missed at school. They dined on the finest cuisine, and as the train made its way through mountains down to the gleaming Côte Basque, they were enthralled. Biarritz is on the border of Spain, on the Bay of Biscay, at the Pyrenees. It was a favorite residence of Napoleon III and Empress Eugenie, and from the 1920s it had become one of the most fashionable resorts in southern France. Every summer, Biarritz welcomed the Continental elite, and Marguerite, Ruy, and the boys were greeted by an international group of sophisticates who never questioned the relationships within their "family." Rich would later remember meeting the composer Ravel, who was part of the social milieu of their childhood.

Ruy bought the boys a dog that accompanied them everywhere. They were soon bored by the Biarritz Club de Bains, where, aside from a friendly, very attractive couple, Max and Mado Deutsch, they found the society too restrictive. The Deutsches not only were extraordinarily good-looking, but also possessed two of the finest automobiles of the period—which intrigued the boys. He drove a black, silver, and gold Deusenberg convertible, and Mado's was a V-16 sports coupe. The Deutsches entertained the family and taught Rich and Bob to dance the fox-trot and Charleston. Rich was a natural dancer, and when he was applauded for his performance, he looked to his mother for approval. His brother noted how much Rich seemed to need both to perform and to please Marguerite. Max and Mado also invited other families with children to their home so that the two boys would make new friends for the summer.

Rich and Bob later discovered that the Deutsches were Jewish, and when Hitler invaded Austria, they quickly returned to Vienna to save the family's home and treasures. They were never heard from again.

Looking for a more relaxed place to play and swim, Rich found the servant's beach, which seemed to them like another world. The two boys, accompanied by Edouard and the dog, felt liberated there and played with huge beach balls, picnicked, and, above all, swam in the beckoning water. Rich and Bob were both excellent swimmers, but they also indulged in what was to become another favorite pastime, singing. Looking back on that summer, Bob Haymes felt that two of the most important aspects of the brothers' lives began here: swimming and singing. And Rich had ample opportunity to observe the young servant girls, to whom he was clearly attracted even at his tender age.

Their beloved Edouard again served as co-conspirator as they drove into Spain to San Sebastian for a day to see the bullfights, so brilliantly described by Ernest Hemingway just a few years earlier. It was a thrilling trip; they relished the beauty of the mountains and sea, with the setting sun and the first shining star in the distance. They relived the bullfight on the drive back, playing toreadors, and, under Edouard's supervision, taking turns at the wheel of the car. Again, Rich thought of his mother, telling his brother how much their mother would have loved San Sebastian and expressing his sadness that she couldn't be with them.

Back in Biarritz, they could not conceal their elation, and Marguerite, perhaps jealous, told Ruy that Edouard should no longer be allowed to chaperone the boys, but Ruy took their side against her. After one of these discussions, Marguerite would make it clear that she and Ruy had to leave, and the two of them would depart for their ritual evening with the international set.

The perfect summer was coming to a close. The boys had been given new bicycles and Rich rode his first horse in Biarritz, the start of his life-long enjoyment of riding. On the night before they were to leave Biarritz, the boys heard the voices of Ruy and Marguerite, sometimes shouting at one another. They heard her slam the door, and shortly Ruy came into their room, tearfully asking them if they loved him. They responded that of course they loved him very much—and offered to help him. He confessed that he wanted to marry their mother and asked them to intercede for him. Rich was noticeably disturbed, and his eyes had that familiar anxious, fearful expression. The boys went to their mother with Ruy and begged that he become part of their family. Marguerite was enraged, telling them that it was not their concern and refusing to speak to them about the matter. When they returned to their room, they heard the sounds of a continuing argument throughout the night.

The next day, the boys and their mother boarded the train to Paris—with not a word exchanged about Ruy and his possible place in their future.

At the house on Rue de Varenne, everything was changed. The servants seemed shocked, and the boys soon learned that they had all been discharged; they left quickly without being allowed to say good-bye. The boys were now alone again, finding their own food, leaning on one another for support as they had so frequently in the past. Marguerite told them only that they would not be returning to the College de Normandie, but, instead, would be going back to the United States. They did not learn that the three of them would be traveling alone until they boarded the boat train that would take them to Le Havre for embarkation. Their mother would not reply to their questions about Edouard, Ruy, and Marte, their maid-housekeeper. Rich tried to excuse his mother's behavior, but Bob was furious and blamed Marguerite. He declared, "I hate her." Rich tried to convince his brother that Bob really loved his mother, that she had her reasons which they might not know, but had to accept. To Bob's repeated shouts of "Why?" Rich could only shrug and admit that he didn't know. Once again, Rich felt caught between the need for the mother that Marguerite could never be and the awareness that her behavior was inexplicable. It was clear now, as it had always been, that Rich wanted to be able to justify his mother's actions, but it was becoming increasingly difficult for him to do so—and his conflicted feelings resulted in his experiencing ever more pain and anxiety. When he grew older, Dick Haymes would express his conviction that he would find love and happiness, and yet he would inevitably contribute to the destruction of that possibility, just as his mother had done in his early years. Perhaps he felt more comfortable with the familiar uncertainty he had lived with for so long; certainly he would express his belief in the kind of love that might be found in a perfect marriage each time he set out on matrimonial seas, only to endure the disintegration of each relationship—in the way that Marguerite's relationship with Ruy had crumbled before his eyes. Ruy was the only father figure in his life as well as in Bob's, and when their relationship was so abruptly severed, they felt as though a part of them had died. And they were not permitted to mourn, for Marguerite would not discuss Ruy with them. She would never discuss any of the decisions that caused consternation in her children. Some time later, they learned that one day in Biarritz, Marguerite found her younger sister, Gwen, who was visiting, in bed with Ruy—both of them drunk. Perhaps she used that episode as an excuse, for the fact was that she was still married to Benjamin Haymes and was getting support from Bob's father, who was growing increasingly angry at her liaison with Ruy, who was providing for her and the boys the kind of luxury—mansion, servants, limousines—that he resented. Perhaps he felt as well that his son should not be raised in a clearly adulterous household, despite having fathered his own child out of wedlock.

This transatlantic crossing was unlike the one that had taken them to the Continent. The boys had their dog for comfort, but they badly missed Ruy and, still in shock, looked everywhere for him on the ship. They could not know that a pattern had begun that would be repeated until they were independent of school and of their mother's support. Bob remembered the years following that painful return voyage as "packed with uncertainty, unsettling changes, and some very cruel lessons." From 1929 through the mid-1930s, they felt like "hapless nomads" with no ties, no roots, and no identifiable home. But they did feel very American, an identity they believed that no one could take from them. Their residence in New York City was 14 East Sixtieth Street, in a smallish apartment, very different from their magnificent Paris home. The mystery of their lost possessions and furnishings in the home on the Rue de Varenne was later discovered to be the result of Marguerite's putting paintings, furniture, and the boys' toys in storage, never to reclaim them. No longer did they attend lavish dinners and observe elegant soirees where their mother held court. Indeed, their only excitement lay in visits to the Central Park Zoo. Marguerite's benefactor—Robert's father—visited them regularly, and the boys noticed her tension whenever he appeared. He was a formidable figure, in his mid-sixties, six foot two inches, with white hair and cold blue eyes. He would occasionally pick Bob up, but was distant toward Rich. When he would arrive, the boys would be sent to their room, leaving Marguerite and the general alone; then they would be sent for, and Rich would invariably be scolded for his playful behavior and threatened with an even stricter school than he had ever imagined.

Soon the family once more embarked for Europe, spending the first summer of the Great Depression in Cannes. The general's finances had not been adversely affected by the economic crisis, so their life resumed its pattern. Marguerite had a new lover, Victor, and the boys soon resumed their water sports. Rich had now become a first-rate diver, doing all of the twists, turns, and somersaults in the air that the Olympic athletes would make memorable for viewers of Leni Reifenstahl's classic film, *Olympia* (1936), some years later. Bob won a swimming race for the under-ten group, and Rich was awarded a medal and a watch for his diving championship as his envious brother looked on.

Richard Haymes looked older and more sophisticated than a boy entering his teens. He was tall, very well-groomed, thin, and well-tanned. He seemed to possess an innate sense of style. In the evenings, as they all sat around the pool at the club, he would be dressed in white flannel pants, with either a bright red or navy polo shirt closely fitting his torso. His hair was no longer curly, but was combed close to his head and kept in place by a scented lotion. He was quite conscious of the effect he would have on others and often posed dramatically, with a foot resting against the dashboard of the latest fashionable car or on the bar at a restaurant. His studied nonchalance was enhanced by casual touches—turned up collars and the scarf or tie that added an unexpected touch of elegance—much like a young Jay Gatsby.

When they next returned to New York City, in 1931, they lived at 1 East Seventy-ninth Street. The boys were sent to Franklin Marshall Academy in Pennsylvania. By the end of the school year, they received a letter from Marguerite, in Paris. The general had provided funds for her own designer dress shop on the Boulevard Capucine; it was called Marjorie-Lou. She did not send for the boys for the summer, but made a brief visit and found a place for them to board at a farm in Fairfield, Connecticut, where Rich lost his virginity to the farmer's daughter, appropriately, in a hayloft.

The next year, 1932, was an unhappy one for the boys. Marguerite was completely caught up in her new dress business in Paris—both as designer and merchant—so she placed them in a private home in Norwalk, Connecticut, owned by an unpleasant couple named Paine, after one interview with them convinced her that they would prove perfect guardians for her two sons. They were to attend the Mitchell School, located two miles down the road. Here, the boys did not need to worry about strictly enforced codes of discipline. Rather, they were now in an experimental, or "progressive," school, where there was virtually no instruction and the boys soon realized that they could work whenever it struck their fancy.

But the Paines were another matter: narrow-minded and miserly. The boys were permitted to use only four inches of water in a tub, there was no heat at night, and they froze in the attic room where they slept. Mr. Paine's brutality was revealed when Rich, by accident, happened to enter the bathroom before the Paine's unattractive daughter had left. After she cried out, Paine grabbed and tied Rich to a post and started to whip him. Now Bob could come to the aid of his older brother. He grabbed a treasured ship model and threatened to destroy it if Paine did not immediately release his brother. Rich had already been struck in the face and was bleeding, but Paine let him go—and from then until the end of the school year, the boys studiously avoided any contact with their brutish host.

But they were again confronted by Paine, in mid-June, when he informed them that he had not been paid for their board in three months and that he would have them taken to Norwalk City Hall. The boys immediately assumed they would be placed behind bars and began making plans to escape. That morning, as they were about to leave, Marguerite pulled up in a Chrysler convertible with her French beau. Bob described them both as somewhat inebriated; Marguerite was dressed as though she were about to attend a garden party. She hugged them as Rich sobbed with joy and relief at this last-minute reprieve. Even Bob was glad to see her, as it prevented their anticipated removal to a jail cell. Marguerite seemed genuinely delighted to see her sons and clearly, neither then nor later, had any conception of the pain her thoughtlessness had too frequently inflicted on them.

After another exciting summer in Cannes, the boys were returned to the United States, to the strictest school they had ever attended, the

Peekskill Military Academy, located on the Hudson River not far from Sing Sing prison. Rich did not fit in, and once again he was the object of his classmates' jealousy and anger. He paid dearly for the fights he got into, by carrying his heavy rifle around the quadrangle at all hours, day and night, no matter what weather conditions prevailed. But he had been saving money, even borrowing from the one friend he had made; and one night, after he got off the bus, he walked ten miles in freezing weather to New York City to the apartment of Marguerite's lover, Victor, who took him in but within days returned him to Peekskill. During his absence, Bob had been whipped by a sadistic teacher demanding to know where his older brother had gone. He remembered spending much of his time at Peekskill in the infirmary from beatings from both his teachers and bullying schoolmates. Perhaps the saddest part of their unfortunate stay at Peekskill was their loneliness at the holiday seasons when they waited expectantly for their mother to whisk them off on another of her exciting jaunts. But, to their everlasting sorrow, she did not appear, and they spent their vacations in deserted dormitories. Almost fifty years later, noted jazz critic Gene Lees remembered his interview with Dick Haymes in the mid-1970s: "He gave me the impression that he and his brother Bob, who became a successful songwriter, . . . were bounced from one private school to another by a mother who couldn't be bothered with them. I caught a glimpse of two little boys clinging together for warmth in a very lonely world."

On another occasion, when the boys waited for her to pick them up at the end of the school year from the École Nouvelle in Lausanne, Switzerland, a furious teacher drove them to Marguerite's apartment, which was not far from the school, and deposited them with their mother, who was ensconced with her latest lover, a huge Frenchman, Paul. After the teacher left, Marguerite offered a lame excuse, blaming a problem with her car. Again, Rich was overcome with conflicting emotions, joy and relief on the one hand and desperation for love and reassurance on the other. For Bob, this episode was simply Marguerite's latest example of gross self-absorption and neglect, and it solidified his hatred of her. He never for-gave her and was incensed, even at his age, at another of her romantic escapades that would result in inexcusable neglect—even, as he saw it, betrayal of her sons.

In 1934, both boys were sent to another harsh and punitive school, a Jesuit secondary school, Loyola, in Montreal, where the teachers rou-tinely used sticks to beat the boys' upturned palms until they bled. Undoubtedly, the constant uprooting of the two young boys and the enrollment at so many schools (including one in Paris) contributed enor-mously to their difficulty in sustaining close relationships in years to come. In later years, the brothers were outwardly charming but emotionally reserved. Years later, friends of Dick Haymes would remark on how diffi-cult it was to penetrate his reserve, but once one became his friend, he offered his trust and companionship wholeheartedly.

Summers were now spent in Westport, Connecticut, where Rich became known for his success with a seemingly endless line of willing young women. He sang to appreciative audiences at the Long Shore Country Club, as he had done on several cross-Atlantic trips and occasion-ally in one of the private clubs in Cannes, St. Tropez, and Monte Carlo, where such members of the elite society as the Kennedys and Marlene Dietrich spent their summers.

After the experience at Loyola, Rich wanted to try to get summer work in the movies. He managed to get to the West Coast, hitchhiking part of the way, and actually did find stunt work in some westerns; he even used his proven diving ability to perform the unforgettable fall from the highest mast in *Mutiny on the Bounty* (1935). A leg injury in a fall from a horse prevented his doing any further stunt work. Now both boys were in Hollywood, and Rich briefly attended a refreshingly permissive Hollywood High School, while Bob was sent away to another Jesuit school, St. Robert Bellarmine, in San Jose, which had its familiar share of brutal instructors, one of whom struck the boy across the mouth for daring to play the piano in the mess hall.

In the summer of 1936, the boys were alone in a beach house in Manasquan, New Jersey. Rich was now seventeen, and Bob thirteen. As in the past, Marguerite left the boys, and Victor dropped by occasionally. But this would prove to be a particularly important summer for Rich. He would sing on the beach, accompanying himself with a four-string guitar, and relished the applause of his growing audience, including the young women who once again flocked to him. He would remember years later that he made his professional singing debut at the Monmouth Hotel in Spring Lake, near Manasquan, giving a few performances with the local Johnny Johnson band.

The summer was not to end without a truly terrifying event. A hurricane struck the East Coast, and their house was quickly flooded. The boys escaped to the garage, where they huddled for many hours on crates, praying that someone would find and rescue them. Bob could never forget how strange he felt his brother's behavior was: Rich sat on the crate reading *Gone with the Wind* by candlelight. Soon, a sheriff, checking all of the beach houses, arrived and drove them away, amazed and angry that they were alone.

By the late 1930s, Marguerite's dress business had failed and the family now had to settle permanently in America. Some years later the boys discovered that she had married a Frenchman and was legally Marguerite Hemon. They moved to California in 1937, to a house on Lookout Mountain Drive, off Laurel Canyon Road, near Grace Hayes, a friend of Marguerite, whose son, performer Peter Lind Hayes, would help Rich get a bit part in a new movie, *Dramatic School* (1938). The film was a poor imitation of the highly successful *Stage Door* (1937), which had provided an unforgettable role for Katharine Hepburn. Rich was one of the boys attending the dramatic school, spoke one line, and showed his athletic skill in a fencing scene—but only if the viewer were to seek him out among the other good-looking young extras. Rich realized that such bit parts were not the answer, and Marguerite, after a heady social life with such stars as Ida Lupino, Ginger Rogers, Mickey Rooney, and Louis

Hayward, was ready for another move. She was disappointed that she was unable to find a role in a Hollywood movie and gave an excuse for leaving California: she was to study with Maurice Jacquet, one of Debussy's protégés. She said that she was preparing for a concert tour featuring Debussy songs, an excuse that was probably not truthful, yet was not really unbelievable, since she was always considered a fine interpreter of Debussy's music. As for Rich, the closest he came to the film studios was as chauffeur for a character actor, Chick Chandler. He had also worked briefly as an unsalaried disc jockey for the Mutual station KHJ in Los Angeles, but he knew it would prove to be a temporary respite. In his efforts to become part of the popular music scene, he had organized a quintet, the Katzenjammers, opening at the Little Eva, a nightclub on Sunset Boulevard. But in the era of big bands, a quintet proved inadequate to the needs of the club, and they quickly disbanded.

Back in New York City, Rich focused on his singing, and Marguerite proved an able singing teacher/coach. Bob was returned to Loyola, which he left after writing a scathing essay, "My Theory on the Anthropomorphic God," that offended the Catholicism of his priest-teachers. He simply walked out and never returned.

When he arrived in New York City, Bob found that his brother had changed. He no longer wanted to be called Rich: "That's kid stuff, Bob. Everybody knows me as Dick now. So stop calling me Rich." The name was not the only change Bob perceived. Dick was now cool, aloof, and, in Bob's eyes, arrogant. The only part of him that remained unchanged was his apparent need for his mother's love, which Bob believed would always remain unsatisfied and would force him into affairs with many women in coming years. For Bob, his return home meant the end of his childhood and certainly a shift in the relationship that had sustained him throughout his life. He and Dick remained close, but never as they had been through sharing so many years of disruption, disappointment, and excitement as well. Bob was always grateful to his brother for helping to create fantasies that would spare Bob the reality of their desperate, needy childhood.

Strangely, it was Bob who saw the reality of those years more clearly than did Dick, until over a decade later when the old, conflicted feelings about his mother made him increasingly bitter. But now, it was clear that Dick, having played the role of father as well as brother, wished to be truly independent, to find his own identity through developing his considerable gifts as a singer and actor. He would never stop seeking that identity, however elusive it might be.

As young men, the differences between Dick and Bob were apparent. Bob was two inches taller than Dick's six feet and had dark hair, dark blue eyes, and a round face. Dick was blond, with light blue eyes, prominent cheekbones, a turned-up nose, and he dressed in English tweeds. Neither looked like the much smaller man, Benjamin Haymes, whose picture was displayed by Marguerite. She never discussed Dick's father, and Bob never learned who his father was until after the general's death. Their mother neither denied nor affirmed the possibility that Dick might be the offspring of a member of the British royal family. (That lineage would have been highly unlikely, as the Duke of Windsor, as a result of mumps contracted in puberty, was by all accounts sterile.) In later years, Dick would offer contradictory versions of his relationship with his father. He would say either that he didn't know him well at all, or, as many friends would attest, that he adored his father. It is quite possible that since he was so young when he left Argentina—to which he never returned—in the absence of a father throughout his childhood, he constructed the memory of one whom he could worship.

Dick auditioned daily for work with a band, and Bob remembered one day when he burst into the apartment and shouted, "I got it!" The "it" was a few dates with Bunny Berigan's band. Dick's excitement was not just that he had a job, but that it was with Bunny Berigan, who by now, in the fall of 1939, was a legend in the jazz world. Berigan was one of the greatest trumpet players of all time, and his classic, "I Can't Get Started," drew worldwide attention when he re-recorded it in 1937. It remains to this day one of the most popular songs ever recorded, and his rendition was so memorable that the great Louis Armstrong, his longtime friend, would not play it, saying that it belonged to Berigan. Earlier, Berigan had played with Benny Goodman's band, had a popular radio show, and formed his own band, which was initially successful. But his management was careless, and the band was criticized as "loosely disciplined." He had a devastating drinking problem (he would become seriously ill and die in June 1942, only thirty-nine years old; ironically, when Berigan was hospitalized on May 31, 1942, Dick Haymes, now singing with Benny Goodman at the Paramount Theater, would be one of the group called in to substitute for Berigan at Manhattan Center).

At the time that Berigan hired Dick Haymes, his band was in decline, and he was accepting local dates in sites that were distinctly less impressive than those he had played in less than a year earlier. A month after Dick's excited announcement, Bob and his mother sat in the audience at the Loew's Pitkin Theater in Brooklyn. After the movie ended, the curtain rose on the band, a clearly nervous young man stepped forward, and a captivated audience heard a full, deep baritone singing the popular "Night and Day." Dick Haymes was now entering the world of his boyhood dreams.

CHAPTER 2

The Big Band Era

The Doors Open

When twenty-one-year-old Dick Haymes left the Berigan band after several appearances, his road ahead had been clearly marked during the past decade. By 1939, big bands had been electrifying live audiences and radio listeners for four years, although the origins of swing were heard in the 1920s in the work of black jazz musicians. Later, Paul Whiteman had formed a large orchestra, which drew on the earlier tradition but changed the arrangements and sound to appeal to white audiences. It is generally conceded that Benny Goodman's band, playing on the *Let's Dance* radio show, created such a large audience for jazz-oriented swing music in 1935 that the big band era commenced in that year. It lasted until after World War II. The majority of the big bands were composed of from twelve to eighteen musicians and one or two vocalists. A few also included singing groups of trios or quartets, such as the Modernaires, who sang with Paul Whiteman and later achieved new popularity with the great Glenn Miller orchestra.

Some of the earlier pioneer bands included Jean Goldkette's and the aforementioned Paul Whiteman's, both of which featured the legendary trumpet player Bix Biederbecke. Along with the Dorsey Brothers and

Goodman, there were a number of bands composed of black musicians, notably, those of Fletcher Henderson, Duke Ellington, Louis Armstrong, King Oliver, and Chick Webb.

When Benny Goodman opened in California in August of 1935, he found a large, excited group of young dancers waiting for his famed clarinet and the band that accompanied him. Goodman gave them what they craved and more—free, uninhibited swing. He had achieved twenty hit recordings in the previous two years, and his young fans were ready to swing along with him on the floor. His music was influenced by black jazz musicians of the 1920s, as the big band leaders gratefully conceded, but until some years later, when the color line was erased, most bands—both white and black—remained segregated. However, it was not uncommon for many jazz musicians to play together after hours at their favorite clubs and hangouts. They also worked together on selected studio recordings and on radio broadcasts.

Goodman, however, was a leader in hiring black musicians, and his brilliant trio, quartet, and sextets from 1935 through 1941 included some of the best there were: Charlie Christian, Teddy Wilson, Fletcher Henderson, Lionel Hampton, Cootie Williams, and Count Basie all worked and recorded with Goodman. His famous jazz concert in Carnegie Hall on January 16, 1938, included Harry James, trumpet; Gene Krupa, drums; Teddy Wilson, piano; and Lionel Hampton, vibes. Soon all four would go on to form their own bands.

Other bands quickly soared in popularity, notably, Glenn Miller's (sweeter, less jazz-oriented), which in 1940 had *Billboard*'s certification as number one in the country, dominating the jukeboxes and, in that year, releasing more than forty-five top-selling recordings. Miller's competition was formidable: Goodman; Tommy Dorsey's band, with Frank Sinatra, who had recorded the hit "I'll Never Smile Again" (number one on the charts for twelve weeks); Artie Shaw, whose hit "Frenesi" kept the top chart position for thirteen weeks; Jimmy Dorsey; Woody Herman; and at least twenty-five other lesser-known bands that packed screaming young fans into hotel ballrooms, theaters, and supper clubs.

Radio was undoubtedly one of the major catalysts for the era of the big bands and the promotion of their vocalists. From the 1920s, with the airing of musical variety shows, which themselves grew out of vaudeville, radio became a force in the music industry. Just two years after the first radio broadcast in 1920, there were over three million sets in use in the United States (two hundred transmitters were used), and the industry garnered $800,000,000 per year. Radio sound was subtler than that on recordings as it was direct and unprocessed, thanks to the new instrument that would soon change vocal style: the microphone. As one critic has remarked, "What was important was . . . its ability to pick up the lightest pressure of a singer's breath upon his vocal cords for transmission to listeners in the homes hundreds and thousands of miles away, or as employed in a P.A. system, to thousands of listeners in large auditoriums." The microphone gave singers the freedom to act while singing and released them from the necessity to force their voices to reach those in the last row of the theater. Frank Sinatra would make the microphone essential to his appeal. He was virtually tied to his microphone. A critic noted, "To him it was, or became, an instrument on which he played as an instrumentalist plays a saxophone, or a trombone—in other words, an electronic extension of his own vocal instrument." The microphone revealed more of the singer—both voice and emotion, particularly, a sense of vulnerability—than ever before. On his BBC radio program in 1988, host Dave Gelly commented on Haymes and the microphone: "All singers made special relationships with the microphone, but none closer or more intimate than Dick Haymes. Dick Haymes and the microphone understood each other." Gelly commented that Haymes's "impossibly perfect" voice "seemed to belong to some impossibly perfect ideal man—warm, gentle, open-hearted and somehow utterly trustworthy." During the World War II years, audiences yearned for just the kind of emotion that Haymes and Sinatra so effortlessly expressed as they sang into the microphone. A 1940s radio critic, Ben Gross, writing in the New York *Daily News*, considered Frank and Dick "both swell fellows . . . and [they] have a great sense of showmanship. But they have created a trend

that is going to play havoc with straight singers, romantic old maids, sentimental housewives and susceptible teenage gals. . . . These boys don't nasal-
ize as Rudy [Vallee] does. . . . They don't groan in the manner of Bing. . . .
They just stand in front of a mike and suffer . . . [and] they turn on the
heartbreak and the pathos. . . . Maybe it's the war. . . . [M]aybe it's just an
escape, a natural reaction against the harshness of everyday life."

Jazz in the 1920s liberated singers and musicians, and the microphone enabled jazz singers and musicians to reach listeners with a natural
beat and rhythm that approximated the rhythms of normal speech.
Undoubtedly, the black singers' approach to the conversational rhythms
and vocal patterns from Caribbean and Latin American musicians was sin-
gularly appropriate to radio, and they developed a relaxed but extremely
articulate style that was soon adopted by other singers, both black and
white, throughout the United States.

The recording industry, although at first fearful that radio would
adversely affect its sales, soon realized that the new medium would serve to
advertise recordings. Even those performers who were loathe to desert concert halls for bare recording chambers were soon converted. The famous
tenor John McCormack saw sales of his new recording, "All Alone" (by
Irving Berlin), which first aired on radio, sell by the thousands, with the
sheet music sales reaching over one hundred thousand. It was clear that
radio was, indeed, the best friend of the recording industry (although troubles between the two would surface in later years).

The radio variety show was instrumental in introducing new singers
and recordings into American homes. Rudy Vallee was the host of *The
Fleischmann Hour*, a model for the variety shows that would dominate radio
and television two and three decades later. Vallee was also one of the first of
the "crooners"—singers who used a soft, intimate, almost conversational
tone, almost as though they were whispering into the listener's ear. Vilified
by religious leaders as "degenerate" and disdained by concert singers, crooning nevertheless became the entrenched mode of popular vocal expression
by the mid-1930s.

Vallee's show ran for ten years (1929–1939) and then later, as *The Sealtest Show*, from 1940 to 1942. He introduced the performers who would themselves become show-business legends during the war years: Eddie Cantor, Edgar Bergen and Charlie McCarthy, Burns and Allen, Dolores Grey, and many other singers and comedians were first heard on Vallee's variety show—which was first broadcast from the stage of the Paramount Theater in New York City.

Other bandleaders of the 1930s soon had radio shows, including Vincent Lopez, Tommy and Jimmy Dorsey, Jack Teagarden, Glenn Miller, Bunny Berigan, Benny Goodman, and Woody Herman, most of whom simply played late-night music from supper clubs, hotel ballrooms, and other venues removed from the radio studio.

Although other crooners achieved success in this period—Arthur Tracy (the "Street Singer"), Gene Austin, Frank Munn—Bing Crosby, who hosted the *Kraft Music Hall* for eleven years beginning in 1935, was indisputably the single most important influence on radio vocalists and on the big band singers of the 1940s. Frank Sinatra and Dick Haymes, as well as Tony Bennett and Perry Como, cited Crosby as the model, indeed, the inspiration for their vocal endeavors. When the newer crooners were automatically rewarded with radio shows, they were normally of fifteen-minute duration, but Crosby's ran for a full hour. He was the most important, the most revered, and the best-selling vocalist and the most popular and successful screen actor of the early and mid 1940s. His relaxed, loose manner and his charm and humor appealed to audiences of all ages. One writer noted, "Crosby managed to sing into a microphone and make the mike vanish, as if it were eavesdropping on him." Yet Crosby could convey the longing and loneliness that afflicted both the troops and families on the home front during the war years in such songs as "I'll Be Seeing You," "I'll Be Home for Christmas," and the favorite to this day, "White Christmas." Crosby was instrumental in introducing taped transcriptions of radio programs, allowing independent stations to buy the transcriptions and air the shows. Crosby remained on the air, in various programs, through the early

1960s and for eight of those years was the most popular personality on the airwaves.

In 1935, another radio show made its debut, and it was to prove a major force in the recording industry and in the careers of American vocalists. After Barry Wood, the program's first main male singer, *Your Hit Parade* in the early 1940s featured a young Frank Sinatra for a time (with screaming teenagers audibly present in the audience) as well as other aspiring vocalists, and the program soon had scores of imitators and successors, providing listeners with the songs and vocalists for whom their appetites appeared insatiable. *Your Hit Parade* aired the top ten songs, sung by a group of singers, which rotated to include such names as Buddy Clark, Bea Wain, Ginny Simms, Dinah Shore, Martha Tilton, Johnny Mercer, Doris Day, Andy Russell, and Dick Haymes, who always disliked the show and years later actually forgot that he had appeared on it for a month in the late 1940s. But *Your Hit Parade* made Sinatra a major star.

The big bands introduced new songs on radio that became immediate hits, and a band's theme song would inevitably prove popular as a recording: Bunny Berigan's "I Can't Get Started," Harry James's "Ciribiribin," Frankie Carle's "Sunrise Serenade," all made the charts.

One other element in the music world would prove indispensable to bands and vocalists: the jukebox, a descendant of the late-nineteenth-century coin-slotted phonograph machine invented by Edison and Wurlitzer's coin-operated player pianos, which by 1910 had become immensely popular. In 1927 there were several record-playing machines that were electrically operated but did not allow for selection of individual songs. Homer Capeheart introduced a machine that made possible electrical selection of either ten-inch or twelve-inch recordings, with excellent sound. The Wurlitzer Company took over Capeheart's design, and by 1935 there were one hundred thousand of these machines—called jukeboxes—in operation. The jukebox provided twenty-four selections, which were regularly changed to allow for new names to acquire a following. Country music benefited immeasurably from jukeboxes, allowing black singers and small groups to find an audience that could not afford radios. The jukeboxes helped the recording industry in the depression by using many recordings that were less expensive to make than those by the big bands. The jukebox would be one of the driving forces in the careers of the major vocalists of the 1940s.

Popular singing was entering its glory days when Dick Haymes was trying to establish himself in the industry. He made a few guest appearances on a short-lived weekly program, *Smoke Dreams* (1939–1940), that presented popular and semi-classical musical selections in the years when disc-jockey shows that played hit recordings of popular songs were rare, and fifteen- or thirty-minute programs like this provided virtually the only opportunities for people to hear the newest music (the popular variety/comedy shows played few songs). Like his younger brother, Dick felt that he was a natural songwriter, and in-between and after his appearances with Berigan, he devoted himself to songwriting. Clearly, New York City was the hub of the industry, and Dick had his antennae out for whatever possibilities awaited a good-looking young man with intelligence, talent, and strong determination. Such a possibility presented itself during the winter of 1940, when one of the friends Dick had made in the music business, Larry Shayne, who headed Famous Music, a branch of Paramount Pictures, arranged an audition for Dick's songs with Harry James, who was rehearsing with his band at the World Transcription Studio at 711 Fifth Avenue.

Harry James was a fine trumpet player who had started his long career at the age of nine in his father's circus band. He worked with several big bands and began organizing his own big band in 1939, making his debut at a hotel in Philadelphia. Unlike Benny Goodman, Tommy Dorsey, and other more temperamental musician-bandleaders, he was generally well liked and quickly became one of Dick Haymes's lifelong friends. Pianist Al Lerner, however, whose relationship with James was difficult, felt that James was no different from the other temperamental bandleaders. Drummer Mickey Scrima remarked on James's self-centeredness. Lerner felt that Harry James was never known as a smooth talker or even a nice guy by those who knew him and that he alienated nearly everyone around him. James's career as a bandleader was one of the longest, as he returned to touring with newly reconstructed bands after their popularity had waned. His biggest recording hits were with vocalists, like Sinatra, Haymes, Helen Forrest, and Kitty Kallen.

On perhaps the most important day of Dick Haymes's life, the eager young man carried files of songs under his arm and, at James's invitation, proceeded to audition them, accompanying himself at the piano. Frank Sinatra had been James's vocalist since June 1939. (James had heard the young singer on the radio and discovered him in person at a club, the Rustic Cabin, in New Jersey.) On January 26, 1940, Sinatra left the James band after receiving from Tommy Dorsey an offer that would pay him fifty dollars a week more than the seventy-five dollars per week he was being paid by James. Sinatra's popularity had steadily grown, particularly among female teenage fans, soon to be called "bobby soxers." James had hired a young singer, Fran Hines, but knew he couldn't replace Sinatra. James liked Haymes's voice at the audition and immediately offered him a job as band singer, which Dick quickly accepted, at the standard fifty dollars per week salary.

Reporter George Simon remarked, "If ever there was a nervous band singer, it was Dick Haymes." Throughout his life, Haymes would be noticeably tense before a performance. He routinely cleared his throat several times, coughed into a handkerchief, and then, as if summoning reserves of courage, he would approach the microphone with long steps, take a deep breath, and start to sing. Decades later, he would write in his diary about his nervousness before performances and worry constantly about his health, particularly about afflictions common among singers. He would always be subject to bouts of flu, to coughs and colds, many of them exacerbated by hypochondria. But when he began to sing, the self-consciousness disappeared, and his singing quickly enthralled the audience. He was never as comfortable on the stage as Sinatra or Perry Como or, of course, the inimitable Crosby; he was unable to relax sufficiently to establish the rapport of the common man singing to an audience of his friends. His brother-in law,

Peter Marshall describes him as "somewhat stiff and aloof, not free and loose" on the stage, not quite able to touch the audience. Part of his problem, as Marshall notes, was his eyesight: "He was blind as a bat, and wouldn't wear glasses on stage." But despite his slight distance from his audience, his voice and delivery were so clearly superior that his slight awkwardness never affected his popularity—and a few years later, at the height of his fame, perhaps emboldened by screaming fans, his concert tours reflected a far more relaxed entertainer. In his reminiscence of the era, Simon remarked of Haymes, "And how he could sing! There wasn't a boy singer in the business who had a better voice box than Dick Haymes—not even Bob Eberly, whom Dick worshiped so much."

Dick was confident about his ability to attract women, and to charm others, but was always modest about his singing ability, confessing only in the 1970s that he knew he had talent. In addition to Bob Eberly, who made some unforgettable recordings with vocalist Helen O'Connell and the Jimmy Dorsey band, Haymes liked Sinatra, but they were not close, and the only influence he credited was Bing Crosby, who was, according to Dick's son, "his idol."

The life of a big band singer or musician was never easy. Bands traveled throughout the year, on buses that were cold and uncomfortable. They played in remote places, often in run-down clubs, with faulty equipment and inadequate dressing rooms. On one tour, the James band played fifty one-night stands, often sleeping in the bus. And money problems were constant: for salaries, buses and drivers, sleeping quarters, food. On one occasion, James paid Dick his salary and promptly borrowed it back from him.

The singers initially were the second rung of the band, performing after the opening instrumental chorus and perhaps returning for a half-chorus at the end of the song. Tommy Dorsey and Harry James built up the role of the band vocalist. According to Jo Stafford, one of the major singers of the era, Tommy Dorsey created the equivalent of production numbers, using her, Frank Sinatra, the Pied Pipers, and Connie Haines. Paradoxically, the popularity of the band singers ultimately led to the demise of the bands themselves. The era of the vocalists, which followed the big band era, was inaugurated on January 19, 1942, when Frank Sinatra made his first records as a soloist, although the success of many big band vocalists made Sinatra's move a logical step in his career.

When Dick Haymes started to work with James's band, he was the same fun-loving, charming, good-looking, sometimes conceited, but ultimately likable young man who had survived a nomadic, often uncertain childhood. He had always loved to play jokes on others, and life on a Greyhound bus with the other band members afforded many opportunities for the kind of pranks similar to those he and his brother had played. Another legacy from those early years would prove destructive throughout his life: his inability to handle money. His mother's casual finances, her sense that somehow, in some way, money would be there for her, resorting even to deceit to secure necessary funds for her exploits, set an example that Dick would never be able to escape. (His brother also had financial problems on a number of occasions.) Dick Haymes simply did not think much about money: he accepted it gladly when it came in, but he never made money his primary goal. And when he had money, he spent it carelessly, thoughtlessly, as his mother had, never thinking of the future, assuming that it would always be available. So his reputation as someone who borrowed freely from others and gave freely when he could (infrequently, as it turned out) was sealed when he was very young.

Yet, in the early big band years, Dick Haymes was able to find order in the disorder of that life: in front of the band, in the recording studios, on the airwaves, he was professional, dedicated, and determined; and it did not take long for audiences, critics, and other musicians to recognize his vocal gifts. He would always remember his first opening at the Paramount Theater in New York to a wildly responsive audience: "I bowed so deeply in answer to the applause after my songs that I lost my balance, fell off the stage, landing fourteen feet below, bruising seven people in the first row of the audience as I landed horizontally across their laps!" George Simon expressed the prevailing view of anyone who heard Haymes, writing in

Metronome (in September 1940), "Harry's fortunate in having one of the very finest band singers in the business. He's Dick Haymes, possessor of a wonderful vocal quality, who, week by week, improves in phrasing, shading, intonation, and reputation and who, at the rate he is progressing should very shortly rank publicly with the accepted two or three topnotchers in the business. So far as this writer is concerned, he's already there." When the band played at the World's Fair in Flushing Meadows, Dinah Shore and other upcoming singers traveled out to hear Dick, whom many believed was the best male singer of the time. Dick always gave credit to the bandleaders who helped him develop his style and polish his technique. "When I first joined Harry," he said years later, "the vocal chorus was always in the middle of the chart where it was almost obligatory to sit on the bandstand and pick your nose. But then he outgrew that and he started to showcase his people. He'd say, 'Hey, I'm gonna take a couple of sets' . . . and I used to front the band for him at the Lincoln Hotel. . . . But later on he started showcasing. I think the singers were probably responsible for that. And later on he learned dynamics because when I first joined the band everything was at one level and everything was loud, loud, loud. It was a revelation to hear myself."

A few months after Dick started with James's band, Al Lerner was hired as pianist, and the relationship between the two lasted for thirteen years. He and Al roomed together in the Forrest Hotel on Forty-ninth Street in New York City, as well as on the road where they often were joined by one or two others in the same room. Dick remembered those days when he reminisced to Fred Hall thirty years later: "It was a team effort because we were all working for peanuts, you know, and trying to pay the Greyhound Bus company and pay the arrangers and pay the hotel bills. . . . The singer was just a side man; but by the time I left Harry the singers or vocalists, to use the term that was used then, were starting to emerge and become important themselves."

Dick and Al Lerner adopted a dog, Flannagan, a gift from a fan, and later a pair of monkeys—the three pets accompanying them on the bus as they traveled to Chicago, Detroit, Boston, and back to New York City. Lerner remembers one occasion when Dick's carelessness with money almost cost him his life. When the James band was working at the Lincoln Hotel at Forty-fifth Street and Eighth Avenue, and they were staying at the Forrest Hotel, they frequently ate at a little Greek restaurant across the street, which was a hangout for members of the local mob. One evening, when Dick was preparing for a date, he went across to the restaurant to complain about his lack of money. According to Lerner, one of the "boys" offered him fifty dollars, with the proviso that Dick return one hundred dollars to him in a week. Dick's normal disregard of consequences in this instance would prove dangerous, when he failed to pay the money—which he didn't have—and the mobster told him that if he did not pay up by that evening, he would "knock his teeth out." When the band started to leave the Lincoln Hotel after the performance, Dick saw several members of the mob waiting at the backstage entrance. He tried to leave by the main hotel entrance, but they had blocked that door too. In desperation, he phoned the owner of the hotel, Maria Cramer, whom he knew, and, as Lerner reports, pleaded with her to save his life. Dick's plea—and his almost effortless charm—worked, and she gave him the money that would release him from his tormentors. He probably did learn from this episode, as he did not have dealings with members of the mob again (and they were ubiquitous powers in clubs and hotels).

The life of musicians and vocalists on the road was difficult: they drank and most of them found available women along the route. Singer Helen Forrest recalled that "the pace was staggering. And some of the guys like Harry and Dick, who kept a fast pace with the ladies every night might have gotten enough sack time, but seldom enough sleep." James often found nicknames for his band members—and Dick gave him the opportunity on one occasion when he overslept from exhaustion and wasn't in his customary place in the wings as the introduction to his number was played. After receiving a phone call from one of the band members, Dick quickly threw on some clothes and dashed over to the theater, where

James and the band were still playing the introduction. Dick sang, despite needing a shave, a shower, and fresh clothes, but from that day on, James would refer to him as "the Zombie."

Although most musicians found Dick likable, his lack of tolerance for those he considered vulgar or unintelligent was often apparent. Some in the James band, like Mickey Scrima, felt that he simply looked down on people, and those who did not understand him or know him well often regarded his sophistication with resentment. Because Dick was very near-sighted and refused to wear his glasses in public, he often unwittingly snubbed friends, who assumed that he was a snob.

Dick met many women in this period, and in late 1940 he married band singer Edythe Harper, whom he had met in Chicago when he was appearing in the Panther Room of the Hotel Sherman. They dated for two weeks when she told him that she was pregnant with his child—and, of course, he offered to marry her. Shortly thereafter, he discovered that her story was a hoax, and within three months he filed for a divorce, which became final in the summer of 1941. Edythe did not pine, as she quickly remarried Vernon Brown, a trombonist with the Mugsy Spanier band.

Dick's life was to change profoundly in the late spring of 1941. He was singing at the Paramount Theater in New York, where the band was doing six or seven shows a day plus a nightly stint at the Lincoln Hotel. Years later, he would ruefully describe the moment when he met his future wife: "I can only tell you that Joanne Marshall was one of the most beautiful women I'd ever seen and I wanted her the moment I first saw her. . . . I decided to marry Joanne and did. My big problem in my youth was that I was too handsome for my own good. Whatever I wanted I could get—and I knew it. Perhaps I would have been better treated by life (later on) had women and 'things' not come so easily." Joanne Marshall (born Joanne Letitia LaCock on January 31, 1922) was the daughter of a West Virginia pharmacist who had recently passed away. She arrived in New York City with her mother and younger brother (Peter Marshall, later a well-known television personality) in 1940 and worked as a model until she was cast by Al Jolson as one of the showgirls in his Broadway play, "Hold onto Your Hats." When the show closed, she joined a chorus line, the "Samba Sirens" of the Copacabana, a popular nightclub—and the group was performing at the Paramount along with the James band and Dick Haymes, whom she had met the previous day. Later, she would change her name to Joanne Dru when she began her own career in films. She fell in love with Dick, and after a whirlwind courtship, they married on September 21, 1941, in the Episcopal Church on Eighty-sixth Street and West End Avenue. Harry James, serving as best man, proved a steadfast friend, lending Dick five hundred dollars for his wedding wardrobe and honeymoon expenses. Dick and Joanne spent three days in Lakeville, Connecticut, to James's surprise. He had expected Dick to perform on the night of his wedding, but when he returned, Dick, knowing that Harry would be angry, took the offensive, exclaiming, "Where have you been?" James could only splutter, "Where have I been?" But he forgave Dick and good-naturedly welcomed him back to the bandstand. Joanne and Dick took an apartment on the Upper East Side of Manhattan—a high-rent area even then, certainly beyond their affordable range.

One of the best female vocalists of the era, Helen Forrest, joined the James band in November 1941, and she and Dick became close friends as well as highly successful collaborators on many duets that reached the top ten on the *Billboard* charts. She never forgot his generosity when she applied for the job with Harry James. It was very important to her that she be taken on as vocalist, as she had fled Benny Goodman, whom she found insufferably rude and difficult. James told her that he already had a ballad singer in Dick Haymes, but she learned that Dick had gone to Harry saying, "We can both sing ballads. The band needs a girl singer. Let her sing." So she auditioned with the band that night, received a standing ovation, and became one of James's most successful vocalists, both in recordings and on the bandstand.

Helen Forrest also considered Dick the best male singer of the time; she found him better than Sinatra. He "could outsing Frank Sinatra while blowing bubbles. There's no contest for me. He had a better sound and a sweeter voice than Frank. Besides, Frank didn't have the range that Dick had."

Haymes recognized in Helen a kindred spirit and would make faces at her as they waited to sing. She described one of the tricks he, Al Lerner, and some other members of the band played in an effort to relieve the monotony of listening to the same comedian preceding their performances six times a day. They came to the bandstand with loaded water pistols in their pockets, and during the comedian's routine they would spray the musicians and their sheet music. In retaliation, the other musicians bought water pistols and filled them with ink—and thus a war ensued. James was furious, and the band costumes were costly.

The accomplishments of Dick Haymes with the James band during the year and a half they were together are impressive. When he took over from Sinatra, he had to use the arrangements that had already been made, and he found that he had to sing in a higher pitch until the songs could be rearranged. Haymes's voice was immediately distinctive, particularly in the lower register. He began to record with the James band in March 1940 and made about forty recordings as well as many transcriptions from radio shows. Five of those recordings reached the best-selling charts: "I'll Get By" was recorded in April 1941, but found its audience during the musicians' strike of 1943. It would become the number one hit in April 1944 and hold that position for six weeks. "Lament to Love," written by Mel Tormé, and "A Sinner Kissed an Angel" both reached the charts within two months of their release in the spring of 1941, and "The Devil Sat Down and Cried," a novelty song with Helen Forrest and Harry James sharing the vocal, soon followed. Dick and Harry James worked closely, often planning their recording choices while riding on the bus between engagements. Dick remembered that his biggest hit with James, "I'll Get By," originated while they were sitting together, exchanging ideas, and later having them written up. He believed that that recording turned out to be a classic because "it had an easy swing feel, as opposed to it always having been sung as a dramatic ballad, rubato style, by various saloon singers." Similarly, his recording of "Ol' Man River" with the James band was very different from the popular song that had first been heard in the Broadway musical *Show Boat*. His version was triple the tempo of the usual recordings—and it was soon imitated by other performers. Dick would speak of the early recording sessions with wonder that any of them survived the grueling schedule. They would finish work at 2:00 AM and arrive at a studio in the early morning often without having slept. He recalled that the average recording date lasted three hours, and it depended on the availability of the performers and the studio. He said in the early 1970s, "I, to this date, hate recording—I think any singer, if he admits it, hates to sing in the morning. But sometimes it was just absolutely necessary. One of the biggest records I had with Harry was a tune called 'You've Changed.' Now that was a morning session and it was supposed to be for the girl singer and she couldn't cut it. Now her register was down in the rupture department in my register. [The arrangement called for extremely low notes—RP] But had it not been morning I never could have cut it. In other words, I got down to those low E flats. . . . [L]ater I had the reputation of having the low notes of all time. But it was really a combination of fatigue and the hour of the day."

Shortly after December 7, 1941, after hearing Franklin D. Roosevelt's declaration of war following the Japanese attack on Pearl Harbor, several members of the band rushed down to the local army recruitment office, eager to join the armed services. Dick's tendency to make quick decisions without thinking of the consequences led him to an action which would later haunt him during the most troubled period of his life, providing fodder for his enemies, including gossip columnists and sensational tabloids. He remembered vividly that day at the draft registration office in Pennsylvania during a tour of one-night stands. When he was classified 1-A later on and ordered to report for examination and induction into the army, his advisors urged him to sign an affidavit of non-belligerency (being a citizen of Argentina, a non-belligerent country). He knew it would mean that he might not ever be able to become an American citizen, but young and thoughtless of consequences, his main concerns were his personal situation (his wife was pregnant) and a career that was still in the formative stage. Further, Dick's declaration was a common practice for resident aliens, the law having been on the books for many years. One of the main reasons, both then and later, for trying to obtain deferments was concern for one's family. We might, in hindsight, ask what his advisors were thinking, but Dick rarely questioned those he had hired to perform the tasks which he had neither the experience nor interest in attempting. Perhaps he didn't make it clear to others that his goal was to become an American citizen. Ironically, as he realized, had he joined the U.S. Army, he would have become a citizen in six months.

He was haunted by his decision, particularly when in the following year he had to appear at the Immigration Office in Los Angeles to register, as all aliens were required to do. He said, "I was carrying a heavy burden—the burden of that letter. I'd never backed down from anything in my life." When he told the clerk at the Immigration Office of his feelings, he was told that he could write a letter rescinding his exclusion affidavit. The clerk offered to dictate it, remarking sympathetically, "You don't need this hanging over your head."

Dick signed the letter and immediately felt better. Shortly after the letter was filed, he received his reclassification from Selective Service and was again 1-A. But after his physical examination (in 1944) he was re-classified 4-F because of hypertension. Later in New York in 1945, he was again classified 1-A and ordered to Ellis Island for another physical. (By that time, Haymes had become well known as an actor and singer.) "I think the draft board and politicians were keeping close tabs on well-known personalities who were not in the service," he said. At Ellis Island, he was kept in bed, under surveillance, presumably to make certain that he didn't take anything to cause his blood pressure to rise. "It was like being in captivity," he recalled. Again, he failed the physical and was reclassified 4-F. There had been no publicity about his letter of exclusion or his later rescission. As far as he was concerned, the matter was concluded. Later, he said, "It all blew up in my face."

As recently as September 2000, the same issue was raised, this time in connection with then New York City mayor Rudolph Giuliani's proposal to erect a statue of Frank Sinatra on a traffic island at Forty-fourth Street and Broadway in the heart of the city. The *New York Times* reporter suggested that a monument in front of the armed forces' busiest recruiting station would honor a man "who avoided the World War II draft and spent much of his life trying to live it down." In Sinatra's case, a deferment was granted based on his claim that he suffered from a punctured eardrum, although his request in 1943 for exclusion from the draft included ailments like neuroses, fear of crowds, undernourishment, and exhaustion. Sinatra would, throughout his life, try to compensate for not having served in the war, as he entertained troops in Italy at the end of the war and made special recordings for servicemen.

Dick Haymes left the James band at the start of the new year. Harry and he would later joke about Dick's leaving and Harry's reaction (Dick joked that Harry fired him, but Harry replied that he hadn't, that he just let him go), but it is clear that they parted on amicable terms. Dick's intention on leaving the James band was to start a band of his own, and, indeed, he had so many connections that he quickly formed his own big band. He also performed with other bands, including two appearances with Charlie Spivak's band, and in February sang "A Sinner Kissed an Angel" and "This Is No Laughing Matter" on *Accent on Music*, one of the many radio shows devoted to the latest popular songs and singers. His effort to secure independence as a big band leader, however, was unsuccessful because, one by one, his musicians were drafted, and he soon realized that his best opportunity would be as lead singer with a major group. After a few months, he was hired by Benny Goodman to take the place of Art London (later singer Art Lund) at the Paramount Theater in New York on May 27, 1941.

Dick had heard that Goodman was one of the most difficult bandleaders. He certainly was a strange man, unable to forget an impoverished childhood, famously rude, and he believed, some say, in having his musicians angry with him so that they would perform more effectively. He suffered from a back problem, which undoubtedly contributed to his unpleasantness, but some of his actions are inexplicable. He would fire musicians for no discernable reason, and Helen Forrest described his habit of staring at the foreheads of performers who displeased him with a piercing look—his "ray" as they named it. "He didn't fire anybody," she said, "He'd force you to quit by giving you that ray. It was just awful." In the 1950s, he would suffer a nervous breakdown, retire, and become an elder statesman of music, playing his famous hits on many occasions. He played at the Brussels World's Fair in 1958 and in the Soviet Union in 1962, and his behavior was offensive to everyone with whom he came into contact.

Remarkably, Dick Haymes and Benny Goodman had a good relationship after Dick indicated to Goodman that he would not tolerate the bandleader's attempts to intimidate him. Every time Dick would get up to sing "Serenade in Blue," Goodman would stand next to him and join in on the melody. Finally, one night Dick stopped singing and said to him, "Look, Benny. You want to play it, be my guest," and walked away from the microphone. Goodman ran after him, "like a pussycat," asking "What's the matter, pops, what's the matter?" Dick replied, "Why don't you shut up and let me just sing my song and stop helping me with your goddam horn, you know." Goodman, surprised, said, "Man, I didn't know I was bugging you." Dick believed that Goodman didn't know how unpleasant he was. "I think Benny is guileless. . . . I think he's on cloud nine all the time and he gets the baby stares. And if he happens to be staring at you and you were self-conscious about it, he wasn't giving you the 'ray,' he was looking at nothing really, he was thinking of something." Dick noted that working with Benny wasn't fun, for all of Goodman's attention was devoted to finding the best clarinet for himself. One or two other players tended to dismiss Goodman's eccentricities and often found him helpful, but they were certainly a small minority.

Although Dick Haymes would remain with Goodman's band for only three months, they made four recordings together, three of them best-sellers: "Idaho," "Serenade in Blue," and "Take Me." Like other musicians and vocalists, Dick Haymes entertained soldiers at the Stage Door Canteen, appearing with the Goodman sextet and singer Peggy Lee. Many of these appearances were broadcast via shortwave radio to overseas troops.

While performing with Goodman, Dick—and everyone in the business—learned that Sinatra was going to leave his successful stint with the Tommy Dorsey band. In an acrimonious contract dispute, Sinatra did leave Dorsey to become an independent vocalist, and Dick was hired to replace him at a salary of almost $150 per week. He joined the band on September 3, 1942, during the second week of Sinatra's two-week notice, so for one week the two singers worked together, even sharing a hotel room. Dick regarded this week as an important training period, and when he was introduced to audiences on the Raleigh-Kool radio show, first by Tommy Dorsey and then by Sinatra, the two singers made the transfer as Sinatra sang his last song for Dorsey and, in very glowing terms ("a fine guy, wonderful singer"), introduced Haymes, who responded, "I don't know if anyone can really take your place with this band, but I'll be in there trying." The relationship between Sinatra and Haymes at this time was friendly, and Sinatra would later sing a humorous song about the new singers "breathing down my neck"—Dick Haymes, Dick Todd, and Como—a riff on Johnny Burke's "Sunday, Monday or Always."

Both Sinatra and Haymes credited Dorsey for helping them to develop as singers by observing his breathing control as he played the trombone. The Dorsey band was, as Haymes said, the "Tiffany's of the orchestra world." Dorsey, he felt, was a star maker, relying on the strongest possible assemblage of supporting arrangers, musicians, and vocalists, many of whom would achieve fame while working for Dorsey. Like the other bandleaders Haymes had worked for, Tommy Dorsey could be difficult, particularly in his strict code of behavior for musicians. He did not tolerate lateness or laziness, but he and Dick, despite some disagreements, got along very well from the outset. The band was playing seven shows a day, moving from one theater to another without a day off. If a musician was late, Dorsey would warn him once or twice and then would let him go. Many musicians simply could not keep up with the pace; Dorsey didn't mind if they performed with hangovers, but he drew the line when a musician tried to hog the limelight on the bandstand. Dorsey saw himself as a creator of an ensemble and believed that everyone benefited from being given the same opportunities to perform before audiences.

The Dorsey band with Dick Haymes and a vocal group, the Pied Pipers with Jo Stafford, was hired in 1942 by MGM studios to provide the musical background for a new film going into production, *DuBarry Was a Lady*. Dick was uncredited in this mediocre adaptation of a Broadway musical, but he was featured in close-up while singing a novelty song, "Katie Went to Haiti," with the Pied Pipers. He provided the background singing for a calendar-girl sequence, introducing each season musically. He looks very young in the film—and silly, as did all of the musicians, dressed as they were in wigs and costumes from the era of Louis XVI and Madame DuBarry.

Joanne had accompanied him to the West Coast, where, after filming, he appeared with Dorsey at the Palladium in Los Angeles for nine weeks. Their first child, Richard Ralph Haymes, was born on July 24, 1942. From the fall of 1942 through the following spring, Dick Haymes appeared weekly on the Raleigh-Kool radio show broadcast from Los Angeles with Tommy Dorsey and his band, Jo Stafford and the Pied Pipers, and occasional guests. The program was directly tied into the war effort, and a series of programs featured at the opening and closing a jingle, "Dig Down Deep," urging listeners to buy war bonds. The show featured a vocal by Jo Stafford, then a Dorsey band number, followed by a medley with Stafford and Dick Haymes, and then a vocal featuring Haymes alone. Dorsey and his band would perform the last song, and the jingle would conclude the show. Dick's songs, including such popular standards as "There Are Such Things," "That Old Black Magic," "Let's Face the Music and Dance," and "My Silent Love," might be repeated from week to week. The music was superior, but there was no effort to offer listeners anything they might not expect. A special show, "Uncle Sam's Christmas Tree," was broadcast on December 25, 1942, at the United States Naval Base in San Pedro, California, and sponsored by the Coca Cola Company. In this marathon show which featured almost every big band, Dorsey's was the last to perform. Dick sang "There Are Such Things" and joined the band for "Marie" and "White Christmas";

the announcer paid homage to the naval forces, and, with its marching finale, the show was typical of the patriotic fervor conveyed by most of the music shows of the period. Clearly, for Dick, the radio shows and the last months with Dorsey were not breaking new ground for him, and a strike by the musicians union prevented him from making new recordings. Indeed, to his regret, he never made a recording with the Dorsey band.

The recording ban started when Judge Learned Hand ruled that the copyright was not infringed by the playing of a record on the radio, despite the labels, which read, "Unlicensed for public broadcasting." James Caesar Petrillo, head of the American Federation of Musicians union, ordered musicians to stop recording on August 1, 1942. Petrillo was shortsighted, of course, not recognizing that radio was popularizing recordings, leading to increased sales. The major result of the strike would be the rise in popularity of individual singers, at the expense of bands and musicians. Dick Haymes, along with Perry Como, Kitty Kallen, Rosemary Clooney, Peggy Lee, Kay Starr, Georgia Gibbs, and Margaret Whiting, as well as Jo Stafford, all began their rise to success as independent vocalists in this period. They didn't need musical backup—as they proved—performing a cappella with such groups as the Song Spinners and the Mills Brothers substituting for musicians.

Dick was restless with the Dorsey band, feeling that he had gone as far as he could singing with big bands, and he became increasing depressed as they toured. He had discussed it with Joanne, who agreed that he needed to try to make it on his own, as Sinatra had. In San Francisco, at the Golden Gate Theatre, Dick walked away from the bandstand in the middle of a song. He would describe his action as experiencing a nervous breakdown, but the incident leading up to that moment is one of the most amusing in his big band career. He remembered, "We were working so hard that days were telescoping into the next and we became sort of ridiculous. Tommy was getting pretty tired too, and during my big 'heartthrob' ballads, he decided to give me hotfoots. You know what a hotfoot is, you stick a match in-between the shoe and the sole and light it, and of course, I twigged to what he was doing. Once was funny, twice was funny, and . . . after the second show I said, 'Look, Tom, please don't do it anymore because it louses my song up and it hurts!' So he said, 'OK, OK, OK.' So he did it the third show. I stopped the band—and you don't do this to Tommy Dorsey. I just cut the band off. I turned around and said, 'Cut.' And I turned back to the audience and said, 'Ladies and gentlemen, we've got a comedian for a bandleader, Mr. Tommy Dorsey, and I'm now handing in my notice. I quit.' And I walked off the stage." Dick could hear Tommy's steps running after him and was expecting an outburst from the bandleader who was known for his terrible temper. He made it to the elevator, to the eighth floor backstage, Dorsey missing the elevator as the doors closed before he could enter. Dorsey ran up the fire escape next to the elevator, and Dick thought, "Oh, my God, he's in a terrible temper," so he got into his dressing room but left the door open, picked up a chair, and when Dorsey got to the door said, "You cross that threshold and you'll never blow that stupid trombone again, because I'm gonna hit you right in the mouth with this chair." Dorsey started to laugh and Dick joined him, while the show below was continuing. Dorsey said, "What do you want?" and Dick replied, "I want to quit, Tom, honestly, I do." The result was that he did quit after finishing that week and the following week, allowing Dorsey time to find a replacement. And in a particularly magnanimous gesture, Dorsey said to Dick, "Do you have any money for clothes and arrangements?" Dick remembered, "I said, 'No.' He said, 'Well you got it.' And he helped me out and got me started and I paid him back and we remained friends till the day he died."

Years later, Dick told a friend that when he went to Tommy Dorsey's wake, he was overcome with grief. When he noticed that Dorsey, lying in his coffin, had new glasses on, Dick wiped his tears away and said, "You don't need these, Tommy," and removed them. Later, he said, he felt "like a real fool."

When he left Dorsey, Dick might also have suspected that the popularity of the big bands was waning. Within a few years, the big band era would end. In 1944, perhaps the most popular leader, now Lieutenant

Glenn Miller, died when the airplane he was in apparently crashed as it crossed the English Channel. It was never found. His loss shocked the nation and affected the morale of musicians and their public. The gas shortage prevented people from traveling to hear the bands that were touring. At Hershey Park in Pennsylvania, only 750 turned up to hear Woody Herman, and the Park closed for the duration of the war. Radio and juke boxes were available everywhere, so listeners were never cut off from the music they loved—but now the music increasingly featured vocalists. Although the big band leaders would try to resume after the war ended, their grosses for each performance fell sharply. Dorsey, who once could command $4,000 per night, and Goodman, who might take away $3,000, were reduced to a total of $700. The halcyon days would be over, and by the summer of 1946 eight of the leading bands folded. The era of the independent vocalist was getting under way when Frank Sinatra left Dorsey and within the next few years would define the music industry. But the era of the big bands would never be forgotten. Peter Reilly, a critic for *Stereo Review*, wrote in 1979, "We did have a 'golden age' of pop music as civilized and sophisticated as anything ever produced by any Western country, and for about forty years, it was probably the most popular and universally identifiable American cultural export."

After making the decision to leave Dorsey and big band singing forever, in February of 1943, Dick borrowed money to send his wife and child back to New York City to live close to her mother while he remained in Hollywood to try to find work—any work except singing with a band. It was painful to scrounge for money as Sinatra's popularity soared through regular appearances on *Your Hit Parade*, which Dick felt "was a joke as far as singers were concerned."

In California, Dick was virtually impoverished. He lived in a furnished room where the rent was overdue. He was unable to find an opening in movies, nightclubs, and radio programs and was close to breaking down psychologically. Joanne and their son, Richard ("Skip"), were being helped by relatives, but he knew that couldn't continue much longer. Joanne had a good friend in the popular singer Helen O'Connell, noted for her major successes in duets with Bob Eberly for the Jimmy Dorsey band, and she spoke to Helen about their plight. Helen persuaded her agent, Bill Burton, to take on Dick Haymes as a client, and Burton immediately wired Dick $175 to cover his return trip to New York. (Dick had split with his former agent, "Bullets" Durgom, to whom he owed a considerable sum. He and Durgom settled in 1948 for $17,500, and they would work together on other projects several years later.)

By the end of March, Burton called Dick and told him he had booked a split week for him, three days at the State Theater in Hartford, Connecticut, and three or four days at the Adams Theater in Newark, New Jersey, for a total of $500. To Dick's surprise, in his first appearance as a solo artist he shared the bill with Shep Fields, known for his Rippling Rhythm band and for his best-selling recordings, "South of the Border" and "Jersey Bounce." Dick was aghast at the sixteen saxophones in the band, and he did not urge Burton to attend any of his performances. But one night Burton phoned him and said he would be there for that evening's performance and would bring someone with him. That "someone" turned out to be Dario Vernon, the owner of a popular New York nightclub, La Martinique on West Fifty-seventh Street. Dario liked Dick's performance and hired him for two weeks to support his headliner, comedian Jackie Miles. Dick had little time to prepare new arrangements for the small nightclub orchestra, but he was helped by friends, including musician "Toots" Camarata, noted trumpet player and arranger for Tommy Dorsey, later a conductor for Ella Fitzgerald, Bing Crosby, and Haymes, and, finally, music director for Walt Disney studios.

Dick's two-week booking at La Martinique on West Fifty-seventh Street, beginning on May 19, 1943, lasted for three months, so stunning was his success. Brought in as an added attraction for Jackie Miles, he was now the headliner, the foremost competitor to Frank Sinatra, who was also drawing a huge audience at the Paramount Theater. Sinatra had just finished an engagement at the Riobamba Club, also on West Fifty-seventh

Street, which competed with La Martinique. The day after his opening, columnist Earl Wilson saluted the new singing star: "The lady members of the Booze Who have a new male singer to swoon over. Dick Haymes opened at La Martinique last night and from where I sat, which was at the ringside, . . . he seemed to be the long-sought threat to Frank Sinatra." Other columnists quickly took note of the two leading singing sensations, with bold headlines announcing "The Battle of the Baritones." Of course, as both Dick and Frank knew, there was no battle, but the publicity kept them in the public eye. His new fame from his performances at La Martinique brought him the rewards he had long been seeking. In rapid succession, Bill Burton arranged three contracts for Dick Haymes, with Decca Records (despite the recording ban), with the Bourjois Company for a radio show, *Here's to Romance*, and, at last, the movie contract he had long coveted, with Twentieth Century–Fox for two pictures a year for seven years. These three successive and lucrative contracts were astonishing to everyone working in popular music and movies. Even Sinatra had not made such a sudden and auspicious ascent to the highest rungs of the show business ladder, although in later years he would become the centerpiece of the American mythology of success.

The Petrillo strike turned out to be fortunate for Dick, for it resulted in his first solo hit, "You'll Never Know," recorded with great secrecy during Dick's second week at La Martinique. Dick Kapp (of Decca), Bill Burton, and Haymes thought that it would be a good idea to make a recording using a vocal chorus to back him up. This effort was, indeed, a battle of the baritones—but only in terms of timing. Word had spread of the plans for Haymes to record a cappella. Manie Sachs, a well-liked figure in the music industry and a close friend of Frank Sinatra, rushed to the Meadowbrook in New Jersey, where Sinatra was appearing after he had finished at the Paramount. Sachs had a contract in hand from Columbia records, dated two days before Dick signed his contract with Decca. On June 7, in a studio at Columbia, Sinatra recorded "You'll Never Know" backed by the Bobby Tucker singers (Tucker was an accompanist for Billie Holiday).

Haymes's "You'll Never Know" quickly climbed to the top of the charts in the summer of 1943 with sales of over one million records. The other side of the hit record, "It Can't Be Wrong," reached the second position on the best-selling charts and stayed there for four weeks. Dick Haymes was now a star among the male vocalists—easily rivaling Sinatra, whose recording of the same song was never as successful as his. During the musicians' strike, Haymes made seven recordings with the Song Spinners, each of them among the best-sellers of the year. These recordings are regarded by some music critics as the best of the pseudo-orchestral efforts, notwithstanding excellent recordings by Perry Como, Bing Crosby, and the Mills Brothers.

When people asked him how it felt to be an overnight success, he would refrain from describing the hours he'd spent on a Greyhound bus and some of the run-down clubs where he'd performed over the past few years. He felt overwhelmed and uncomfortable with the adulation he was receiving from his enthusiastic fans. (A Dick Haymes fan club had been started in 1942, and they began to publish a newsletter, the *Haymes Herald*, in 1944). Success worried him; he felt confident about his recording career, but less so about the radio and film commitments. A coast-to-coast radio show in the early 1940s meant two live broadcasts each day, one for each coast. He recalled it as a constant treadmill and was disturbed by the tenacious and exuberant fans, particularly after he made his first film. He said that he couldn't go from one place to another without police escorting him in and out of his limousine. He recalled that he did not like that life and the adulation did not thrill him. "It did exactly the opposite—it embarrassed me because I didn't feel worthy. It wasn't the return of Jesus, you know, it was just a boy singer that all the teenagers wanted to tear his clothes off, that's all." He was particularly uncomfortable with the fans who shrieked during performances at the Roxy Theater in New York City. He felt that they weren't listening to his singing, that a turn of phrase would evoke sighs, shouts, or screams and the situation would become chaotic. It seemed to him, looking back, that there was little room for artistry in those performances.

Dick always cared about his performance as a vocalist, and his reception by critics of the 1940s was just the beginning of the international recognition of his consummate artistry. Barry Ulanov, in his important history of jazz in American, sees Dick as more than a conventional romantic baritone: "For one thing, he exploited the luxurious lower reaches of his voice . . . [and] he sang with a delicacy and deftness that came only from jazz, the brisk jazz the James band was playing in those years. He made lovely records of 'I'll Get By,' 'Minka,' 'You've Changed,' and 'You Don't Know What Love Is,' giving good songs additional distinction by the strength of his feeling and the uninterrupted length of his phrases." Will Friedwald, reviewing Haymes's recording career, praises Haymes for not resorting to gimmicks, as Dean Martin and Perry Como so often did: "He developed a voice so fine and pure, and had a gift for interpreting love songs so convincingly and meaningfully, that the blasé arrangements Decca gave him never mattered and his personality even rendered his accompaniments a nonconsideration." When we listen to the recordings from the early 1940s, we hear a smooth, young voice, with a somewhat higher range than he would display in his best years—for many listeners, the mid-1950s, when, ironically, his popularity was just a memory. The arrangements for the big band singers are geared to the musicians, and the vocalist is simply one part of the whole, commanding no more than a third of a two-to-three-minute performance. With "You'll Never Know," from the popular film musical *Hello Frisco Hello* (1943), we hear the Dick Haymes voice that would electrify listeners, now free to linger over the low notes, displaying the feeling the lyrics demanded (he would say that he really learned how to act through singing), his phrasing and articulation achieving a new level of distinction.

During his years with the big bands, before he achieved fame as a singer-actor on his own, Dick Haymes recorded more than thirty-five songs with James and four with Goodman. Seven of them were top-selling hits. The training he received—working with the three greatest musician-bandleaders of the era, traveling with the musicians, finding the strength for seven shows a day for weeks on end, recording in the early morning hours—was a rough road, and he had drawn upon the same strength he had been forced to summon from the time that he was a young boy, uncertain of where he might be the next day. Undoubtedly, his longtime pattern of acting based on the necessity of the moment, with scant thought of consequences, was as helpful here as it had been then. He was young, handsome, with a lovely wife and child; he had overcome seemingly insurmountable obstacles, and at last the world seemed ready to embrace him. He packed his family for the trip to California, scarcely prepared for the success that would forever change his life.

CHAPTER 3

"That First Wild Wind of Success"

When the Haymes family left New York for California in October of 1943, three of Dick's most recent recordings were certified hits: his July 3 recording of "It Can't Be Wrong" was now second on the charts, the July 31 recording of "In My Arms" had reached number seven, and "You'll Never Know" was at number one, having sold more than one and a half million copies. Dick's royalty on that one recording was eighteen thousand dollars, in sharp contrast to the twenty dollars per side for his big band efforts. For the first time in his life, he had no money problems and could look forward to fulfilling his commitments to radio, Decca records, and Twentieth Century–Fox Studios.

Dick was very anxious about his overnight success. He remembered years later that on his way out to California with his family on the Super Chief, his main worry was, "I've gotta make it. Will I make it? Will I be good enough? Do I stand a chance?" He was particularly nervous about his forthcoming radio series, as it would be live—and broadcast twice for the two coasts. He realized that there would be no opportunity, as there was in recording, to make alterations and corrections in his delivery.

The family bought a lovely home in Longridge Estates, in Van Nuys, California, in the San Fernando Valley. They purchased the home from composer David Rose, and in one of Marguerite's séances at her son's (she regularly practiced mystical techniques), she predicted that it would be sold back to Rose, as it would be. Although they considered it a modest investment, it included a swimming pool, tennis court, music room, along with two convertible automobiles. Although the fan magazines reported dutifully on their lives, the bases for those pieces were press releases drawn up by Fox Studios. One magazine reported that Dick and Joanne did not like Hollywood nightlife, whereas, in reality, they were swept up by the glamour of nightclubs and parties, often resulting in periods of exhaustion for Dick, who had to keep up with a demanding schedule. As in all celebrity success stories, the early interviews and magazine stories establish a persona that will forever haunt their subject. Dick was portrayed as a devoted family man who preferred to spend his leisure time in the family's swimming pool—and, indeed, photos of a closely knit family accompany every article. Dick promoted a singular myth for fan magazines—that before he was twenty he had sold a series of short stories to the prestigious *Atlantic Monthly*. He even described them as based on the mysterious life in the sewers of the Paris beggars ("hoboes fascinate me"), and the magazines remarked on their timeliness in the light of recent reports that the French underground used the elaborate sewer system during the German occupation of Paris. No record exists of such stories, but Dick and the studios were clearly trying to establish the persona of a sophisticated, even erudite young man. (The likelihood is that Dick did write short stories during his teens and would like to have had them published in an upscale magazine. It is to his credit that he cited the *Atlantic Monthly*, however inaccurate his account of their publication.) The public portrait of Dick Haymes is not far from the truth: he did speak three languages, did read widely, and had certainly traveled in his youth. But once the public persona takes hold—as his did—it made him far more susceptible to later criticism than other stars who did not succumb to the nation's infatuation with strong family images during wartime.

Even the fan magazines admitted several years later, after that image had already begun to unravel, that once the couple arrived in California, the party circuit began, and Dick and Joanne were caught up in the fever of celebrity nightlife. Dick admitted, "There's a rush act in Hollywood but when you first arrive you don't know that. You're excited by the glitter and you think you must go to every party that's given. You tell yourself that "you must be seen here and there. The races call you. Palm Springs calls you. Home becomes a place where you phone the cook and say you won't be back for dinner. Joanne and I did Hollywood like that." Joanne would remember, "We never did a sensible thing and probably never will." But she was going to have another child in the spring of 1944, and so her activities were somewhat curtailed for the next few months.

Richard Haymes Jr. remembers the early years at Longridge, the big white house and the nanny, Mrs. Estes, whom the children called "Noonie"— for him, a surrogate parent—who took care of them. He remembers that his parents had separate rooms, his father's filled with leather furniture and horse paraphernalia—saddles and leather bridles, for Dick was an avid rider—and his mother's stately, opulent bedroom which reminded him of either the private quarters of Queen Elizabeth or Scarlett O'Hara's lush bedroom. Richard remembers that the family had a lot of money and gave lavish parties. When they moved to Encino a few years later, the parties were held around the swimming pool, where the distinguished guests gathered. Richard (called "Skip" in those days), after playing at the pool with the guests in the afternoon, was sent to bed by 6 PM, just as the drinking was beginning. He remembers that all of the "action" was at the pool and that he enjoyed the parties voyeuristically from his bedroom window that provided a clear view of the celebrants.

When Dick arrived in California, he had already been titled "King of the Jukeboxes," and newspaper articles and fan magazines heralded him as the rival to Crosby and Sinatra. Columnist Louella Parsons intoned, "Haymes Joins Crosby, Sinatra Ranks." He won a West Coast disc jockey's popularity poll in 1943 (over both of his rivals), and in the competitions that were routinely set up by the media, he quickly became the foremost contender. One reporter noted that crooning is divided into two sections with Haymes "heading the juke-boxers and Frankie Sinatra breathing incense limpidly over the radio and spilling over into Haymes's juke domain. They say in Hollywood that in every household where there are two or more dancing youngsters there's sure to be controversy about which is the better singer—Haymes or Sinatra. They say you can't sell a Haymes fan a Sinatra record and vice versa." In the sheet music magazines that were popular, like *Song Hits* and even one titled *Sing with Dick Haymes*, his new status was repeatedly proclaimed in such headlines as "Meet the Juke Box King." A fan magazine article titled "Rival of Crosby and Sinatra" continued, "Dick Haymes, Juke Box King, is off to a flying start in Hollywood and threatens to be keen competition for Bing and Frank." One studio press release in 1945 noted that Fox was grooming the young singer (whose face was unfamiliar to most audiences) for the same kind of success that they had built for their other young actors, Henry Fonda, Tyrone Power, and George Montgomery. Richard Haymes Jr. recalls that his father (like his uncle Bob) was too intelligent to be "into the whole show business thing the way Sinatra was. . . . I think Dad felt he was a generic star. He was a very spiritual man, not religious in the doctrinaire way, but saw it as his Karma to play the role of Dick Haymes, the big star."

Perhaps most dramatic for the Haymes family was the sudden change in its financial situation. Dick had earned two hundred thousand dollars in eight months from his film contract (twenty-five thousand dollars per picture), record sales, and radio host salary. His new recordings routinely sold widely, and in his first year in California he had ten charted recordings, followed by a streak of hits—another ten—in 1945. His financial freedom did not change Dick's habits, however. Peter Marshall, Dick's brother-in-law, looking back over the early years in California, believes that success came too suddenly for both Dick and Joanne; they were "children in paradise. . . . Dick was a man-child. He was one of the highest salaried Americans for two years, and he'd spend money as soon as he got it." Marshall notes that taxes were very high, and Dick never thought in terms of the Internal Revenue Service that later in his career would pursue him ceaselessly. He had "no sense of saving or investing." Once, Marshall recalls, a friend had a lot on Ventura Boulevard available for a ten thousand dollar investment. Dick refused (the lot eventually became the site of a successful supermarket) and chose instead to invest in a nightclub on Catalina Island that, he boasted, "made [him] a v.p." The club soon closed, and Dick's investment was lost. As Marshall, who was extremely fond of Dick Haymes, recalls, his brother-in-law had no common sense, and people took advantage of him: "If he lent you one hundred dollars, he never expected it back. If you lent him anything, you'd never get it back." Marshall attributes Dick's approach to money to Marguerite Haymes and her adventurous life; she somehow found whatever income was needed for her next escapade. Marshall recalls a story about Dick's attempt to follow the advice of his manager to be thriftier when traveling and living in hotels. Dick had been ordering room-service drinks—three or four drinks for the two of them. His then manager, Mort Good, admonished him, "Dick, that's a waste of money. Buy a bottle and just order ice." True to his instincts, Dick did buy a bottle, but not from a liquor store. He simply called room service for a bottle, accompanied by a bucket of ice. Dick's disregard of financial matters was evident in his exceptional generosity. When he had money, he bought lavish gifts for his wife, his children, and his friends. Often, after a concert, he might be so moved by one of his fans that he would take off his watch and give it to an audience member who came up to speak to him. His managers soon learned to carry a supply of watches for such occasions.

Dick Haymes's exceptional good nature during these early years of success was apparent in the medium that had largely created his appealing persona: radio. Before he started work on his first film, his radio show, *Here's to Romance*, sponsored by the Bourjois Company's Evening in Paris Beauty Products, began broadcasting on CBS at 10:30 ET on Thursdays, with Dick as the MC in Los Angeles and Buddy Clark serving as host in New York City. The announcer was Jim Ameche and the orchestra was led by

Ray Bloch. Dick's previous radio performances were very different from his role on *Here's to Romance*, where he was showcased. When he appeared with Tommy Dorsey and his orchestra, Jo Stafford, and the Pied Pipers in 1942, he was simply part of a prearranged format, with no opportunity for him to offer deeper, more probing arrangements or to reveal the versatility that would characterize his performances on radio, where he would be the star. The formula did not vary, and, as we know, Dick's unhappiness led him to leave Dorsey.

The difference in the quality of his performance on his own program was palpable. He was totally self-assured, charming, in the Bing Crosby manner, unafraid of the ad-lib, completely at ease with his guests, and clearly widening his range both in the choice of his material and in his delivery. His generosity to others was noticeable, as in the broadcast where he introduced "'A Lovely Way to Spend an Evening' which was sung by my good friend Frank Sinatra in *Higher and Higher*" (1943, Sinatra's first film-acting role). Some members of the audience, aware of the "battle of the baritones," laughed after Haymes mentioned his "friend" Sinatra. He then proceeded to offer an original rendition of Sinatra's hit, adding a caressing note to the repetition of the key phrase, "to spend an evening," and extending "lovely" to convey the depth of feeling suggested by the lyrics. So sensitively did his radio performances convey the mood of the wartime years that in June 2004 a television dramatization of some stories by Sam Shepard, "See You in My Dreams," featured Dick Haymes's radio performance from the mid-1940s of the title song ("I'll See You in My Dreams").

Haymes hosted the program from California for several months, even as he was making his first films for Fox. His next radio show, the Auto-Lite *Everything for the Boys/The Dick Haymes Show* was immensely popular, starting in June of 1944 and continuing until July 1948. (The title of the program was changed to *The Dick Haymes Show* in October 1945, after the war had ended.) Haymes's radio career lasted for more than a decade, *Club 15* following from 1949 through 1950, *The Carnation Show* in 1950, the NBC *Bandstand* in 1956 and 1957, and *Make Mine Music* with the Percy

:_:_:_:_:_:_:

Faith orchestra on CBS Sunday mornings in 1958. Most radio programs in the 1940s would be on the air for thirty-nine weeks, with a thirteen-week hiatus.

Through the decade and into the early 1960s, Dick Haymes would be a guest on innumerable radio and television programs. In his early radio shows, the sponsors spared no expense in securing the most popular guests for the Auto-Lite programs: Judy Garland, Betty Hutton, Dorothy Lamour, and Jimmy Durante were just a few of the film stars who appeared with regulars, singer Helen Forrest (replaced by Lina Romay and then Martha Tilton when Forrest left the show in 1947), conductor Gordon Jenkins, and the singing group Four Hits and a Miss or the Swingtet. The program was aired Saturday nights for thirty minutes, and for a time it was the highest-rated radio program in the country. A music historian describes *The Dick Haymes Show* as one of the last "blockbuster" popular music programs on network radio. Helen Forrest said that working on the show was fun because of the host: "Dick was terrific and made work fun." Dick always loved to joke, and his ad-libs often threw her off, making her laugh on the air. He knew that her laughter was infectious and that listeners would warm to her—as they did. In fact, on occasions when she laughed in public, people would approach her and say, "You must be Helen Forrest." She remembered how his female fans would write and phone Dick and wait for him after each show. Dick and Helen often toured to promote the show, and their duets on records resulted in six best-sellers and, in total, over a million copies of sheet music. Commenting on the popularity of the show, one newspaper, noting that sixty-five people were responsible for the radio show, praised the baritone voice "that has brought him up the ladder from coffee and doughnut money to a six figure income in less than three years."

Both singers entertained troops throughout the country and visited military hospitals. On one occasion, Helen Forrest became so distraught at seeing the badly wounded men that she was unable to sing. Dick was sensitive to her distress, advising, "Just don't do it, Helen You can't do it, so stop trying. You tried. It's not your fault. It tears you apart."

Gordon Jenkins remembered the work that the radio shows entailed: "We had to do a whole half-hour of new music every week, plus the writings that my colleague and I had to do . . . had a big orchestra and plenty of rehearsal time." Jenkins believed that Haymes "probably had better breath control than anybody [he'd] worked with, with the possible exception of Tommy Dorsey. . . . Dick would take a big one and he'd just go on indefinitely. . . . He never made any trouble of any kind. He was possibly the least temperamental."

Popular singers of the period, Dick Haymes among them, made many recordings that were sent abroad directly to the troops. Like Sinatra, he was troubled that because he did not serve in the military his career had soared; and also like Sinatra, he compensated by becoming an indefatigable entertainer for servicemen. Servicemen in the United States and abroad were now among the most enthusiastic of his radio listeners. Thus, when Twentieth Century–Fox started production on Dick Haymes's first film, *Four Jills in a Jeep*, they knew that there was a large audience eager to see the young man who had rapidly become one of the three most popular recording artists and radio entertainers in the country. Sinatra's first film, for RKO, apart from his singing, was mediocre, as were several of his MGM films, and his acting skills were undeveloped. Crosby, of course, was a master, in films as well as in all the other areas of entertainment that he had conquered over the past decade. Dick Haymes knew that his future depended on joining the ranks of Hollywood movie stars, and he was delighted that in the Fox studio he seemed to have found yet another new home. Years later he would remember that the studio was like "going to a nice university. Everybody was friendly. Nobody competed." He remembered that those were the days when Darryl Zanuck ran the studio, and there were trees in a courtyard and an attractive commissary. There was no jealous competition that he recalled. Dick said, "[It was] a very sensible studio. I can't think of any head cases coming out of 20th the way they came out of Metro."

During the war years, only Metro-Goldwyn-Mayer had greater film rentals and stars with more drawing power than Twentieth Century–Fox.

There was no overseas market, but production costs averaged $1 million per film, and attendance was very high. Because of wartime cutbacks in the use of film stock, production at Fox was cut from fifty features to thirty-one (in 1943), and B films were reduced far below twenty to twenty-five, which was the prewar norm. From 1939 to 1947, Fox produced more Technicolor films than any other studio. Color was particularly effective for the kinds of mainstream American subjects Zanuck promoted, among them the musicals that featured Fox's leading stars of the genre: Alice Faye and Betty Grable. (Zanuck served in the military after the outbreak of the war, returning to the studio in 1943.) The main emphasis throughout the early to mid-1940s was on drama, romance, and musical comedy, most of them becoming box office successes, if not memorable artistically. Zanuck had upgraded the quality of Fox productions before the war years, releasing *Young Mr. Lincoln* in 1939 and *The Grapes of Wrath* in 1940. By the mid-1940s, it had become one of the major companies in the industry, leading all other studios in gross box-office receipts ($185,673,000 in 1945) and releasing such important films as *How Green Was My Valley* (1941), *The Ox-Bow Incident* (1943), *Laura* (1944), *The Black Swan* (1942), and *The Gang's All Here* (1943) with the studio's major star, Alice Faye. Faye had been with the studio since the early 1930s and had appeared in such successful black-and-white musicals as *In Old Chicago* (1937) and *Alexander's Ragtime Band* (1938). By the early 1940s, after her marriage and motherhood, she cut back on her film work, but did make the highly successful *Hello Frisco Hello* (1943), where she introduced the song that would virtually make Dick Haymes's career, "You'll Never Know." Faye could not record the song, as the studio did not allow their stars to enter into recording contracts, but wartime audiences who longed for the peace and tranquility that she expressed so tenderly on the screen remembered her moving rendition fondly. Unlike Metro-Goldwyn-Mayer, which had a separate blue-ribbon musical unit led by Arthur Freed and featuring such renowned musical stars as Gene Kelly, Fred Astaire, and Judy Garland, Fox did not have a separate unit and its musical stars were not as popular as Metro's, and most critics would agree, not as technically skilled. Apart from

Alice Faye, Fox musicals of the 1940s featured Dan Dailey, June Haver, and their biggest star, Betty Grable, who had joined the list of top-ten box office players in 1942 and would become number one in 1943 as well as the highest-paid star in Hollywood. She remained one of the top-ten stars for ten years, reaching the second position in 1947–48, when her salary had climbed to $325,000 per picture—almost equivalent to the millions of dollars contemporary stars receive today. By the mid-1940s, she would become the highest paid star in Hollywood.

The budgets for Dick Haymes's first two films for Fox were moderately high: $1,125,000 for *Four Jills* and $1,635,000 for *Irish Eyes Are Smiling*, the latter in Technicolor. By contrast, his next effort, *Billy Rose's Diamond Horseshoe* (1945), with the leading Fox star, Betty Grable, would cost $2,535,000, making it the studio's most expensive film of the year; its success undoubtedly persuaded Fox to invest $2,245,000 for Haymes's next effort, *Do You Love Me?* (1946), a mediocre film that nevertheless was also a box office success. Dick had been paid $25,000 for his first screen role.

Fox mobilized its publicity department, issuing press releases and slightly fictionalized biographies of its potential new musical star, Dick Haymes. Newspapers and fan magazines picked up the stories and repeated, almost verbatim, the studio's version of Haymes's career, which appealed to readers steeped in the mythology of self-made, hard-earned success, another in the never-ending saga of American dreamers whose dreams came true (ironically, at this time Haymes's Argentinian citizenship was mentioned rarely, and, if so, casually). Announcing the release of *Four Jills in a Jeep*, *Movieland* noted, "Dick Haymes, the radio singer . . . has what it takes to make a place for himself on the screen and you'll be screening-hearing more of him." The *Milwaukee Journal* headline read, " 'You'll Never Know' Boy Shines on Screen Soon," noting that the song "brought him a fat Hollywood contract. . . . And, more important to those million juke fans, it gives them their first good opportunity to size up the man behind the voice." Fox circulated stories that Dick Haymes and Perry Como were signed up for future productions "at big money," and Haymes's description as "King of the

Jukeboxes" was cited by virtually every reporter. The official Fox press release stated, "He has a million fans who have never seen his face. . . . [I]n *Four Jills in a Jeep* he becomes a face: an actor as well as a singer. He has a huge following eager for a glimpse of him: they are the Haymes fans who buy his records by the hundred thousand hot off the mould. He has also a smaller public to impress, the people who don't know about him at all. It's a somewhat trying position. Dick Haymes the actor has to live up to Dick Haymes the singer." The release went on to describe him in the most flattering terms, introducing the notion that fans would perpetuate for decades: "He has the eternal youthfulness which made the Duke of Windsor a world favorite during the years he was known as the Prince of Wales." Then the press release dramatically evoked the mythology of Dick's rise from virtual poverty after he left Dorsey to his sudden ascension to the top of the *Billboard* charts. Perhaps because they had touted Haymes widely, Fox cannily controlled his appearance in the film. *Four Jills in a Jeep* was clearly the vehicle provided to an aspiring Fox musical star, introducing him to a new audience, but waiting for his next two films to mold him into a genuine star. For Dick, with the radio show, the studio work, the press attention, and the fan letters, there was little time to think about whether or not he could achieve success in films. Fox said he could, and Dick had no reason to doubt those who now controlled his career. His voice would be his—but for the rest, the studio could make him into a movie star. Of that, he was certain.

Among the talented performers in Fox musicals, there was no male singer—only a few actors with pleasant voices (like John Payne) who could serve as romantic foils to their female stars. But perhaps the most important impetus for the first Dick Haymes feature was the war and the role of entertainers who traveled throughout the world to visit the troops. In addition to performers like Haymes, Sinatra, and Helen Forrest, a notable group of entertainers, Kay Francis, Mitzi Mayfair, Martha Raye, and Carole Landis, had made a USO tour in 1942–43 that was widely reported in the press and particularly in the fan magazines. The studio did not foresee the press criticism which would call *Four Jills in a Jeep* a "bald-faced attempt to capitalize" on the tour, so self-serving that GIs walked out on one showing. The *New York Herald Tribune* critic, Otis Guernsey, decried its self-praise as "almost sickening"; and Bosley Crowther in the *New York Times*, in addition to describing the film as "a raw piece of capitalization upon a widely publicized affair," dismissed it as a "claptrap saga" that seemed to have been tossed together too quickly.

Of course, a good deal of the criticism reflected contemporary sensitivity to films using the war effort for any reason but to promote patriotic fervor at home and to bolster the morale of the soldiers. MGM's *For Me and My Gal* (1942) was not criticized for its blatant use of patriotic fervor by entertainers, but today that particular aspect of the film might make us cringe (fortunately, Gene Kelly's brilliant debut and the perfection of his performances with Judy Garland make the theme of the film easy to overlook). The criticism now seems overstated and almost irrelevant: what is interesting, and valuable, are the musical performances by Dick Haymes and Jimmy Dorsey and the extraordinary cinematography by one of the only five cinematographers honored by a star on the Walk of Fame, J. Peverell Marley, who had worked on the first of his 117 films in 1923.

The film opens with an on-screen statement about the entertainers, their bravery and commitment, and after the first credits, in extra large letters, "And Introducing in his First Motion Picture Dick Haymes as Lt. Dick Ryan." The special dance numbers were staged by Don Loper, and the director was the experienced, if not great, William A. Seiter, who would later direct Dick Haymes in *Up in Central Park* and *One Touch of Venus* (both 1948).

The first sequence is directly aimed at the war effort. Set in a CBS studio, it is a command performance for the troops, featuring the brightest name on Fox's roster, Betty Grable, singing "Cuddle up a Little Closer" from her recent hit movie, *Coney Island* (1943) as soldiers are shown listening at their bases with rapt attention. Kay Francis, who had aged considerably from her starring years, is trying to put together a group to entertain GI's overseas—and eventually succeeds as Mitzi Mayfair, Martha Raye, and Carole Landis join her. Comedy is introduced by Phil Silvers playing a liaison soldier who arranges for them to move from place to place. Probably the silliest aspect of the film is the ersatz romances between Kay Francis and a colonel (who is also a doctor) and between Carole Landis and an officer whom she weds in the film. Martha Raye's comic routines are unexceptional—too broad, as usual—and Carole Landis is both beautiful and stiff as a performer. There is little doubt that the introduction of Dick Haymes provides the best reason to look at this film, and he is aided considerably by Peverell Marley's fine cinematography.

In a major musical sequence in a large hall with a staircase in the center and two large columns on either side (they keep the film frames closed so that our attention doesn't wander away from the performers), Jimmy Dorsey's band plays a fine jazz number, with several soloists featured, the rendition made even more impressive by the situating of the band between the two columns. We see Dick Haymes walking in, then Raye performs "Mr. Paganini," and the camera moves over a half-dozen beautiful women to the top of the staircase where a very young, very handsome and poised young man in uniform, filmed in medium close-up, begins to sing "How Blue the Night." In a seemingly effortless performance, Haymes's voice is commanding: his low notes better than they had ever been, his articulation perfect, and, above all, his ability to convey the sincerity of the feelings expressed in the lyrics makes this an unforgettable moment in the film—or in any film.

Dick Haymes sings his second song, "You Send Me," as he looks at Mitzi Mayfair—a genuine courtship in song, once again sung with confidence and mastery of every note. In the last line, in contrast to his effective low register through most of the number, he ends backed by a choral group, "Don't ever send me away from you," on a higher register that, because of the contrast, introduces a note of hope and longing. Dick Haymes would always say that he learned to act through singing—and here it is apparent.

The romance between Dick Haymes and Mitzi Mayfair is played for comic effect, in contrast to the traditional heavy-breathing love affair of Carole Landis and John Harvey, who plays her officer/lover. When Dick arrives on a motorcycle and looks for Mitzi, he takes her aside to a table in a little bar and hums before he sings "How Many Times Do I Have to Tell You?" which is, of course, his declaration of love. Marley composes this as a two-shot throughout, filmed medium close-up, so that the feeling is conveyed with genuine intensity to the film viewer. Indeed, when Haymes stresses the word "miss" in the line, "How many times do I have to say I miss you," we can see how accomplished he is as an actor through his singing.

Clearly, from the brief description above (and I did not linger on Carole Landis's love story and wedding, the most artificial episodes of the film), this is not a major film, nor, as a black-and-white venture, is it an elaborate production. Costs were clearly kept reasonably low, and the film was plainly intended to boost morale among soldiers and civilians—even though that intent backfired. But today, it is enjoyable primarily as Dick Haymes's auspicious debut; indeed, Fox was so confidant in his ability that he began immediately to work on his next film, *Irish Eyes Are Smiling*, and was already scheduled after that as the leading man with the studio's premiere star, Betty Grable, in the lavish *Billy Rose's Diamond Horseshoe*.

One of Twentieth Century–Fox's most popular and reliable forms of the movie musical was based on the careers of lesser-known musical figures, both composers and performers. These films were generally set in the past and allowed the directors and cinematographers opportunities to create colorful and often fanciful worlds that had a special appeal to wartime viewers both at home and in the armed forces. The costumes and settings were especially appealing in Technicolor, which the studio used in almost all of its period musicals.

Irish Eyes Are Smiling, also released in 1944, was directed by Gregory Ratoff, the colorful Russian actor/director (he would later direct Dick Haymes in *Do You Love Me?*); and among the other creative participants were Natalie Kalmus as color consultant, Hermes Pan, dance director, and Alfred Newman, music director. The producer was the famous writer Damon Runyon, with whom Dick struck up a close friendship. This film would be the first starring vehicle for June Haver as well as for Dick Haymes, and Fox promoted it heavily. The studio was always looking for an actress similar to

Betty Grable, who had succeeded Alice Faye as the top Fox musical star, and June Haver would become second only to Grable, especially after Alice Faye left the studio in 1945 after a feud with Darryl Zanuck.

Irish Eyes Are Smiling is based—very loosely—on the life of Ernest R. Ball (1878–1927), composer of such popular songs as the film's title, as well as "Mother Machree," and "Let the Rest of the World Go By," written in 1919, which would become associated with Dick Haymes as his personal theme song in many of his radio performances throughout the 1940s.

The plot, unfortunately, is plodding and predictable, but the musical numbers, in the best Fox tradition, are expertly staged and sung, the costumes are impeccable, and the supporting cast, notably Monty Woolley, Anthony Quinn, Max "Slapsie Maxie" Rosenbloom, and opera greats Leonard Warren and Blanche Thebom, add sparkle to the ensemble. The film opens in a music school in Cleveland, where young Ernest Ball is fired for writing songs the school regards as demeaning (e.g., with a popular, ethnic appeal). He then takes his songs to a burlesque house where he meets a scrappy Irish showgirl, Mary "Irish" O'Brien, played by June Haver. Mistaking her for the star of the show, he plays and sings for her ("I'll Forget You") when the star walks in and, seeing Mary in her dressing room, has the young woman fired. So the "boy meets girl, boy loses girl, boy gets girl" plot begins—and Ernest and Mary will be at odds until the end of the film.

A major scene, set in New York City at Broadway and Twenty-eighth Street, is colorful and intriguing as we view horses and old cars in a bustling street. Ernest is determined to find Mary, but is unsuccessful and takes a job plugging songs. After a poorly received number, he takes off his coat and sings his own song, "Let the Rest of the World Go By," and the audience cheers. This moment is a highlight among Dick Haymes's musical performances in film. He begins singing loudly and firmly, and then, when the audience begins to listen, he softens his tones and is joined by a choral group. Haymes brings out the song's themes of longing and hope, his low notes familiarly rich and his face conveying the sense of the lyrics. In its typical rags-to-riches montage, Ernest Ball becomes a success, as his songs reach the Palace Theater, to be sung by a leading mezzo-soprano, Lucille Lacey (played by Beverly Whitney) and the newspapers headline, "Newcomer takes Broadway by storm."

Later, Haymes's rendition of "When Irish Eyes Are Smiling" is thrilling—conveying the depth of his love for Mary. But she is gone, and the remainder of the film details his efforts to find her, her realization that his feelings are genuine, and the machinations of everyone to reunite them.

After a final lavish number featuring June Haver, "Bessie in the Bustle," the lovers are reunited and the final sequence opens with a still frame of an "Album of Memories" by E. R. Ball. The book opens and the frame comes to life, first with an Irish jig, and then with the title song and "A Little Bit of Heaven." The film ends with a spirited rendition of both the title song and "Let the Rest of the World Go By" as the scrapbook closes.

Unfortunately, screenwriters Earl Baldwin and John Tucker Battle were unable to write dialogue that might energize the sagging plot. However, viewers knew in advance the kind of film they would be watching; the appeal was clearly the music and the star performances, and, on this level, *Irish Eyes Are Smiling* succeeds. It is true that June Haver was not the ideal romantic foil for Dick Haymes that Betty Grable and Vivian Blaine would prove to be. Ideally, there should have been additional occasions for Haymes to sing and act, for his role demanded him to react to silly devices in the narrative rather than to play a commanding role. Fortunately, Fox probably realized that he was under-used in this film, for in his next role, opposite Betty Grable, there would be little doubt that Dick Haymes was an authentic Hollywood leading man, just on the verge of genuine stardom.

Shooting on *Irish Eyes* was completed by December, and before starting his next film, Dick left for New York City for a brief engagement at the Roxy Theater. Joanne remained at home because of her pregnancy. (Helen Joanna was born on May 13, 1944.) By the time he returned to the studio to start work on his next film, his star had risen even higher. His new recording of "Put Your Arms around Me" and "For the First Time" sold 250,000 copies in the first week of its issue, and his income had soared well above two hundred thousand dollars since the previous April, only one-eighth of that from his film salary. And in his appearance at the Roxy, his fans matched the convulsive welcomes that teenagers had been giving Sinatra for several years.

Haymes barely had time to relax before shooting began on *Billy Rose's Diamond Horseshoe*. The title was drawn from the famous nightclub on West Forty-sixth Street in New York City, in the heart of Broadway's theater district. Billy Rose, the legendary show business entrepreneur, had founded the establishment in 1938. It quickly became noted for his then unique formula of cheap food and drinks and scantily clad chorus girls, maintaining its popularity for decades.

The film, as so many other musicals of the era, has a weak and utterly predictable plot. But it is enormously entertaining, primarily because of its two stars and a colorful and talented supporting cast. Betty Grable is the focus of the film, and she delivers on every level: as a dancer, singer, winning actress, and charismatic beauty. In his role as an aspiring young doctor who wants to try show business, Dick Haymes has his best role to date, youthful, charming, graceful, and infinitely appealing in his vocal performances. Clearly, he has acquired greater ease and confidence than he exhibited in his two previous film appearances. He works particularly well with Betty Grable, and the rapport between the two is palpable. He does not fade next to her vibrant personality, but rather offers a wholesome and winning "boy next door" charm that succeeds in releasing the more vulnerable aspects of her persona. The casting is ideal, and Fox would try to repeat the success of this first pairing of the two performers. As we shall see, the personal relationship between Dick and Betty Grable would develop as they worked more closely over the next few years. And it would become more complicated, as she became the wife of one of Dick's best friends, Harry James.

The film opens with young Joey (Dick Haymes) going to the nightclub, Billy Rose's Diamond Horseshoe, to see his father, Joe Davis, who stars in the show. He sees the poster of Bonnie Collins (Grable) outside the club and walks in. Grable appears in center stage, and from the moment Joey looks at her, he is in love—and his admiring stare conveys not only his admiration, but his sexual longing as well. Indeed, it is the sex appeal of both stars that propels the film.

The conflict as to whether young Joey will go to medical school or enter show business is as artificial as the musical numbers, but perhaps that is part of the charm of the film. Audiences knew that the lovers would triumph, but the enjoyment of the film—and others similar to it—is simply watching it play out, particularly when the performers are so talented.

Unquestionably, the interaction between the two stars and their individual musical performances carry the weight of the film. Dick Haymes had already performed admirably in two films, the first successfully introducing him as a film performer to his adoring fans and the second offering him a more lavish and sophisticated venue. Clearly, the studio had plans for him, and his third film would cement his position as a major new Fox star, the musical equivalent of the studio's most romantic male lead, Tyrone Power, who became a good friend of Dick Haymes during their years at Fox.

When Haymes sings his first song, "I Wish I Knew," it is the first effort in his courtship of Grable. (The song would become a hit recording for him in 1945.) He uses the microphone here as he did on stage—as a supporting player in his entourage. Indeed, his handling of the microphone is the equivalent of Grable's dancing, and as he pours his heart out to her in song, it becomes a major element of his charm and sex appeal. The next step in their courtship is accompanied by one of Haymes's most successful songs, one that would be identified with him throughout his career, "The More I See You." The two young people are on a boat on the Hudson River. She has been cool, teasing him so that she can acquire a fur coat from Claire (Beatrice Kay) if she spurns Joey and forces him to leave the nightclub, allowing his father to marry the older woman who has been shunted aside by the doting father. The plot is all pretext, but the song is genuine: when he begins to sing, she is eating popcorn and ignoring him. He notices a fan on the bench and waves it behind her head, creating a chill that forces her to move closer to him. As he sings, "Can you imagine / How much I love you," he places his arm around her; and at the climax of the song, she looks dreamily into the distance. With quiet conviction, he has told her of his love, and she has revealed her own feelings for him. The delicacy of this moment is extraordinary—one of the finest in musical films of the era, done with minimalist precision by two genuinely gifted performers.

There are several other spectacular numbers, at their best with Grable's singing and dancing (the choreographer was the brilliant Hermes Pan), but the last number unites the two lovers in one song in an unusual placement: Grable is on stage with the other performers, and Haymes is in the wings (he has become a physician), and the director, George Seaton, daringly cuts away from what would normally be the final grand musical number to Dick Haymes, standing in the wings, quietly reprising "The More I See You" in a more upbeat but no less poignant expression of love. The film ends with a kind of double vision: the performers on center stage and Haymes's voice caressing the final notes of the song as he holds the microphone almost as though it were his lover. The brilliantly staged show numbers, the almost surrealistic filming of Cavallaro's piano and other instruments, the comic and satirical musical acts, all are finally subsumed in the tender and melodic ballad that provides a moving conclusion to the many exaggerated antics that often seemed to overwhelm the delicacy of the love story.

After the release of *Diamond Horseshoe* in the spring of 1945, Dick Haymes was truly a household name. The *Los Angeles Times* headlined, "Dick Haymes Has Role Depicting Own Career," seeing in the film a parallel with the star's acceptance as a popular singer. The leading movie magazines devoted four- and five-page spreads to the parents' doting on their son and newly arrived daughter, swimming, riding, and enjoying "wonderful sun-drenched hours" together. After each film, Dick would make concert appearances in New York, Boston, and Chicago. He, Helen Forrest, and Gordon Jenkins did one of their Auto-Lite shows from the Roxy, bringing excited young Haymes fans to the New York City theater.

On one such occasion, some Sinatra fans actually scratched him, so jealous were they of his booming popularity. Reporter Diana Gibbings in the *New York Times* noted how much Haymes's performance at the Roxy resembled Sinatra's, and for good reason:

> Mr. Haymes has been clever enough not to deviate in character from the well-trodden path. Teenage attachments, after all, are not distinguished by a craving for originality. His approach to the microphone, for instance, whether in his current NBC show or before the footlights at the Roxy, is a mixture of bonhomie and an awkward diffidence becoming to a college sophomore. He shuffles from one foot to another when accepting applause, and wears a suit whose outsized shoulder pads usually find favor at campus barbecues. As one bobby soxer unexpectedly remarked, "He puts it on kinda thick." Mr. Haymes' singing, however, is by no means as callow as his mannerisms. He is gifted with a natural rich baritone which he uses expertly and whose range and quality are more than adequate for the popular ballads (sung sweet and slow) and occasional folksongs which remain the limit of his public repertoire. He does not as a rule attempt to evoke a querulous sigh from his feminine audience with rhythmic affectations. He sings his numbers straight, and that is what they like about him.

Clearly, his awkwardness—a genuinely shy response to fan's feverish adoration—made him even more popular with them and conveyed the essential boyish charm that Hollywood would exploit in his subsequent films.

At the end of a Chicago performance in August at the Oriental Theater, where he had closed a record-breaking two-week engagement, Dick jumped into a taxi so that he might make a quick getaway from the waiting crowd. He was actually driving the cab when a teenage girl flung herself at the moving vehicle, landing between the hood and the fender. Dick was appalled that she had actually risked her life, saying that he would gladly have given her the autograph she desired. He would write his name thousands of times during an engagement that scheduled six shows a day. Fans would line up, and he would dutifully sign anything they presented to him: photos, autograph books, scraps of paper. On that day, he was too exhausted for the signings, and, as a result, he was pursued by the ardent fan. When asked by a reporter what it was about Haymes that appealed to her so much, one of the girls responded, "It's the way he looks at you that gives me wings . . . no frills, no sobbing, no strangling of the microphone." He had an indefinable "something" that set the young women on the edge of their seats when he began to sing. The fan pointed out that when in the final bars of "I Wish I Knew" he hunched his shoulders and crooned, "If I'm a fool just say so," just about everyone in the audience jumped up simultaneously, screaming, "No, no, Dick! Not that!"

Dick was very attentive to his fan groups, writing them to acknowledge their letters and gifts and explaining why he couldn't answer them immediately. As he told one fan, after finishing the filming of *State Fair* in early 1945 and then going immediately into production for *Do You Love Me?* he was scheduled to begin shooting *The Shocking Miss Pilgrim* in early 1946. He wrote to Virginia Haywood, the president of his fan club, "For the past few weeks this has been more or less my schedule: at 6:00 AM I get up and an hour later finds me at the studio where I work until 6:00 PM. My evenings are spent in radio rehearsal and in meeting my record dates. I find but little time for my own pleasure—one of which is keeping closer contact with you and my other friends." In every letter to his fans, he mentions how he enjoys riding with Joanne and spending time with his two children on Sundays. He apologized to Virginia for belatedly acknowledging the anniversary of the club. A popular teenage fan magazine, *Calling All Girls*, featured an article on Dick's special appeal to the young girls who were attracted to the performer and might want to join the fan club.

In addition to his regular performing schedule, he appeared as a guest on many radio shows, including Jack Benny's show, where, along with Andy Russell, Dennis Day, and Bing Crosby, they formed a quartet to perform a commercial (and Dick interjected a plug for his Auto-Lite show). *Variety* reported every rumor about his career, many of them planted by his manager to create interest in more dramatic film roles. It stated that Dick Haymes would make a gradual switch from singing to dramatic star and that in his next film, *Mine on Sunday* (which was never produced), he would sing only one song. After that, the article continued, he would do two pictures a year, one with music and one without.

During their residence in Longridge, the Haymes family experienced a major disruption to their seemingly idyllic life. In the spring of 1945, the studio announced that Dick and Joanne would be having a trial separation to attempt to work out their marital difficulties. The public was assured that there would be no divorce. Dick moved to a hotel in the San Fernando Valley, and Joanne and the two young children remained in the house. Within a few weeks, their problems were resolved and Dick returned. He was quoted as stating, "We had some misunderstandings, but a few lonely days apart convinced us how unimportant they were." Soon the magazines picked up the story; with a headline undoubtedly suggested by Fox, "Marriage Is Worth Saving—Dick Haymes," the story vaguely referred to misunderstandings and jealousies that for a few months threatened to derail their marriage. The article suggested that the Haymes's experience might help other troubled marriages, a typical moral "spin" that magazines used to excuse their blatant sensationalism. Publicly, Dick blamed himself for being old-fashioned, believing that his wife, who had for some time been interested in resuming her aborted career, should stay at home with the children. Clearly, as the children were cared for by others, the reason lay elsewhere. He admitted publicly that he was domineering and opinionated in his approach to their problems. He attributed the episode to "the dangerous time in a marriage . . . when the first flame dies down . . . when a husband and wife . . . love each other less deliriously. There is a letdown, like getting back to a normal temperature after running a fever of 105. This may happen any time from fourteen days to fourteen years after a wedding, depending on the individuals concerned." He attributed their problems to difficulties in adjusting to their seesawing fortunes. He then recounted his loneliness without the family for four months (somehow the separation has been extended by the magazine) and showed a thoroughly conciliatory husband eager to be part of the kind of home life for which every man longs.

What were the real reasons for the short breakup? Clearly, one of them was, indeed, Joanne's desire to return to her career. She was signed for her first film, *Abie's Irish Rose* (1946), which was produced by Universal and Bing Crosby Productions and proved a box-office disaster, but she then signed with Howard Hawks, of Warner Bros. studios, who directed her in several highly successful westerns. The other issues affecting their marriage were never mentioned in the press. Dick's weaknesses, as his son and others attest, were women and drink. In these early days of success, his drinking was not the problem that it would become in the next decades, but his attraction to women and theirs to him was little changed from his teen years. As Helen Forrest wrote, "I never saw women go wild over a man the way they did over Dick. Oh, maybe more swooned over Sinatra, but I doubt they melted when they met any man the way they melted when they met Dick and he gave them that grin of his. Most women who met him would do anything for him." She continued, offering probably the key reason for their separation, "I lied for Dick. I don't know many men I'd have lied for, but I lied for him. When he was married to Joanne Dru, he made me his alibi. I went along with him even though I really liked her. We used to rehearse songs for the show at their place and I felt terrible about betraying her, but I couldn't help doing what Dick wanted me to do. He'd tell her we were on business for the show and I'd cover for him if she'd call. We'd go to the Brown derby or some place for lunch or dinner and sit down and I would stay put and he would go out the back door. . . . I covered for him for three years."

A fan magazine story, "Who Said Divorce?" alluded to the night that Dick was having dinner with a group of friends at a restaurant after his radio show, and he was seen laughing and chatting with an attractive young woman who had come with one of Dick's friends. The story indicates that the harmless chat was reported to Joanne. "We saw Dick having dinner with a strange girl . . . or perhaps she was with someone else in the party . . . or perhaps he was table-hopping . . . or something," the friend reported. Joanne heard the same kinds of reports every few weeks, until she finally confronted Dick—and they fought over her efforts to return to her career. The magazine report suggested that Dick's attraction to other women was a scarcely veiled Hollywood secret, and the "official" account was actually a public relations effort to cast his philandering in a more palatable form for his many fans.

Forrest remembers that years later, after Dick's death, she and Joanne talked about it and about how Joanne had trusted her. Joanne understood, telling Helen that she always knew how he was with women. She realized in retrospect that the first flush of success so overwhelmed them that they never really spoke about the tensions that were present in their marriage, even after he returned to their home.

Dick was delighted to be reconciled with Joanne and the children, and the pictures of the reunited couple show them as happy with each other as when they were first married. Several fan magazines dutifully reported Dick's "confessions" about his role in the separation, with no mention of his straying and great emphasis upon the importance of home and hearth to this "average American." He was still working at Fox on the film with which he would forever be associated, *State Fair* (1945), and he could finish the film without the incessant questions by the media. He was back at home, driving his slick Lagonda convertible to and from benefit performances ending with dinners at the Brown Derby or Romanoff's, where he would invariably pay the check, usually with crisp new bills.

State Fair was a remake of the 1933 film that starred Janet Gaynor and was directed by Henry King. The 1945 version has the only score that Richard Rodgers and Oscar Hammerstein II wrote directly for a film, and one of the songs, "It Might as Well Be Spring," won an Academy Award (sung by Dick Haymes at the ceremony in 1946). The film is pure Americana, but without the obvious self-parodying of another American classic, *The Music Man*, which opened as a Broadway show in the next decade. Released as World War II was ending, the film is a celebration of our country: middle-American values of home, family, true love, the land, and, above all, confidence in the possibilities that the future held. Rodgers and Hammerstein had stunned audiences several years earlier with their Broadway smash hit "Oklahoma," and they imparted many of the same qualities of the show to this film, with the notable absence of outstanding dance performances (despite the presence of Hermes Pan as choreographer). The studio assembled a top cast: Jeanne Crain, Dana Andrews, and Vivian Blaine, along with Dick Haymes, who had shown such promise in his earlier Fox films. The supporting cast was outstanding as well: Charles Winninger, Fay Bainter, Percy Kilbride, Frank McHugh, and Donald Meek. Direction was by the experienced director of Betty Grable and Alice Faye musicals, Walter Lang, and the musical direction was by Alfred Newman.

When Jeanne Crain sings "It Might as Well Be Spring" (actually it is the voice of singer Louanne Hogan) before the family leaves for the fair, she expresses the restlessness and longing for the excitement that only true love will provide—the essence of great popular songs of the era. The melody, at different tempos, provides much of the background music for the film. Dick Haymes's first important song is "It's a Grand Night for Singing," after he has met the sophisticated band singer Emily Edwards, and he picks up the chorus as they dance together at the nightclub where she is performing. Haymes looks very boyish throughout the film, as the director clearly intended; he sings beautifully and moves gracefully. His role is genuinely endearing to audiences—he *is* the boy next door—but, unfortunately, he lacks Dana Andrews's dark, simmering sex appeal. As well as he performs and sings in this film, Haymes's boyish image would persist in the public's imagination, as *State Fair* became one of the major musical hits of the era.

He sings part of "That's for Me" and introduces "Isn't It Kind of Fun," which is a typical courtship-in-song that he carries off as well as in his earlier films. But clearly, the focus is on the Margie/Pat love story, as Wayne, after discovering that Emily is married, albeit separated from her husband, after a drunken revel with the song plugger, played by McHugh, returns home to take up with his college sweetheart, played by Jane Nigh. Both Andrews and Blaine are city bred, and both are attracted to the girl and boy from the middle-America farm. The contrasting romances add some tension to the script, but because Emily is married, there is no possibility that her romance with Wayne will survive in these years of the strict Hollywood censorship code.

Haymes's last song is a reprise of a few bars of "It's a Grand Night for Singing," but he is so likable, and his voice so rich and melodious, that many film viewers believed that his part was equal to Andrews's. He always looks attractive, in a wardrobe that accentuates his fine physique and graceful mobility. But it is clear, from the contrast between the two, that at this point he has neither the acting skill nor the extraordinary good looks of Dana Andrews, who had filmed one of Fox's most successful suspense thrillers, *Laura* (1944), and would go on to star in a major postwar film, *The Best Years of Our Lives* (1946). (Ironically, Andrews's career would falter after his success in the latter film.)

Dick Haymes's recording of "It Might as Well Be Spring" would go on to become one of his top recordings, reaching the *Billboard* charts in November of 1945 among the top-ten hits and later competing with the equally popular recording by Margaret Whiting with Paul Weston's orchestra. (The Haymes version would remain on the charts for twelve weeks, reaching the fifth position; Whiting's would last for eleven weeks, reaching number six.) The song became one of the staples of his repertory and remained so throughout his career. In March 1946, Dick would sing "It Might as Well Be Spring" at the Academy Awards ceremony, where it won the Oscar for best song in 1945.

Louanne Hogan remembers working with Dick Haymes. They had met earlier when both sang for Tommy Dorsey: "I remember going to Montana or Utah [with the band] traveling on the Pullman cars, with no heat whatsoever. I remember Dick and I sitting there, clinging to each other, freezing to death." She remembers working with him on *State Fair*, and after the film was released, when he was touring the country, he would always mention her as having done the singing for Jeanne Crain. He even said that her rendition was superior to Margaret Whiting's hit recording of

"It Might as Well Be Spring," a conclusion that Hogan does not entirely support. [In the 1970s, Louanne Hogan was working in a department store, and Margaret Whiting recognized her and said in front of onlookers that Louanne's version of the song was better than her own!] She still remembers how devoted Dick was to his family: "He used to show me pictures of little Skippy, his baby son."

In the same year, Alice Faye was making what would be her last film for Fox, *Fallen Angel*, and her last film until her appearance almost two decades later in an inferior remake of *State Fair* (1962). Much of her footage was cut from the final version of the film, and the focus was on Linda Darnell as Darryl Zanuck tried to build up the younger performer. Perhaps the most painful decision was to drop Faye's rendition of the song "Slowly." She felt that the film had been ruined and left the studio without picking up her personal belongings from her dressing room. Dick Haymes's recording was used in the film, and it would go on to become another hit record, reaching the twelfth position on the charts. After the release of *State Fair* and Haymes's ongoing success as a popular singer, his future seemed assured.

After the film's release, Dick and Margaret Whiting performed for a week in Boston at the RKO Boston Theater. They shared the same manager, and Bill Burton booked the two thinking that their best-selling recordings of the same song would make them a particularly exciting combination. For Margaret, it was an important engagement, coming at the beginning of her career, and she was excited to work with Dick, whom she liked personally and whose work she appreciated. They started at 9 AM and worked until 10:30 or 11:00 PM, beginning the week with six shows per day and ending with nine. They would walk together from their hotel to the commons, the theater, and, if possible, back to the hotel. But the major problem was getting out of the theater, for she remembers, "The girls were so nuts about him." He got along very well with musicians. "He was a natural, a great singer. He'd just open up his mouth." But she cannot understand why he is forgotten today. She also remembers his sense of humor. "He was so funny;

I can still hear that laugh of his." He was, she recalls, deeply in love with his wife. He tended to keep people at a distance, talking mostly about music, and she recalls that in Boston he did not seem as nervous onstage as others reported that he was. "He was happy, singing, joking, never had a chip on his shoulder then, but did later." She says that he had "class. He was a connoisseur. He must have been a great lover." She never had a problem working with him, even under the pressures in their Boston booking. "He was happy, singing and then shouting, 'Whoops! That's a good one!'"

Dick and Joanne realized that the stresses of their dual careers and the constant nightclub rituals left them little time for their home, children, and, above all, relaxation. In the summer of 1946, they sold the Longridge home and bought a ranch in Encino on almost four acres. Dick wrote to his fans, "Our new farm is really a complete dream home: it has on the property a nice home as complete as one could wish for, a nice nursery home for Pidge and Skipper [the children would live in separate quarters from their parents], a guest house that sits next to the pool which we can also use for a rumpus room or rooms, a tennis court and a barn for my horses with large corrals and a big work ring encircling a permanent pasture." His brother, Bob, worked with him for weeks on preparing the grounds and helping with the move. After the family moved in, the guest house was usually occupied: Bob was there with his songwriting collaborator, Marty Clarke; Peter and his wife, Nadine, would also stay in the guest house; and another friend of Dick, Eddie Pike, was there as well. Buddy Bregman, the record producer, remembers meeting Dick and Joanne at the Racquet Club in Palm Springs when he was very young. Dick and Joanne would invite him to their home, and he was thrilled to go up in Dick's Navion plane. He remembers what a superb pilot Dick was. Bregman would spend a dozen weekends with the family, playing tennis with Peter Marshall and his wife. Peter, noting the expense of the lavish dinners and parties at the Haymes ranch, was concerned and advised Dick, "You've got to cut down." Dick responded in his usual jocular fashion by posting signs, "One glass of milk per person." Marshall believes that the couple's lifestyle came too quickly for them to comprehend and to manage. Dick's son suspects that his agent, Billy Burton, was stealing a good deal of money from his father, for the actor/singer paid little attention to financial matters. The money was coming in steadily, more than he could spend, and Dick assumed it would continue forever. His approach to money was consistent with that of his mother; eventually he would have to face his disregard of financial matters.

His son remembers the playhouse on the ranch grounds, the corral, the path behind the house that led to a chicken house, the lavish bar with saddles for stool seats, and, above all, the Christmas celebrations when he received "a sea of presents" that took him more than a day to open. He remembers that he adored his father but that they would get into rows when he sometimes awakened at 4 AM (he was only four years old), and his father, with a hangover from the evening's pool party, would be angry with him. Dick was never abusive to his children or to his wife, but he did have a temper, and his son, looking for attention, would defy him, seeking to provoke his anger—and in that way get his attention. Indeed, both Joanne and Dick were loving but distant, both focused on their careers. Dick constantly vocalized in the house, and Richard Jr. remembers that he had a dream where he flushed his father down the toilet while he was vocalizing. His daughter Pidge (her given name is Helen, after singer Helen O'Connell) remembers an incident when she was very young. She had a doll, Liza, that she carried everywhere. Her brother mischievously threw it into the pond. She cried and told her father. Dick, angry at his son, took him to his room and made him stay there for the remainder of the day. The punishment seemed too harsh to the little girl, so she went up to her father and falsely confessed, "I did it." Clearly, Dick, never having had a father, and having had a mother who had no skills as a parent, did not know how to be a loving yet firm father. He was better with his daughter, who was not a difficult child, and their relationship in the future would prove far less abrasive than that between Dick and his son.

After the move to the ranch, Dick turned down a concert tour to be with his family, but Joanne was at work again filming *Red River* on location in Arizona. Here she met actor John Ireland, who would in a few years become her second husband.

Dick was still the favorite singer after Crosby—and still rivaling Sinatra. He won the *Motion Picture* 1946 poll as best crooner, over Perry Como and Andy Russell (Crosby and Sinatra were ineligible), and regularly scored among the top four in *Downbeat* polls. He was asked to appear on *Your Hit Parade* as a Saturday night regular, but he signed a three-year renewal with Auto-Lite. He was making a new film, too, as Fox quickly cast him in a musical with his friend Harry James and the beautiful star Maureen O'Hara.

Originally titled *Kitten on the Keys*, the film opened in 1946 as *Do You Love Me?* Seeking to capitalize on the names of its stars, the studio was attempting to recapture the audiences that during the war had flocked to theaters to see Betty Grable, Alice Faye, Sonja Henie, and others who appeared in the immensely popular Technicolor musicals. Unlike *State Fair*, it had a sophisticated veneer, but lacked the charm and appeal of that film's outstanding Rodgers and Hammerstein score.

Maureen O'Hara's career was assured by the time she made this film, although perhaps her two most popular hits, *Miracle on 34th Street* (1947) and *The Quiet Man* (1952), had yet to appear. This film was a departure for her: she did not perform in musicals, and although she had a superb, well-trained voice, here she is simply a beautiful centerpiece. The action—such as it is—belongs to Haymes and Harry James, both at the peak of their careers. Maureen O'Hara did not like the film; she would not go into details, but although she loved working with Dick Haymes, with whom she became very friendly, I suspect that she thought the producers were not using her talent well—particularly, her voice. She remembers the friendship between Dick and Harry James and his wife, Betty Grable, and she speaks highly of Dick's professionalism on the set, his warmth and cooperation with the cast and crew.

As a contract player, Haymes did not question his roles. He had no reason to quarrel with a film that cast him as the leading man (Harry James could not be taken seriously as a romantic rival), and he had the opportunity to sing and to charm his leading lady. Sadly, his talent—which shines here— was not given a screenplay worthy of him or of the other cast members, and the film is, as a result, flimsy (Maureen O'Hara shares this view). Released soon after *State Fair* (1945), it is particularly disappointing, for the earlier film had an unforgettable score, good direction, and a decent screenplay. Throughout the film, Haymes and James offer several solos—each one extraordinarily fine, even though the music is not up to the level of Rodgers and Hammerstein.

The most appealing aspects of the film are, first, New York City (maybe today, after the events of September 2001, we are sensitive to the city as backdrop in many films of the past) and then Harry James's music and, above all, Dick Haymes's singing. In this film, he is relaxed and romantic, playing a "groaner" in the mode of Sinatra (he's dieting to get skinny and the girls flock to him in a scene reminiscent of Sinatra's early appearances in concerts). He sings "As If I Didn't Have Enough on My Mind," half of "The More I See You," and, in addition to the title song, a light, swinging "Moonlight Propaganda," featuring dancing, a Central Park backdrop, and a romantic kiss as the two lovers, Haymes and O'Hara, discover their feelings for each other through the music and the song lyrics.

The film is forgettable, but Dick Haymes is not. He is assured, relaxed, good-looking, and his voice, diction, phrasing, and delivery are perfect. Throughout, he maintains his dignity and charm, and I could not help wishing that the film were better written, that the studio had aimed higher in producing a vehicle with such talented players. Even Betty Grable appears at the end—a joking allusion to her marriage to James—but, finally, the film is mediocre and unmemorable, as *State Fair* and *Billy Rose's Diamond Horseshoe* are not. For Maureen O'Hara, the role is a throwaway. She could and did do better. When we recall her luminous performance in *How Green Was My Valley* five years earlier, we wonder why Fox would cast her in a film where she had nothing to do. Incidentally, she and Haymes had no chemistry between them, as he did with Grable, and she with John Wayne. And Harry James simply was no actor.

So, unfortunately, Dick Haymes gave one of the most charming and effective performances of his career in a film that is otherwise just a pleasant, slight, and forgettable confection. Perhaps, had producer George Jessel and director Gregory Ratoff found a clever scriptwriter, *Do You Love Me?* might have been the vehicle that would ensure Dick Haymes's future as a movie star. Nevertheless, it did well at the box office, with gross domestic rentals of three million dollars, the sixth highest Fox film of its eighteen major releases in 1946. *State Fair* was tied with *The Dolly Sisters* as the top box-office success of 1945 with four million dollars in domestic rentals. Yet the production costs for *Do You Love Me?* were almost two hundred thousand dollars higher than those for *State Fair*.

During these years of Dick Haymes's early success, his brother, Bob, was trying to launch a movie career, but was far less successful. With the exception of one of his last films, an Abbott and Costello vehicle, all of his roles were in B movies produced by Columbia Pictures, and all eminently forgettable. In a 1945 film, *Blonde from Brooklyn*, he appears as a good-natured young singer, with a round, innocent face, albeit a weak mouth, and a first-rate voice. Indeed, it is clear that Bob Haymes was a good singer—not in the class of his brother or of any of the very popular baritones of the period, but clearly skilled in his delivery, notably in his articulation and in the force of his lower register. In *Abbott and Costello in Hollywood* (1945), he is the young leading man who makes a number of appearances in-between the antics of the two stars. Again, his voice is excellent, but his presence on the screen does not seem natural. In later years he would become a successful songwriter and work in television. He and Dick were close in these years, but there would be long periods when they didn't communicate at all. Nevertheless, when Dick needed his brother, Bob would be there for him, as he had been for Bob during their peripatetic childhood.

And what of Marguerite Haymes as her elder son's career soared? As one might expect, she was a prominent figure on the Hollywood scene. She became a friend of Carole Landis, sent out press reports stating that she was going to open a chain of voice studios in major cities throughout the United

States, and sat for many interviews with fan magazines, embellishing her own career and her role in her son's success. In 1945 she published a book, *The Haymes Way*, subtitled *Make the Most of Your Voice*, in which she outlines the principles that will help the average singer achieve his or her potential. The inside cover offers an often fictionalized account of her musical career. Then she offers advice—how to sing "the Haymes Way." The tone is consistently encouraging and upbeat, offering aspiring singers generalized advice relating to relaxation techniques, posture, practice, microphone use, and various musical exercises. On the back cover, Marguerite, looking young and attractive, sits on a couch with a large book beside her in front of two oversized pictures of Bob and Dick. At the foot of this page are two endorsements from her sons. Bob says, "Words can never express my gratitude and appreciation for the understanding and guidance you have always given me in my career. Thanks a million and the best of luck." Dick writes, "Here's hoping everyone will gain from the great opportunity offered in this book, all that I have from your wonderful coaching and constant help. The best of luck and my sincere gratitude." Both sons felt they had been cajoled into those endorsements, and both resented Marguerite's use of their names, their words, and pictures. Undoubtedly Marguerite's training as a singer had influenced her sons, but both of them always believed that she consistently used their success to further her own ambitions and always exaggerated her role in their achievements.

Dick was not unlike Marguerite, however, in some of his interviews with the press and the fan magazines. He wanted to win an Oscar, noting that he had asked Darryl Zanuck to star him in *The Foxes of Harrow* (the part went to Rex Harrison in the 1947 film), and he declared his interest in the kind of swashbuckling films that starred Tyrone Power and Errol Flynn. He had reportedly asked Darryl Zanuck to cast him in the role of Johnny Nolan in the film adaptation of Betty Smith's best-selling novel, *A Tree Grows in Brooklyn* (1945), but Zanuck felt he was too young for the role of the alcoholic father. James Dunn received an Academy Award for the role, and Dick always regretted his own missed opportunity. He reportedly studied the work of Cary Grant and told the press that he and his wife were starting a local stock company for aspiring actors either in Encino or downtown Los Angeles. They would rent the theater, buy the equipment, and Dick would act in each play and direct a few. He further noted that he had started his own record company, the Beverly Publishing Company, with a partner, Larry Shayne: "While we haven't crashed through with a big hit, we have kept out of the red." There is no record of the company or of any of its releases.

He recorded two songs with the top performers of the day, Bing Crosby and the Andrews Sisters, and he was already scheduled for a repeat film performance with Betty Grable in *The Shocking Miss Pilgrim*. New film roles and his greatest triumph as a singer lay just ahead. But early success, as F. Scott Fitzgerald wrote, leads to "the conviction that life is a romantic matter." Dick Haymes could not know it, but his early success would prove, like that of so many young celebrities, including F. Scott Fitzgerald, a "single gorgeous moment" that would gradually fade into a "wistful past."

CHAPTER 4

The Perils of Celebrity

The Shocking Miss Pilgrim reunited Dick with Betty Grable, who was now married to his good friend Harry James. The two stars grew very close working on the film. James and his band were on a summer tour of the Midwest, and, according to Helen Forrest, Dick and Betty were together at the close of each day's shooting. Forrest reports that when James returned from his tour in August and discovered that his wife and close friend were dining intimately at a restaurant, he "stormed" in waving a pistol, which fortunately did not go off. Dick would never then admit to having had an affair with Betty Grable, but late in life he confessed to Forrest that, indeed, they had during the making of the film. His relationship with Harry James remained cool for years until they were reunited when they performed together in the late 1970s, years after James's divorce from Grable in 1965 and her death in 1973. Affairs between costars were not unusual in the Hollywood of the 1940s, nor are they today, but the postwar social climate did not permit the kind of sensationalizing of star dalliances that is now ubiquitous. Dick Haymes and Betty Grable were, for the fan magazines, good friends, as he was with Betty Hutton, Maureen O'Sullivan, Lana Turner, and others with whom Helen

Forrest asserts he also had brief affairs: "I used to say, 'Who is it this time?' And he'd grin and say, 'You really don't want to know, do you?' and I'd grin and say, 'No, I don't.' And I didn't." Forrest credits Dick Haymes with having more genuine charm than most of his contemporaries. "He could melt your knees with a smile, cause your heart to flutter with a touch." From his earliest years, women found him irresistible, and his position as a leading Hollywood star enhanced his appeal. Clearly, the marriage would eventually succumb to the pattern of infidelity—even to the point where Joanne Dru would accept the overtures of her costar, John Ireland.

During the next year—from 1946 through 1947—Dick Haymes's recording career would continue successfully, scoring ten additional hits, two of them duets with Helen Forrest and two reaching top-five positions on the *Billboard* charts: "Oh, What It Seemed to Be" and "Mamselle," the latter from the Fox hit dramatic film *The Razor's Edge*. *The Dick Haymes Show* on radio was highly successful, recruiting the most important Hollywood stars as guests. A particularly appealing feature was a new family-style skit with Haymes playing the part of clean-cut Harry Burton. In addition to his own radio show, he appeared as a guest on many of the most popular variety and musical programs as well as on the dramatic series *Suspense*, also sponsored by Auto-Lite, that replaced his show in July of 1948. The next year, he would headline the nightly *Club 15* show sponsored by Campbell Soups, where he would share the spotlight with singer Evelyn Knight, the Modernaires, and the Andrews Sisters.

Haymes would continue to make appearances throughout the country, consistently drawing large, enthusiastic crowds to the Roxy in New York City, to the Gate Theater in San Francisco, where he performed with Helen Forrest, and to the Steel Pier in Atlantic City. The son of the owners of the latter venue, George Hamid Jr., remembered that Haymes was the Pier's biggest draw in 1946: "Dick Haymes was the hottest single attraction in the country. And he played for us at the pier and was hotter than Sinatra and hotter than Perry Como." His career seemed to be on the right track, although closer scrutiny by him or by his manager would have exposed the vulnerability of his work in films.

Although it is not unusual for films today to earn over $50 million on opening weekends, the highest attendance records were set in 1946. Although admission fees were minimal, the year-end total profits for all studios reached $1.5 billion, with approximately 80 to 90 million people attending movies every week. Twentieth Century–Fox was very profitable, nine of its features that year grossing over $3 million. Indeed, it led all the other studios in profits that year, its films a mix of melodrama (*Leave Her to Heaven*), light comedy (*Centennial Summer*), westerns (*My Darling Clementine*), film noir (*The Dark Corner*), and, of course, the Fox staples, musicals (*Three Little Girls in Blue*). Two new musicals starring Dick Haymes were in production in 1946, *The Shocking Miss Pilgrim* and *Carnival in Costa Rica*, and the studio expected both to equal or exceed revenues from similar films that Fox had been releasing regularly.

Although *The Shocking Miss Pilgrim* would perform passably at the box office, its production costs ($2,595,000), were far too high in relation to its earnings ($2,250,000). It did not prove as profitable as Betty Grable's other, more successful film that year, *Mother Wore Tights*, where she was paired with a new Fox actor whose chief talent was dancing, Dan Dailey, who did not aspire to the same kind of romantic leading man status as Dick Haymes. By 1947, Darryl Zanuck, like other studio heads, was convinced that the public would respond to lavish productions, and several of the most expensive films of the year would prove unable to offset those costs. Unfortunately, the two films that starred Haymes were not box office hits; Betty Grable could attract audiences even to a slight film, but *Carnival in Costa Rica* would prove to be a great disappointment for Fox, Zanuck, and, of course, Dick Haymes.

The Shocking Miss Pilgrim is a synthetic story about a graduate of a business college that trained "typewriters" for Remington and Company, which pledged jobs to all the graduates who would go into the business world and use the new typing machines. Cynthia Pilgrim (Betty Grable) secures a job with the Pritchard Company in Boston, where her boss is John Pritchard (Dick Haymes), a handsome young man who is prejudiced against women working in an office. The plot lines are clear from the outset: he will have to accept the new independent woman, and the two will ultimately fall in love. As a further hurdle, after he learns to accept a woman as an office worker, he must learn that his wife is entitled to continue her career.

As they had in *Billy Rose's Diamond Horseshoe*, Haymes and Grable worked well together and there was an obvious chemistry between them. The music—by George and Ira Gershwin—is excellent; Grable sings "Changing My Tune" effectively, but the two most popular songs are the duet, "Aren't You Kind of Glad We Did?" (later banned by the radio networks for too-suggestive lyrics), and the ballad, "For You, For Me, Forevermore," both recorded for Decca in September 1946 by Haymes with Judy Garland, accompanied by Gordon Jenkins and his orchestra. Ira Gershwin had combed his late brother's files and came up with these few songs. He screened the film before it opened and liked it, but the reviews were not good, and Grable fans rejected the film's restrained new image of the wartime pinup girl—in long dresses and tightly coiffed and darkened hair—so unlike the singing and dancing star of so many lush musicals. A recent critic, however, softened the harsh appraisal of the 1940s, conceding that it "bubbled with charm" and "deserved a better reception."

Dick Haymes is relaxed and confident in his role, and when he waltzes with Grable and they sing complementary tunes ("Waltzing Is Better Sitting Down" and "Waltz Me No Waltzes"), the grace and ease of both performers are seductive. But the highlight of the film is "For You, For Me, Forevermore," a genuine courtship song that provides Dick Haymes another opportunity to display his acting skills through his singing—his rich baritone caressing the lyrics and expressing with conviction the feelings that the dialogue merely suggests.

Carnival in Costa Rica, which was released in 1947, would be Dick Haymes's last film for Twentieth Century–Fox. His leaving the studio was undoubtedly the result of both the poor performance of the film and the attempt by the studio to cut the high production costs incurred by the eighteen films released that year. Further, audiences were beginning to decline, and of the musicals, only those featuring Betty Grable were regarded as potentially profitable. One of the solutions for the studio was to release from contract some of the stars whose films had failed at the box office. Unfortunately, Dick Haymes would be among that group. The only musical stars to remain with the studio into the 1950s were Betty Grable, June Haver, and Dan Dailey, Grable's frequent costar.

Even before the film opened, Haymes must have suspected that it would be unsuccessful. He expressed interest publicly in becoming a director and a producer and indicated that he was less than satisfied with his film roles, even that of the young brother, Wayne, in *State Fair*, where the biggest challenge was to convincingly portray an eighteen-year-old when he was almost thirty. He planned to try musical comedy, where he might really "sing out," and to broaden his base of performance.

Carnival in Costa Rica's production costs were $3.2 million (its sets alone were the fourth highest of the year for Fox, almost 7 percent of its budget), and the domestic rentals were only $1.0 million. In addition to *Mother Wore Tights*, *I Wonder Who's Kissing Her Now*, a musical about the career of a turn-of-the-century composer, Joe Howard, and featuring June Haver, turned a modest profit. Its leading man was Mark Stevens, a Fox contract player with passable musical skills.

The failure of *Carnival in Costa Rica* should not be blamed on Dick Haymes. From the outset, the conception and the execution of the film are deeply flawed. Gregory Ratoff, now a good friend of Dick Haymes, once again is his director. His costar is Vera-Ellen, who would become a fine partner for Gene Kelly in *On the Town* (1949), one of MGM's classic musicals. Essentially a dancer, she is out of her element in duets with Haymes (her voice was dubbed), and the two are thoroughly unconvincing as a romantic couple. The second leads are Cesar Romero, a familiar figure in Fox musicals, and Celeste Holm, in her second film after an auspicious stage run as Ado Annie in the hit Broadway musical "Oklahoma." The production numbers are gaudy and, for all of the fluttering costumes and lavish sets, unattractive.

Although he is the romantic lead, Haymes is swallowed up by the pyrotechnics of the production, as virtually any actor or musical star might be (perhaps Danny Kaye, with his irrepressible comic sense, could have survived). Clearly, this film would not add to his luster as a film star, but he was still featured in the popular press, which praised him for having developed into a "restrained and sensitive actor."

During the final year of his association with Fox, Dick Haymes's life story was featured in innumerable magazines—the facts highly glossed, but the image unvaryingly favorable. He was often pictured on one of the Palomino horses he raised at his ranch; his apparently loving wife and children were featured, and he consistently referred to his exciting plans for the future—notably, in new business enterprises. One of the most common threads in these pieces was his generosity, his befriending others, often supporting them and providing them with work and opportunities to make careers for themselves. Among that group were Eddie Pike and Marty Clarke, who had been his schoolmates. (Clarke would go on to collaborate with Bob Haymes as a songwriter.) He had kept in touch with Pike, who served in the war, and on the basis of Pike's description of D-Day, he secured him a job as a writer. He hired Clarke to help with his new firm, Beverly Music. He helped singer Matt Dennis start his singing career, although Dennis's songwriting efforts, unlike his own years ago, were as promising as his voice. (Dennis would write such classic songs as "Will You Still Be Mine?" "Let's Get Away From It All," and "Everything Happens to Me.")

His stand-in, Bob McCord, in a lengthy memoir printed in June 1948, tells a remarkable story of Dick Haymes's kindness and generosity. They had met on the set of *Four Jills in a Jeep*, where McCord had been pulled from his work on a potato field to serve as an extra whom they needed to ride a horse. Their shared interest in riding led Dick to invite McCord to spend a weekend at his home in Longridge. Both men were at the time expecting a second child, but McCord's finances were limited, working as a ranch hand. Because their measurements were so similar, Dick suggested that Bob McCord work for him as his stand-in on his next film, *Irish Eyes Are Smiling*. After the filming ended, McCord had no job, so Haymes hired him as his personal secretary/assistant. McCord notes that all of Dick's protégés performed well for

him: "His old boyhood pals Eddie Pike the writer and Marty Clark, the composer, ride the boom with Dick not because he is their pal, but because they
can produce, and he knows it." Alec Milne, who taught Dick to fly, became
prosperous as a pilot-instructor on the basis of Dick's recommendations.
McCord accompanied Dick on tours, handling the details of travel, setting up
appointments for interviews, and helping with the fan mail. He quickly
became part of the Haymes family establishment, firing domestic workers
whom Joanne had hired but didn't have the heart to discharge, exercising
the horses, and, on Dick's days off, swimming with him in the family pool.
Dick even made McCord become a pilot, so enthusiastic was he about flying,
and he personally came to McCord's house to install a playground he had
purchased for McCord's children. McCord concludes by praising his boss as
"an overgrown kid playing Santa Claus," a man who has stood up "under
all the pressures—fame, money, adulation, to a degree which had wrecked
many another young star—and stayed regular."

Dick Haymes's public image had never been better, as his generosity
was touted even by the studio, which sent out a press release about his
efforts on behalf of a talented eighteen-year-old singer, Joanell James, for
whom he secured a break in a new film. A teenage magazine, *Sweet Sixteen*,
carried a flattering cartoon history of Dick Haymes's life, celebrating "the
Young Man with a Voice" and concluding, "To millions of Americans, Dick
Haymes is . . . the best."

Newspapers reported some of his other activities: in April 1948, he was
the first person to pilot his plane from Van Nuys Municipal Airport to
Washington, D.C., over Skyway 1—the first of a proposed network of similar sky routes, consisting of distinctive ground markers to guide private pilots
on cross-country flights. He would finish his trip by flying to New York,
where he would broadcast for the next two weeks. A notice that he lost his
driving license for two weeks for speeding was buried in small print in the
Los Angeles Times in June, as was the settlement of the financial dispute
between Dick and his former manager, George (Bullets) Durgom, to whom
he paid $17,502. The birth of their third child, Barbara Nugent, in September

1947 provided many occasions for photographers to snap the apparently idyllic family enjoying treasured moments together. It was reported that Dick received the news of the birth of his third child in his airplane, flying back home from San Diego, where he had been entertaining troops. In March of 1948, newspapers showed photos of the baby's camera debut that were reprinted throughout the country. The focus throughout these years was on Dick Haymes's success—as one article described it, "Haymes & Company is one of the most Horatio Algerish tales every to come out of movieland."

When Fox dropped Dick Haymes from its roster of contract players, he had no difficulty in securing a two-picture deal with Universal Studios. The publicity department of the studio was working feverishly to sustain the popularity that his recordings were still enjoying. *Variety* reported that between June 1947 and June 1948, Haymes's recordings sold more than those of any other popular singer, almost seven million, with his royalties reaching $215,000 during that period. In fact, his most successful recording, "Little White Lies," which sold more than two million copies, remaining on the charts for twenty-three weeks, was released in April 1948, just one month before the opening of his first Universal film, *Up in Central Park*. That hit record became Haymes's signature song, resisting efforts by any competitors, then or later, to surpass his version. He remembered that the song was recorded at the end of a four-side session with Gordon Jenkins and his orchestra and the singing group Four Hits and a Miss. They had an hour of studio time left, and all of them wondered what to do next. Jenkins suggested "Little White Lies," but Haymes was not inclined to do it until they both agreed to imitate the old Tommy Dorsey recordings, like "I'll Never Smile Again." Haymes never loved the song, but was pleased by its popularity, even though "it was a spoof on Dorsey." He said, of the recording session, "Nobody was a genius, it was just an accident."

Publicists, playing on the heavily promoted popular image of the star, suggested using the Haymes San Fernando Valley ranch as the setting for photo shoots of him and his family, and one ventured that papers might report "A Day with Dick Haymes," focusing on his career in movies, radio, recording, music publishing, flying, breeding and riding horses, along with other activities. Noting that crooners and musicians are the busiest persons in the performing arts, they stressed the business activities of Bing Crosby, Harry James, and others. Many of the publicists' notes indicated that audiences would respond to articles stressing his and Joanne's happy marriage, and one even ventured to suggest that their five-year-old son be put into a scene in the new film.

While Dick was working on his first Universal film, Joanne was making director Howard Hawks's *Red River* (1948), which became an instant classic, featuring Montgomery Clift and John Wayne. Her next film, another western, to be released the following year, was *She Wore a Yellow Ribbon*, directed by John Ford. It too was widely praised and was a box office hit, giving her increased prominence as a star. For Dick, although publicly praising his wife's career, it cannot have been easy watching her succeed in A-level films while his own film career was clearly on a downward spiral.

In 1947, the publicity machines at Universal-International pictures were starting up to devise a major campaign for the newly planned film adaptation of a moderately successful 1945–46 Broadway musical, "Up in Central Park," produced by Mike Todd. The Sigmund Romberg–Dorothy Fields score, critics felt, was the most memorable aspect of this unserious exposé of Boss Tweed and his gang in New York City in the nineteenth century. In 1946, it had been rumored that Fred Astaire might be interested in directing the film, planned as a big-budget Technicolor extravaganza. But somewhere along the way, those plans were dropped and, instead, the film released in early 1948 is a tepid, somewhat lumbering black-and-white adaptation with little to recommend it save the valiant efforts of a talented cast.

What happened in the interim is uncertain—at least the files I studied at the Universal archives at the University of Southern California are not clear. But if we remember that big musicals were already on their way out after World War II, and that Universal was not in the same league as

MGM or Fox, it is clear that they were hedging their bets on this film and that they were guided by a preview audience's indifference to the musical numbers. So they simply cut most of the songs—the more colorful numbers from the original print—and what is left is the outline of a story with some excellent singing by Haymes and Deanna Durbin (who goes on much too long in most of her numbers) and an engaging performance by Vincent Price as Boss Tweed—a far cry morally and physically from the historical figure. There was only one song from the original Broadway show that was a hit, "Close as Pages in a Book," and for some reason it is heard only as background music to open and close the film.

The plot concerns Boss Tweed's rigging of a mayoral election by hiring disembarking immigrants to vote in the name of persons who were dead or otherwise unable to make it to the polls. Deanna Durbin is Rosie Moore, and her father is played by Albert Sharpe, who had acquitted himself with distinction earlier on Broadway in *Finian's Rainbow*. Dick Haymes is John Matthews, a muckraking *New York Times* reporter who tries to take down Boss Tweed and in the process falls in love with Rosie.

There are only a few musical numbers in the film; and at least for Durbin, they are not particularly appealing. The memorable musical moments are provided by Dick Haymes in a duet with Durbin in "Carousel in the Park" and, notably, his one single number, "When She Walks into the Room," delivered with charm, grace, and fine voice. The picture is not helped by Durbin's appearance: she is decidedly overweight, and there is no chemistry between her and Haymes. Part of the problem was that she was going through a divorce (indeed, she said she could not make publicity appearances for the film because she did not feel up to it), and this would be one of her last film roles.

The publicity notes for the film indicate that the studio saw the film as a potential moneymaker. They issued press releases describing Haymes's prowess as a private air pilot; and some of the press agents offered suggestions that there be a celebration on the mall of New York's Central Park (with then Mayor O'Dwyer attending), that Hearst newspapers publish items about Boss Tweed's secret love life (thus tying in with Tweed's infatuation with Rosie in the film), that the three principals enact Currier and Ives prints, and, for Dick Haymes, that he actually cover an assignment for the *New York Times*. They also thought of tying in his career with those of Tony Martin, Frank Sinatra, Dorothy Lamour, and Harriet Hilliard, all performers who had graduated from singing careers to acting in films.

The Universal publicity files indicate that Dick Haymes was, in 1947, still at the height of his public popularity and busily engaged in many enterprises subsidiary to his acting and singing. When we try to chart his decline in popularity, certainly this film and the one that followed provide obvious answers. The reviewers noted that admirers of the stars would be disappointed at the lack of opportunity provided by the film for their singing, and all noted the evident silliness of the plot. For Dick Haymes, there would be no film like *From Here to Eternity* to rescue his film career, as there was for Sinatra, and the poor reviews of this film and his next, *One Touch of Venus*, which opened in August of 1948, clearly point to his dim future as a movie star.

The negative reviews of his first Universal film might have served as a lesson to be more selective in future roles had Haymes not contracted for both of them at the same time. But the question remains, why did Dick Haymes take a second-lead role in the 1948 adaptation of a more successful 1943 Broadway musical, "One Touch of Venus"? The obvious answer is probably the money he would receive, but his seventy-five thousand dollar fee was fifty thousand dollars less than that paid to Ava Gardner and Robert Walker. Haymes did get his name above the title, but it was the third name after the other two. And he is little more than Robert Walker's sidekick in the film, but his voice transcends the banality of the film—as it did years earlier when he sang (uncredited) with the Pied Pipers in *DuBarry Was a Lady*.

Robert Walker, a brilliant actor (Hitchcock really knew how to use him in *Strangers on a Train* a few years later), plays a dithering department window trimmer in a role that cries out for someone like Hugh Grant, who does this sort of thing perfectly. Ava Gardner, looking like a very earthy, sexual goddess, is rivetingly beautiful—although her acting skills are minimal. The two most talented musical performers in this film, Dick Haymes and Olga San Juan, are given little to do; and unless you are particularly interested in either of them, their parts are forgettable. (The preview audience questionnaires did not indicate that even one viewer singled out Dick Haymes either for praise or criticism, suggesting that he did not register with the audience.)

Once again, the songs suffer here as they did in *Up in Central Park*. The music, by Kurt Weill, was cut to just a few songs, the dancing disappears from the film, and the song lyrics, by such notable writers as S. J. Perelman and Ogden Nash, had to be rewritten to satisfy the censors.

Some of the fault—for both musicals—must lie with the director of these two Haymes ventures, William A. Seiter; but clearly, the studio's desire to economize and hedge its bets with musicals underlies their mediocrity. Both should have been in Technicolor, and both should have included important dance numbers, and the presence of only three out of the Broadway show's sixteen songs indicates that there was not much confidence in the musical film at the outset.

Yet, for those who have studied the artistry of Dick Haymes, somehow the film is not disappointing (except for his secondary role). He sings the important ballad "Speak Low" beautifully, as a duet with the dubbed voice of Eileen Wilson for Ava Gardner, and later thoroughly outclasses everyone else in another duet that cuts between two couples in a waltz, "Don't Look Now but My Heart Is Showing." There are several close-ups of Gardner, as we might expect, but Haymes does get one medium close-up singing this song; he looks handsome and his deep baritone contrasts sharply with Walker's unsteady, wavering tenor. But for his career, this role, I believe, led to Dick Haymes's final years in film.

Yet the publicity people were still at work trying to capitalize on Haymes's continuing popularity with the public. A possible news release announces his plans as producer-star with his partner-manager, Bill Burton, and his undertaking a round-the-world flight in one of his own airplanes. Although the publicity department devoted most of its efforts to promoting

Ava Gardner, there were suggestions for Dick Haymes's publicity: a photograph of his latest child; a story on the studio's grounding Haymes for the duration of the film (clearly, from flying his planes, for insurance purposes); possibly a release on his new producing plans; a layout story of the family at home (along with another suggestion that one of his two children be given a small role in the film); a possibility that he would christen one of his new planes "Venus," with Ava Gardner breaking the champagne bottle; and, finally, life stories (how he started as a band singer and graduated to independent star and film actor); and a comparison of Haymes with his foremost contemporaries, Crosby and Sinatra. Those are the "angles" that the publicists viewed as likely to attract the public's interest.

The reviewers commented on how few opportunities Dick Haymes was given to sing in this film. Although his acting is acceptable, the role is undemanding, and he looks awkward or uncomfortable in several scenes. His waltz with Olga San Juan shows him as a graceful dancer (as we remember from *State Fair*), but the question remains as to why he agreed to take this role.

It would be unfair to blame his participation in this film on Bill Burton, his manager. It is clear that Dick Haymes was caught up in the center of Hollywood life with his film, radio, and recording career, trying to do many things at the same time, while keeping up an expensive way of life—ranch, horses, airplanes, potential record and film production companies. It was too much and he was pulled in too many directions at the same time. Many performers both before and after Haymes can point to specific decisions at particular moments in their careers—mistakes that somehow led to a painful descent from the heights. *Up in Central Park* was a promising vehicle, but *One Touch of Venus*, coming as it did after the failure of the earlier film, undoubtedly led producers to conclude that Dick Haymes was not the rising star that had shone so brilliantly at Fox. His later efforts could not transcend the mediocrity of these last two films, but fortunately, his voice never lost its power to move his audience—and some of his best recordings were still to come after he left Universal.

The situation at home on the ranch had become increasingly difficult for both Dick and Joanne. Their careers were in conflict, they spent little time together, and when they did reside under the same roof, they argued constantly—with mutual accusations of infidelity. Their three children were spared much of the heated arguments, residing as they did in a separate bungalow. (Joanne told a reporter that they had adopted that plan for the children on the advice of a noted Viennese pediatrician who believed that children must create their own world, and if they are not constantly involved in the affairs of their parents, they are less likely to develop neuroses.) Further, Dick broke with his longtime manager, Bill Burton, for several reasons. Burton claimed that Dick was not reliable, that he missed engagements, and Dick felt that Burton was not guiding his career in the direction it should be taking—and he always had the suspicion that Burton was taking money from him. His financial situation was at best unstable: his generosity and thoughtlessness regarding his income would now haunt him. Although his recording career provided his basic income, he was forced to tour more frequently to supplement the salary he had come to depend upon during his years as a Fox contract player.

Ironically, as his marriage to Joanne Dru was collapsing, he was honored at the Golden Gate Theatre in San Francisco as 1947's model father (as were Bob Hope and Bing Crosby in past years). But by the Christmas season in 1948, the announcement had gone out to the press that the Haymeses were separating prior to a divorce. The story, as reported by Louella Parsons, the Hollywood gossip columnist, was, according to Dick, that they were kept apart by their commitments to their careers. "I haven't really seen her for three months," he said. "When I came back from New York she left the next day for location." Just a few months earlier, Joanne had told a reporter how happy she was staying home and taking care of the children, and that Dick told her to feel free pursuing a career. She concluded the interview by affirming her marriage: "Don't marry a crooner—unless (1) you can find one to make you as happy as mine has made me, and (2) you find one of your own—because *this* one I'll keep!"

The public statements reflect the mixed emotions of the couple. Joanne would say years later that they never should have split, and Dick remembered those troubled days with deep regret: "It was just a series of egoistic mistakes on my own part, the breakup of my marriage, breaking up with my management with Billy Burton. I just went through a dark, satanic period, that's all, and started drinking too much and started being disinterested."

Dick had, indeed, started to drink, primarily in an effort to escape the tensions at home. Invariably, as a youngster, he had looked to his mother to rescue him—to no avail—but the need for a comforting female to lift him out of his despair would remain with him to the end of his life. During this difficult period, he would find what he believed was the answer to his desperate need for love and affirmation, and, above all, relief from his tensions, in a beautiful woman who would accept him just as he was and ask for nothing more than a life of pleasure—tennis games, parties, nightclubs, and, as he later admitted of his extra-marital relationship with Nora Eddington Flynn, "torrid sex."

Although columnists would assert that Dick and Nora met in Palm Springs at the hotel where both played tennis, the Racquet Club, clearly they had met earlier when she was married to film star Errol Flynn, whom Dick admired and liked as a friend. Flynn's lurid sexual escapades were the subject of rumors and covert gossip for years; on one occasion, he would be taken to court for statutory rape, a case that gossip columnists avidly followed. While married to his last of three wives, Flynn was living with a seventeen-year-old girl. Nora had married Flynn as a very young woman, and after enduring his many infidelities, she decided to leave him, moving with one of her two daughters to a house in West Los Angeles. She had not yet told Flynn that her departure would be permanent.

Dick Haymes was an honorary vice president of the Racquet Club, where he and Nora began a romantic liaison. Nora described Dick as "very sweet, very gentle, very devoted." Their marital problems provided a basis for their relationship, each finding in the other an emotional outlet for tensions that were destroying their marriages. Eventually, their secret was revealed in gossip columns, and after Nora went to New York City, where Dick was performing, their marriages soon dissolved. Years later, Dick admitted that Joanne had tried to salvage the marriage, telephoning Nora to ask her when she would "return" her husband. He remembered that Joanne refused to admit that their marriage was coming to an end. For Dick, the new relationship was filled with hope and possibility; he rented a new home on Canon Drive in Beverly Hills, where he would live with his two new stepdaughters (Nora was given custody of her children). The new house had three additional bedrooms for the Haymes children, and the devotion of Nora Eddington, who did not seek her own career, allowed Dick once again to face a future that seemed to hold the promise of personal fulfillment and renewed success in his career.

Dick Haymes and Nora Eddington Flynn were married on July 17, 1949, in the garden of his new home with some seventy guests attending. Both Joanne and Nora had received divorce decrees in Nevada a few weeks earlier, and Dick's settlement to Joanne would provide full future support of their children. One of the popular jokes of the day was that Errol Flynn had bribed Dick to marry Nora so as to relieve him of alimony—but Flynn's public statements at the time indicate how resentful he was of Haymes. Nora would remember, "Dick Haymes was a romantic. He loved love and when he was in love, it was all that mattered." Their marriage released Dick from the quarrels that had plagued the last year with Joanne. He and Nora took up the life of young celebrities—nightclubs, parties, sports, swimming and tennis in particular. Theirs was not an introspective relationship; both loved to be at the center of the social whirl, but neither realized how dependent they both were on romantic illusions more appropriate to couples at least ten years younger—and without the responsibilities of a lavish lifestyle and five young children. Nora suffered a miscarriage early in the marriage, but their active social life was not impaired.

Years later, Dick Haymes would look back critically at this period of his life, remembering that from the start the press, which attended the wedding, was dubious. "I believe they look upon the whole wedding as a charade. Deep in my own disquiet I know it is but a charade." He remembered their honeymoon in Hawaii and their "going through the motions" of being happy. It is clear that Dick was looking for something to relieve the pressures of his now-floundering career. "I am no longer with Fox and I have lost the Auto-Lite show. My career is slipping. I am now sporadically recording, still with Decca thanks to some very faithful friends such as Morty Halitz and Sonny Burke. I have maybe two movies at Universal that are not good and business is falling off on personal appearances. Things don't look good and I know it. Burton and I have broken up and I miss him tremendously." In his aborted autobiography he is even more frank about his marriage to Nora:

> My career had peaked and everything in music was in a state of sus-pended animation, waiting for Elvis Presley and the birth of rock and roll. Some blamed it on television, but I think it was more that the times demanded something new and different. I had picked the wrong woman to marry at the wrong time. Nora was an Irish-American beauty, strictly a Hollywood oriented lady who loved the gossip, glamour and parties of the celluloid capitol of the world. Nora was more liberated than most women of the time and really a few years ahead of the Truman-Eisenhower era.
>
> It was a time when I should have stayed single. I had all the deductions I could use, thanks to Joanne and my children. It was also a time when, unconsciously, I was starting to drink more than I should, probably insu-lating myself against the building pressures in my life without even being aware of it. I'd been and done everything one man can be and do—or so I thought. I was really too naïve to understand Hollywood. My marriage to Nora was all right but it was not a Dick Haymes marriage and was des-tined to fail.

Although Haymes was scrupulously honest about his mistakes in hind-sight, he was mistaken about his marriage to Nora as "not a Dick Haymes marriage." Indeed, it followed the pattern of five of his six marriages: it was swift, romantic, and seemed to promise eternal love and deliverance from the painful necessities of daily life.

However, Dick Haymes had miscalculated the public's response to his divorce and remarriage. Joanne Dru was now a popular film actress, and she was equally notable as a devoted wife and mother. That image, so carefully constructed over the years of their marriage, made her immensely appealing to film audiences and fans. It should not have come as the surprise that it did when in June of 1949, just before the wedding, *Radio Best* magazine published an article, "Who Put the Hex on Haymes?" The subtitles, "Are his marital troubles to blame? What about his romance with Errol Flynn's wife? Is it his emotional immaturity or does he need a course with Dale Carnegie? Maybe Dick Haymes will have to seek the answer within himself," lead into a particularly virulent attack on him as a person, and as a singer and actor, even criticizing his appearance. In celebrity culture, such destructive attacks were hardly unusual, even in the 1940s. They have become commonplace today. But the level of malevolence must have startled Haymes. And clearly, had he consulted with advisors of stability and maturity, they might have been able to reign in his flagrant pursuit of a new love which might damage his public image. Of course, he did not consult anyone—Bill Burton was no longer his manager—and, as he had done all of his life, he simply followed his instincts. Up to now, they had led to success.

The article, copiously illustrated with photos of Joanne and the children at home that contrast with several of him and Nora out on the town, cleverly lays the blame on Haymes himself: "Can he, despite his current marital troubles, his headline-creating 'romance' with Nora Eddington Flynn, his mysterious break with his longtime mentor, friend and manager, Bill Burton, and his incredibly heedless public relations, overcome the apparent hex on his career? Can Dick come back as the top personality he once was? No one knows." The sharpest thrust follows: "For if anyone put a hex on Haymes, it seems it was Haymes himself—a fellow with one of the richest, lushest baritones in show business and an unbelievable knack for losing friends and alienating people." The writer hypothesizes that he may come back stronger than ever, but concludes that for now he is just marking time. Only his records are successful, and this when other singers like Sinatra, Perry Como, Gordon MacRae, and others "are outdistancing him on the screen."

The article concedes that Haymes lost his Auto-Lite show because of the ratings. Al Jolson's very popular show was his competition as a result of the success of the biopic, *The Jolson Story*, which resuscitated his faltering career. According to the writer, Haymes turned down several other good radio opportunities because of his self-destructive ego and refused to head a New York television show which involved commuting between the East and West Coasts. Then the article attacks his acting—although praising his comedy sense in *One Touch of Venus*—noting that his "dramatic range runs the gamut merely from A to B" (a famous line written years earlier by Dorothy Parker in a critique of Katharine Hepburn).

The writer of this piece interviewed Joanne Dru the previous January—she is clearly favored—and quotes her as saying, "Dick is a pretty mixed-up boy. He's been badly advised, he's had some strange friends and he seems to have gone off at an unfortunate tangent; yet I know that he loves our three children devotedly. As for me, I'd take him back gladly any time he wants to come back." Accounts of Dick's trips with Nora follow, and the writer speculates on how Dick will manage to support his family and to pay a reputed five thousand dollars per month in alimony to Joanne.

Like many articles on celebrity culture, this piece is transparent in its effort to appear analytical. First, it devotes several paragraphs to the brilliant managerial skills of Bill Burton and then criticizes Haymes for his "poor judgment in dropping his long-time pilot at a critical point in his career, just as he has shown poor judgment in his handling of his public relations, in his attitude toward the press, in his inexplicable rudeness towards the little people whose job it was to work with him." Ironically, the writer does not list the favors that Dick performed for those same people, the generosity that the fan magazines once celebrated. He has, the writer concludes, lost the good will of the press, an indispensable commodity in celebrity culture. The article then slyly berates Haymes for insulting many of his associates: Helen Forrest, who never said that Haymes treated her other than with warmth and consideration, and others to whom he might have given a gold watch one day and then not spoken to them a short time later. There is no mention here of Haymes's notoriously poor eyesight that, as we know, was the reason for his apparent slighting of acquaintances. After listing all of Dick's successes, the article moves to its conclusion, hammering at his personal failings and his "emotional immaturity" with a series of questions designed to deliver the final blow to Dick Haymes, the celebrity who is "not the most popular man in Hollywood today." Is it his "roving eye"? His "mercurial enthusiasms and even more sudden shifts of interest? His frequent callousness to people who can't hit back?" After a grudging acknowledgment of Haymes's great talent, the writer condescendingly remarks, "And as for television, while certainly not the most photogenic personality on the air, he is at least no more frightening to the video cameras than, say, Milton Berle" (the popular comedian with a cartoonish face). Finally, the question, "Can Dick Haymes ever come back?" is answered by another question. "Richard, got a mirror in the house?"

In response to such highly critical articles and comments by gossip columnists, Haymes gave an interview to *Radio and Television Mirror* titled "Now I Can Sing Again." Here, he tries to present himself sympathetically to an audience that has not heard his side of the story of the divorce and romance with Nora. The article quotes Dick copiously about Nora's rescuing him from despair, her love restoring his confidence in his ability. Before meeting Nora, he says, both he and Joanne knew that their eight-year marriage was over, that his career had become a bore, that the future looked "dirty, sullen grey . . . hopeless." Dick carefully explains that his main concern is for the five children involved in the two families, but he maintains that his and Nora's love was so important that all other problems melted away. And he concludes that it is better to break up unhappy marriages than subject children to the atmosphere of unhappy homes. He tells Nora that the public response to their love could be devastating to his career, but she replies that she does not care—her love is unconditional. The article then goes on to describe their "blissful" life—with Nora's two children and frequent visits from his three. He is revitalized, getting up early, playing tennis, and staying in evenings without friends dropping in (he carefully ignores the many photos of himself and Nora enjoying Hollywood nightlife). He declares that he has decided to simplify his business efforts, to cut people from his payroll who are simply living off his concert earnings, and to scale back his appearances. He rejects the lush life he once led and is delighted that Nora stays at home with the children. He ends on a positive note: his new radio show, *Club 15*, has allowed him to shed the juvenile persona that had characterized him for years, his recording career is going well, and he will not pursue film work unless the roles allow him to play more mature characters. He notes that he is going into the Cocoanut Grove with his own show. Because of Nora, he concludes, his life has taken a new direction, and he will be eternally grateful to her.

Although Dick and Joanne believed that their divorce would have a minimal effect on their children, Richard Jr. was six years old and keenly felt the impact of the great change in his life. He remembers his mother, not an angel, but rather like a character out of a Jane Austen novel. She could get along with everyone in her personal and professional world, indeed, was adored by her friends and even social acquaintances. As she had told her brother Peter, and years later she confessed to her son, "I should have stuck with your Dad." Richard Jr. believes that if people like his parents knew then what they know today about the disillusionment phase of a marriage, where people fall out of first love, they might have made their marriage work. He recalls that he was not happy about the breakup, feeling resentment toward his mother yet, when with his father, longing to be back with her. He remembers that after Joanne married John Ireland, whom neither he, his sister, nor his uncle Peter liked, the property was neglected, the pool filled with leaves and debris, and the ranch no longer seemed opulent. Richard Jr. was hostile to "Big John," as he called Ireland, and wondered if he were to blame for sending the boy to military school. His sister believes that Dick didn't know how much Richard Jr. was hurt by the divorce, but as she notes, "He was incapable of parenting." Sadly, Dick would repeat the mistakes made by his mother that had made his childhood so painful—notably, sending his child away to a school, rupturing the now minimal continuity that existed in the boy's life.

Richard Jr. remembers that Joanne would try to have Ireland discipline her obstreperous child, but although he never volunteered to spank the boy, he agreed to her requests. Richard Jr. recalls vividly that once in their barn when his pants were down, waiting for the blow from Ireland, he looked up and saw his father's photograph in a frame. He never forgot his feelings at that moment, torn between his two parents. John Ireland was, however, a genuinely violent man who would become abusive to Joanne, finally hitting her in the face, breaking blood vessels in her eye in such a severe battering that she filed for divorce by the mid-1950s.

Dick was a stern father who never struck his son or engaged in any form of corporal punishment. The child felt the tension in both parents, and was often angry that his father no longer lived with him. "There was something about him larger than life," he remembers.

His younger sister, Pidge, doesn't recall exactly when her father left, but remembers when he was gone. Joanne and the children moved to Beverly Hills. Her mother was angry at Dick for neglecting to send the money to support the children, but Joanne never spoke against their father to them. Pidge believes that her mother was deeply hurt by his infidelities, which she sees as the primary cause of their breakup. One of Pidge's most vivid memories of that sad time is of the night that the family dog, Brutus, a boxer that Dick loved, went missing from the new home in Beverly Hills. He was later found by the neighbors at the Encino ranch, many miles from his new home.

Richard Jr. enjoyed going to Palm Springs to spend some vacation time with Dick and Nora and her children. He remembers his father drinking steadily as he listened to classical music, switching from Tchaikovsky to Rachmaninoff, Shostakovich, and Gershwin's "Rhapsody in Blue" as his young son lay in bed allowing the music to flood through him, creating a passion for classical music that has never ebbed.

In January 1949, Dick Haymes joined the leading Hollywood stars at the Harry Truman Inaugural Gala. Later that year, his new agency, MCA, booked him to open at the Cocoanut Grove. *Variety* raved, "Dick Haymes is indubitably tops in his class, able easily to capture any audience with his magnificent baritone and a compelling personality. In his first nitery date for seven years he shows a maturity of performancing style, burnished to a high brilliance by excellent timing and staging of his numbers. Alone and with the Four Hits and a Miss he received one of the most enthusiastic opening night receptions any singer has had in a long time."

In an interview with radio host Jack Ellsworth at the Roxy Theatre in New York, Dick talked about his plans to appear at the Hippodrome in Baltimore to fulfill a promise, and then to return to the sunshine of the West Coast. He told Ellsworth about plans for a combination radio and television program, and the problem of dealing with the coaxial cable that did not reach across the continent. Anticipating new technology, he indicated that the program would be filmed. He was quite conscious of the competition within the new medium, and admired Milton Berle for coming up with an idea for a show that attracted so many viewers.

When Dick was signed as host of *Club 15*, a popular radio show originally hosted by Bob Crosby (Bing's brother), his main weekly attraction was the Andrews Sisters, who had become the most popular singing group during the war and remained so for many years. In 1947 they had recorded two songs with Haymes and Bing Crosby, and Maxene Andrews would later claim that Dick "counted" the lines so that everyone would have equal time on the record. As the Andrews Sisters' biographer notes, Maxene's claim is questionable, pointing to the released final cut of "There's No Business like Show Business" as a "nicely balanced group effort," noting that Patty Andrews's solo spots included at least five more lines than either Haymes or Crosby. In fact, Haymes might have altered the arrangement to the advantage of the trio.

After concluding his year with *Club 15* in 1950, Haymes appeared on the Carnation Hour for part of the 1950–51 season. His recording career with Decca resulted in nine additional charted recordings, none, however, reaching the position that "Little White Lies" had in 1948. In addition to radio performances, Dick Haymes started to appear on television in 1949 on the *Milton Berle Show* for Texaco, and in 1950 on the DuMont Television Network's *Star Time* with Benny Goodman and his sextet. In the next year, he would appear on the *Dinah Shore Show*, the *Kate Smith Hour*, and the *Texaco Star Theater*. He reported that he had received over five thousand letters asking him to appear in a western film where he would sing and that he was looking for a script.

A script did come along, but it was not for a western, nor was it for a big studio and expensive production. The little-known film *St. Benny the Dip* was released in 1951, making its debut on October 12, 1951, in Bismarck, North Dakota! It was a far cry from his earlier lavish productions, but in recent years it has been rediscovered by film scholars and respected for its style, production values, and acting. Haymes was approached by Edward and Harry Lee Danziger to star in the film written by George Auerbach. Production began in February 1950, and Haymes taped his last eight *Club 15* radio shows before shooting on the film began.

One of the most unusual collaborations in film history was that of director Edgar G. Ulmer and actor/singer Dick Haymes. Ulmer was a Viennese-born director who had as a youth worked with the noted director Max Reinhardt as well as with such luminaries of early film as F. W. Murnau, Ernst Lubitsch, Fritz Lang, and filmmakers employed by UFA studios in the 1920s when German film was thriving. His greatest claim to fame is *Detour* (1946), which critics have called the best B film ever made.

Probably Ulmer would have remained the brilliant but unnoticed director of films ranked B and below (he is sometimes referred to as a director of Z films) had the French film community not discovered him and found in his films evidence of the hand of a true *auteur*. Before his death in 1972, he had become well known to students of film as a distinctive visual stylist who, with meager budgets, was able to communicate a strong visual personality. In fact, the small budgets tended to stimulate visual virtuosity, and Ulmer soon developed a singular expressionistic cinematic style.

Before embarking on the Haymes project, Ulmer had directed several B films, including *Ruthless* (1948), often regarded as one of the most memorable of the *films noir,* as well as a number of ethnic films and a forgettable science fiction thriller. All of his films were done, by his own choice, for studios ranked at, or even below, Poverty Row—PRC (Producers Releasing Corp.) and Eagle-Lion—or were produced independently and released by United Artists, as was *St. Benny the Dip.* Ulmer's continental background and his choices of films and working conditions would seem to mark him as the most unlikely director for a Dick Haymes film project. But let us remember that Haymes, although he had acquired a reputation as the "boy next door" in his films, was in reality an intelligent, sophisticated man, undoubtedly receptive to the innovative film techniques and virtuosity of his new director.

Given the decline of his film career, Dick Haymes's acceptance of the leading role in this film about three con men is not surprising. The surprise comes in the way he performs, the skill of the director, and the realization that had he had opportunities that utilized him in roles other than as a boyish leading man, Haymes might have had as fine a movie career as Sinatra.

Dick Haymes is at his best in this film. As the con man, he is cool, sardonic, handsome (clearly, he needed a director like Ulmer to show his good looks to advantage), and smooth. He is charming to Linda, the daughter of a drunken musician, and his strength as the leader of the three men is clear. And in his one song (the hymn-like "I Believe"), his voice is firm, deep, and rich. When he begins to sing in the church, he begins in medium shot and then walks to the foreground as he sings, and ends with the other two men standing on the pulpit. Haymes's movement from the rear of the hall to the foreground is slow, deliberate, and in perfect accord with the song. And it is without doubt the turning point of the film.

Despite a weak script, the film is affecting—and largely because of the genuine charisma that Dick Haymes brings to the role. He is not forced into juvenile expressions of sentiment, and a slight awkwardness that is noticeable in other films is entirely absent here. This is a role—not just a part—and he seems to relish embodying the scarred young man who is reluctant to commit himself to the possibility of happiness in marriage. When he tells Linda he's "a guy on the move," he is completely convincing, making his final capitulation that much more moving.

Dick Haymes would make two more films in the next few years, but they rehashed the kinds of roles he had played almost ten years earlier. Only in *St. Benny the Dip* is there a hint of the actor that he could be; but, unfortunately, he never really had the opportunity to grow and develop in roles that would place demands on his skills as an actor. This film offers a glimpse into the kind of career he might have had in films, and despite its apparent limitations, it demands our attention as a sample of Dick Haymes at his best.

St. Benny the Dip was clearly not the solution to Dick Haymes's financial difficulties. He continued to appear in nightclubs in the East, including the popular Bill Miller's Riviera in Fort Lee, New Jersey, where Lena Horne had just concluded an engagement. In July 1951, he decided to try musical comedy, opening at the War Memorial Opera House in San Francisco in the Harold Arlen and E. Y. Harburg musical, *Bloomer Girl*. *Variety* would not be as kind to this performance as it had been to his Cocoanut Grove appearance two years earlier. The review praises the production and staging as well as the performances of Frances McCann, Bambi Linn, Dooley Wilson, and others in the cast; it singles out Dick Haymes for criticism: "little is required of and contributed by Dick Haymes, whose singing is less than effective and whose acting is weak throughout." Haymes was not alone in receiving less than glowing reviews in a musical. *Variety* concludes, "'Bloomer Girl' looks to retrieve much of ground lost by season's opener, 'Girl Crazy,' with Mickey Rooney, which proved a cropper."

Once again, Dick Haymes was invited to sing at the Academy Awards ceremony in March of 1952, along with Danny Kaye, Jane Wyman, Jane Powell, and Howard Keel. He also had an opportunity to resuscitate his languishing film career when two up-and-coming young talents, Richard

Quine and Blake Edwards, approached him to make a picture at Columbia Pictures with Mickey Rooney. He read the script, found it hilarious, and agreed to make it. He later said, "It's a far cry from the big-budget pictures, but it turns out to be a funny little picture with a less than fair score." Perhaps the most important event coinciding with his working at Columbia was meeting Harry Cohn, whom he described as "a legend in the business. He likes me and is talking about future projects." Indeed, Harry Cohn would play a decisive role in Dick Haymes's career and personal life.

In 1953, Dick Haymes made two pictures for Columbia Studios, *All Ashore* and *Cruisin' Down the River*. Both were directed by his friend Richard Quine, who co-wrote them with Blake Edwards, both had water-based settings (the Pacific waterway to Catalina Island in the first, a river in the second), both had some memorable musical moments, and, sadly, both were commercial flops.

We need not look far for reasons for their failure: Columbia Pictures, by 1953, was not the strong studio that had produced Frank Capra's classics in the 1930s and major 1940s films such as George Stevens's *Talk of the Town* (1942) and *The More the Merrier* (1943), Alfred Hitchcock's *Saboteur* (1942), and the memorable Cary Grant/Irene Dunne melodrama, *Penny Serenade* (1941). Of course, Columbia always produced B pictures and westerns, but by the 1950s, it was producing far fewer films and was relying more heavily on the many independent producers with whom it had contracted in the late 1940s. It had formed Screen Gems in the late 1940s and was directing its efforts to television production and distribution.

In 1953, it produced only fifteen in-house films and thirty-three outside productions. Of the former, *The Big Heat* and *From Here to Eternity* would become classics. All the rest are distinctly minor, despite the efforts of such directors as Raoul Walsh and Andre de Toth. (One of the outside productions was the Rita Hayworth vehicle, *Miss Sadie Thompson*, released in 3-D, directed by the capable Curtis Bernhardt.) It had become clear by the early 1950s that television had cut deeply into film audiences, the consent decree had changed the way studios could distribute films, and the rise of independent producers had altered the way studios conducted business. The studio system as it had existed in the previous two decades would be dead within a few years.

All Ashore is a pale imitation of the MGM postwar success that ushered in a new era of film musicals, *On the Town*. Instead of Gene Kelly, Frank Sinatra, and Jules Munshin, it features Ray MacDonald, Dick Haymes, and Mickey Rooney, who tries gamely to inject some life into this limp comedy.

Quine's direction is unimaginative, but the musical arrangements are by Nelson Riddle, who would achieve fame with Frank Sinatra, and they are clearly superior. Indeed, in this tale of three sailors on brief shore leave on Catalina Island, the brightest moments are in the musical numbers— although the songs themselves are not memorable. Peggy Ryan and Ray MacDonald, both versatile performers, sing and dance with energy (sometimes too much), but the film is clearly straining to achieve what the MGM trio handled effortlessly.

Haymes's role is that of a wise-cracking, self-assured ladies' man, and throughout the film, he and MacDonald reduce Moby (Mickey Rooney) to a figure of ridicule. The weak plot is just an excuse for some excellent singing and dancing, and for the antics of Mickey Rooney, who gives a game performance.

For devotees of Dick Haymes, the film is disappointing. He seldom gets the opportunity to sing a solo, and because he plays such an unpleasant character throughout the film, we really do not warm to him as we would in his next Columbia film, *Cruisin' Down the River*. The director is unable to invest him with the kind of charm that Gene Kelly so effortlessly exhibited even when playing egotistical or unsavory characters, as he did in so many of his films. But Haymes is supposed to be the macho hero familiar to viewers of Kelly. Clearly, there is just not enough balance here concerning the offhand cruelty of two sailors toward the third; and Haymes, as the stronger of the two, seems almost a villain throughout much of the film.

The surprise is how well Haymes handles himself in the numbers with MacDonald and Rooney—both experienced dancers. His grace was apparent early in his film career, in *State Fair* (1945), although he did not perform specifically as a dancer. But when he danced with Vivian Blaine— and in later films with Betty Grable and Deanna Durbin—it became clear that he moved with ease and assurance. Here, he is required to dance, and although he does not have the remarkable ability that Sinatra demonstrated in *On the Town*, he keeps up with the other two and, indeed, does not betray his inexperience as a dancer.

Haymes's best number in the film, and the film's best ballad, is "Who Are We to Say?" which he sings with the same full-throated ease he would display in *Cruisin' Down the River*. In the 1950s, as he would later demonstrate in the classic *Rain or Shine* and *Moondreams* albums, Haymes's voice was at its best: rich, deep, and emotionally expressive. As in *State Fair*, he sings while dancing—and falling in love with his partner. Courtship ballads were a Hollywood staple, and nobody did them more effortlessly than Dick Haymes.

The slapstick jokes which make Rooney a comic foil pale quickly and add a somewhat unsavory note to the film. But that is not the only reason for its box-office failure. The movie musical was dying, and an attempt to resuscitate it by adding broad comedy was doomed. Once again, Dick Haymes seemed to be caught in the time warp that would plague so much of his career.

Cruisin' Down the River had an attractive cast including, in addition to Haymes, Audrey Totter, Cecil Kellaway, and singers Connie Russell and Billy Daniels. The Technicolor consultant was Francis Cugat, brother of the bandleader and creator of the famous cover of F. Scott Fitzgerald's *The Great Gatsby* in 1925.

The plot starts with a flashback to the nineteenth century, on the *Chattahoochie Queen* riverboat. Dick Haymes plays a riverboat gambler who defeats the owner of the boat in a double-or-nothing game and, in addition to the boat, wins the hand of the lead singer, played by Connie Russell. The defeated captain threatens revenge on Beauregard (Haymes). The next scene—perhaps the most successful in the film—is set in a New York City nightclub where young Beau Clement is the featured piano singer. Here, Haymes does an assured and full-voiced "There Goes That Song Again," an up-tempo version that should answer critics who contend that he couldn't swing.

The remainder of the film is a typical plot, reminiscent of the old MGM musicals: Beau has inherited the rival as well as the hand of his granddaughter. Clearly, the major interest in the film is the music—particularly the performances of Russell, Daniels, and, most important, Dick Haymes, who is the star.

Haymes is clearly in command of his role: as the mustached Beauregard, he is elegant, poised, and graceful—in the flashbacks, his voice and movements are as fine as they were in his Fox successes. In the modern sequences, he sings a variation of "Pennies from Heaven"—"Riverboats from Heaven"—with a full-throated yet nuanced baritone. Renditions by Connie Russell (a popular television singer) and Billy Daniels's rousing "Sing You Sinners" are noteworthy musical interludes, but the film really belongs to Dick Haymes, whose "Swing Low, Sweet Chariot" is just one of his several notable numbers.

Why then did the film fail? Clearly, the plot is hackneyed, the script is bland, and the direction is routine. Apart from Daniels's "Sing You Sinners" and Haymes's cabaret routine, the director does not stage the musical numbers memorably. Quine was a regular at Columbia, dependable, but unoriginal. (Blake Edwards would become one of the most important and creative Hollywood directors some years later.) *Cruisin' Down the River* is an attempt by Columbia to recreate its past musical successes, but it is stale and unexciting. These two 1953 releases would be Dick Haymes's last major films.

Dick appeared in a few more TV films with Screen Gems, Columbia's subsidiary; and, ignoring the clear signs that his film career had not been revived, he moved with Nora to a new house in Bel Air, one of the most exclusive neighborhoods in Los Angeles. He remembered that move as incongruous, for alimony, child support, and the decreasing amount of work and high living were quickly draining his resources. Although Dick did not like much of the new music that was being recorded (some of the top hits were undistinguished songs that he believed pandered to the audience's desire for novelty, like Patti Page's "How Much Is That Doggie in the Window," Rosemary Clooney's "Come On-a My House," and Guy Mitchell's "Pittsburgh, Pennsylvania"), he was very unhappy that in 1952 Decca had not renewed his recording contract. His last charted recordings were in 1951 and did not move into the top twenty for the year. "I am just about broke," he said. Even his former friend and stand-in, Bob McCord, sued him for eleven hundred dollars in back pay. It seemed as though his situation could not get worse—but Columbia Studios and Harry Cohn had opened the gates to a period of decline and despair that he could not have imagined even in those grim days in Bel Air. The new chapter in the life of Dick Haymes would prove more dramatic than any of his films, and more devastating than anyone could have foretold.

CHAPTER 5

The "Love Goddess" and the Threat of Deportation

Although neither Dick nor his wife, Nora, spoke publicly about the reasons for their separation in the spring of 1953, it seems clear that Dick was once again swept up by his passion for a new love, Rita Hayworth, Columbia Studios' reigning queen, named "the Love Goddess" by Harry Cohn. Nora states in her autobiography, "In 1953 Richard and I decided on a divorce. I have no complaints against him and as marriages go it was a smooth one. It had no ups and downs. Always it was on an even keel. And that was probably the trouble, if you can call it such: for who could follow in the footsteps of the highly unpredictable Errol and keep me from boredom? No one, I guess." Nora's great romance was with Errol Flynn—the subject of her book. Both she and Dick Haymes married for the same reason: to avoid confronting the pain of divorce. And, of course, their partying and drinking prevented them from growing close, the marriage serving essentially as balm for their wounds.

During the most difficult period in their marriage, Dick met the founder of the Self-Realization Fellowship of the Church of All Religions, which he considered a milestone in his "constant search for the first breath [he] drew in this life experience." That is the other side of Dick Haymes— a deep spirituality, which would help him to face his darkest and most difficult moments. He was not traditionally religious, but, perhaps influenced by his mother, he was always attracted to Eastern religions. Ironically, in all of his personal writings, he would express the most heartfelt dedication to spiritual life and leaders and, in the next sentence, discuss his financial problems and latest nightclub bookings.

When Dick was on the Columbia lot after finishing *All Ashore*, he wandered over to the set of Rita's latest film, *Miss Sadie Thompson*. She was rehearsing dance routines, and Dick was captivated by her beauty and grace. He introduced himself to her, and she agreed to have lunch and a martini with him. (Columbia producer Jonie Taps recalled that she arranged the luncheon and that she was present.) Dick recalled, "I was still married to Nora and Rita had just picked up her divorce from Aly Khan. The two of us were rebounding and both lonesome, I'm sure. We filled a mutual vacuum in each other's lives."

As columnist Earl Wilson remembered, Rita told Dick that she was going to New York for the opening of her latest film, *Salome*, whereupon Dick replied, "I'll go to New York, too, just to see you." Dick was true to his word and arrived to meet Rita at the Plaza Hotel in New York City, where, immediately, a camera caught the two about to enter a waiting limousine. The photo appeared in newspapers throughout the country, for like Betty Grable and later Marilyn Monroe, Rita Hayworth was the reigning Hollywood sex symbol, and her every move provided fodder for the tabloids. There is little doubt that Dick fell in love with her as quickly as he had with his three former wives, but in this case, the added element was her celebrity. As Dick said, "Nora was not very happy about it—nor was Harry Cohn, Rita's boss at Columbia Studios. Harry . . . liked to play God with his stars and Rita was his hand-made creation—the 'Love Goddess.' He had always objected to the men in her life unless he personally sanctioned them. I was no exception. Suddenly things began to happen to me that shouldn't be happening. Rita was sure Harry [Cohn] was behind it all."

By 1953, Rita Hayworth's greatest triumphs as a star were behind her. She had started in films as a teenager in the 1930s, Margarita Carmen Cansino, dancing with her father Eduardo, a Spanish immigrant, and other members of her family. She was a gifted dancer and made a number of appearances in minor films. After her first notable appearance in a major role, *The Strawberry Blonde* in 1941, she was a new and important Hollywood property whom Harry Cohn and Columbia Pictures elevated to instant stardom. Before her most famous film, *Gilda*, in 1946, she had starred in more than six major box office hits, dancing brilliantly with both Gene Kelly and Fred Astaire, the two most important male dancing leads in film history. After 1946, her films were not as successful, but she was still Hollywood's reigning beauty, where her success as the number two "pin-up" girl during and after the war (only Betty Grable was more popular) kept her every movement before the public. Her search for love—like Dick Haymes's—was persistent and erratic. Her first husband, Edward Judson, whom she had married when she was nineteen, was a ruthless business man, considerably older than she, who guided her career, mismanaged her earnings, and exploited her beauty, youth, and insecurities for the sake of publicity. Rita had been a victim of incest by her father when she was on dancing tours with him, and as if to compensate for her father's cruelty, she always looked for security in a strong man who would treat her with kindness and consideration. Thus, after she ended her marriage to Judson in 1943, she married the brilliant, egotistical, and mesmerizing Orson Welles, who took control of her career; as director of the unusual film *The Lady from Shanghai* (1948), he changed her signature red hair to platinum blonde. They had a daughter, Rebecca Welles, but the couple's marital problems led to their divorce in 1948. Still seeking the perfect mate, Rita thought she had found him in one of the wealthiest and most fascinating men in the world, Prince Aly Khan, with whom she had a torrid affair before they married in 1949 (she was then pregnant with their child, Yasmin). Aly Khan's money was controlled by his father, the Aga Khan, and Rita's new husband felt free to spend her considerable earnings. He had secured a divorce to marry her and now felt that she had to acquire the image of a princess. He too tried to remake her: French lessons and tutoring in the proper etiquette for mixing in royal circles. Like Welles, Aly Khan committed infidelities that contributed to Rita's self-doubt; and again, she would be headed for divorce, but this one would prove far more complicated. She received her decree in Nevada on January 26, 1953, Aly remaining in Cannes with his new love, actress Gene Tierney. Although Rita was given custody of Yasmin, she was deeply troubled by the possibility that since she had received a default decree, it might not be recognized everywhere—and Aly might want to claim Yasmin at some future date. Thus, when Dick Haymes appeared on the scene, she found in him the charm, support, and devotion that she desperately needed. For Dick, Rita was the woman of his dreams.

It seems clear that both Rita Hayworth and Dick Haymes had been damaged by the absence of nurturing parents as well as by the obvious pattern of neglect they had endured as children. At the time that Dick met Rita, he was unable to face his inner demons, drowning them in alcohol and women. His drinking had escalated during his years with Nora, and his children remember that after three drinks he would become drunk, often succumbing to maudlin self-pity. Rita, too, liked to drink, and neither recognized how dominated their relationship was by alcohol. It is apparent that their attraction for each other, like Dick's for Nora, and Rita's for Welles and Aly Khan, was based on desperate need and strong physical attraction, but each was incapable of moving to the next step, actually getting to understand and respect the other. Despite the myriad troubles they encountered during their brief liaison, their bond would be severed primarily by their mutual inability to cope with persistent personal demons.

Their troubles began in May 1953. Rita was scheduled for location shooting in Hawaii on *Miss Sadie Thompson*. Dick did not want to interrupt their budding romance (he had similarly spent much time in Palm Springs when he was courting Nora), and so he decided to accompany her. Hawaii was not then a state, so as an Argentinean citizen, he had to present the proper papers to enter. He could not find his alien registration card, so on May 21, 1953, he went to the Immigration Office in Los Angeles to apply for a temporary replacement card. He asked at the office if there were anything else he needed and was informed that the card was sufficient. He returned to Los Angeles on June 7 and went to the Immigration Office on July 8 to pick up his new card. He was asked by the immigration official to whom he had spoken in May, Richard Cody, to accompany him to the investigative branch, where he was subjected to detailed questions about his status, in particular, the date that he entered the United States. When he responded that he had returned to the country a few weeks ago, the interrogator showed him a form dated January 25, 1944, asking as an alien to be exempted from military service. He was asked if he understood that, having signed the exemption request, he was ineligible to become naturalized as an American citizen. Moreover, the McCarran-Walter Act, the current immigration law passed as recently as June 27, 1952, over President Harry Truman's veto, required that anyone who was not eligible for citizenship because he had been granted an exemption from military service be excluded—or deported—from the United States.

Dick could not believe what was happening. Why had the government gone back into its files to find the draft exemption record? The McCarran-Walter Act reflected the growing anti-communism in the United States in the early Cold War years, allowing the government to deport any alien who engaged or intended to engage in activities deemed "subversive" to national security. Dick Haymes clearly did not fit the "subversive" profile, so the question of the origin of the deportation effort was legitimate. Both he and Rita suspected that Harry Cohn, who wanted total control of Rita and resented her affair with Haymes, had made a phone call that started the pursuit of Haymes's deportation. In just a few weeks, newspaper reporters and gossip columnists, always eager for any items relating to Dick and Rita, had the whole story; and the words "draft dodger" would come to haunt

A very young Dick Haymes,
ca. 1940. Susan Calter Collection.

Dick Haymes singing with Harry James and Orchestra, 1941. Roger Dooner Collection.

Helen Forrest, Gordon Jenkins, and Dick Haymes, *Everything for the Boys*, CBS Radio broadcast. Roger Dooner Collection.

Wedding of Dick and Joanne, September 21, 1941. Harry James is fourth from right and Peter Marshall is second from right. Courtesy Joanna Haymes Campbell.

ick Haymes, Betty Hutton, and Jack Haley on *Radio*
Hall of Fame, Blue Network, 1944–45. Museum of
Modern Art Film Stills Archive.

Bob Haymes, 1943.
Susan Calter Collection.

ick with Linda Darnell on *Command Performance*, for the Armed Services
Radio Service, 1944. Roger Dooner Collection.

Dick Haymes, Ginger Rogers, and escort at a movie premiere, January 1945. Roger Dooner Collection.

Cass Daley, Dick Haymes, June Allyson, Sterling Holloway, Barbara Stanwyck, Linda Darnell, and Errol Flynn on *Command Performance* for the Armed Services Radio Service, 1944. Roger Dooner Collection.

Marguerite Haymes in the mid-1940s.
Susan Calter Collection.

Betty Grable and Dick Haymes in *Billy Rose's Diamond
Horseshoe*, 1945. Author's Collection.

Helen Forrest and Dick Haymes at Ciro's nightclub, ca. 1945. Museum of Modern
Art Film Stills Archive.

Dick Haymes, Jeanne Crain, and Dana Andrews in a scene from *State Fair*, 1945. Author's Collection.

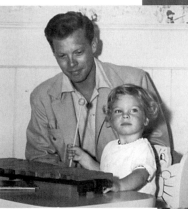

Dick and son Richard ("Skip") at home, ca. 1945. Susan Calter Collection.

Tyrone Power and Dick Haymes, ca. 1947. Roger Dooner Collecti

Dick Haymes and Maureen O'Hara in *Do You Love Me?*, 1946. Author's Collection.

Dick Haymes, Dinah Shore, Al Jolson, Margaret Whiting, and Lou Silvers, music director, on CBS radio, April 1947. Roger Dooner Collection.

Dick Haymes and Al Jolson
at Lux Radio Broadcast of
Alexander's Ragtime Band,
March 1947. Roger Dooner
Collection.

Jimmy Durante and Dick
Haymes, at rehearsal for radio
program, January 1945. Roger
Dooner Collection.

Dick and Joanne Haymes
at home with children
Helen Joanna, four;
Richard Jr. ("Skip"),
six; and baby Barbara
Nugent, March 1948.
Roger Dooner Collection.

Dick, baby Barbara Nugent,
and mother Joanne Dru,
1948. Author's collection.

Joanne with children Richard
("Skip"), Helen, and Barbara
Haymes, ca. 1949. Roger Dooner
Collection.

Dick Haymes and Nora
Eddington wedding, July 17,
1949. Susan Calter Collection.

Dick Haymes, Gordon MacRae, June Allyson, Edgar Bergen, and Dick Powell
(on trumpet) with the Firehouse Five Plus Two band, on radio show, March
1950. Author's Collection.

Ida Lupino and Dick Haymes on CBS radio, February 1950. Roger Dooner Collection.

Steve Lawrence, Eddie Fisher, Brad Phillips, Al Martino, and Dick Haymes at reception for Brad Phillips, WINS radio station, New York. Show *Singing Battle Royal*, October 1952. Courtesy Harriet Wasser.

Dick and Rita Hayworth immediately after their wedding, September 24, 1953. Courtesy of the Academy of Motion Picture Arts and Sciences.

Dick, with new beard, hoping for role in Rita's new film, *Joseph and His Brethren*, never produced, with Rita, ca. 1955. Roger Dooner Collection.

Dick Haymes, his wife Rita Hayworth, and her children Rebecca Welles, eight (left), and Yasmin Khan, five, and the family dog, running along Malibu beach, shown after the deportation hearing was dropped, 1955. Author's Collection.

Dick Haymes wins his
deportation case, May 1955.
Roger Dooner Collection.

Dick and Rita entering Columbia studios
in Dick's Lagonda convertible, 1955.
Author's Collection.

Billy Daniels, Dick Haymes, and Audrey Totter in *Cruisin'
Down the River*, 1953. Author's Collection.

Diana Lynn and Dick Haymes in TV drama, "National Honeymoon," for the Ford Theater, October 16, 1952. Author's Collection.

Fran Jeffries and Dick Haymes, ca. 1958. Susan Calter Collection.

Dick and wife Wendy, ca. 1972. Roger Dooner Collection.

Frank Sinatra, Jr., and Dick Haymes on
Adam-12 television show, March 13, 1974.
Roger Dooner Collection.

Dick Haymes onstage at
the Cocoanut Grove, 1972.
Roger Dooner Collection.

Lord Mountbatten, Monty Hall, and Dick Haymes at Variety Club International Dance, honoring Lord Mountbatten, at the Waldorf-Astoria Hotel in New York City, October 14, 1975. Roger Dooner Collection.

Hollywood Walk of Fame star honoring Dick Haymes for radio career, 6100 Hollywood Boulevard. Walter Boettger Collection.

Hollywood Walk of Fame star honoring Dick Haymes for recording career, 1724 Vine Street. Walter Boettger Collection.

Kobal then outlines Haymes's troubles, accepting the epithet "draft dodger." He then remarks, in a criticism that would become familiar in every biography of Rita Hayworth, "Haymes now set about advising Rita on her career, soon dictating not only the style of her hair, costumes and film roles, but suggesting that he produce and co-star with her in *Joseph [and her Brethren]*." At the same time, Kobal, like every other Hayworth biographer, notes that the actress *looked* for men to rely on, to guide her, to take charge of her career—and James Hill, her last husband, did exactly what Dick Haymes is accused of without the condemnation of historians or commentators. Hill also notes that her marriage to him and to Orson Welles reflected her tendency to marry father figures—or strong men upon whom she could lean. Because Dick Haymes's fortunes had fallen so swiftly in these years, the criticism of his trying to restart his career with Rita's help was ferocious; yet Frank Sinatra, who in the same period used everyone who might help him to secure the role of Maggio in *From Here to Eternity*, was admired by the press for his tenacity.

The biography by Joe Morella and Edward Z. Epstein, *Rita: The Life of Rita Hayworth*, appeared in 1983, and the authors thank the "many people" who have helped, adding, "In some instances names have not been revealed." Hayworth was still alive when the book was published; but, lacking any notes or sources, it is not persuasive, especially when the authors, before mentioning his name, refer to Dick Haymes as "the man certain people in the industry referred to as 'Mr. Evil.'" They reveal their bias clearly when they admit that Welles was unfaithful to Rita and that Aly Khan was neglectful and hurtful, but that the real villain was Dick Haymes, according to vague and undocumented sources.

James Hill never mentions Haymes in his *Rita Hayworth: A Memoir* (1983), but he adds important information about his former wife. He describes their heavy drinking and notes, "Rita had this glazed unseeing look as though I wasn't there. I had only seen a look like that once before. It was during the war, on a machine gunner carrying a Browning automatic who had just wiped out an entire pocket of the enemy." Hill was attempting to do

Dick Haymes. Historians accepted the version of events more favorable to Rita Hayworth—with Dick Haymes emerging as the villain of a drama that would play out for two years.

Any discussion of the relationship between Dick Haymes and Rita Hayworth must take into consideration the many biographies that have been written of her and the continued interest in her by historians of the golden age of Hollywood cinema. A dramatic presentation, "Rita Hayworth: Latin Love Goddess," at the Smithsonian National Portrait Gallery in 2001, marking the publication of a new volume of photographs of Hayworth, is a good example of the mythology that has grown over the years regarding the star and her numerous husbands. No one in the audience could emerge without citing Dick Haymes as the most unsympathetic of the men she married—the actor playing the role tried to convey the distasteful portrait of Haymes that emerged in the early 1950s. The sources for the drama were the authors of the biographies that trashed Haymes as well as the memoir by her last husband, James Hill, that should have raised questions about the negative view of Haymes that was presented as fact. Because Rita Hayworth was so famous and so treasured by moviegoers and film historians, the accuracy of biographers' statements about Haymes has never been questioned.

A number of sensational tabloids purported to give readers the "inside stories" of the lives of celebrities. Actually, the articles used hearsay and speculation to arrive at spurious conclusions that invariably tarred the subjects of their reports. When *Confidential* named Haymes "Mr. Evil," based upon a remark someone had made at a country club, other paper picked up the epithet, and it became part of the mythology of the Haymes Hayworth relationship.

The first of the books devoted to Hayworth, John Kobal's *Rita Haywori The Time, the Place, and the Woman*, appeared in 1977. Kobal's source for negative remarks about Haymes is a *Photoplay* magazine article publish some years after the two had parted (he does not give the date). He qu his source's judgment, "If there was one marriage that was predestine failure before the ink was dry it was the marriage to singer Dick Hayn

Kobal then outlines Haymes's troubles, accepting the epithet "draft dodger." He then remarks, in a criticism that would become familiar in every biography of Rita Hayworth, "Haymes now set about advising Rita on her career, soon dictating not only the style of her hair, costumes and film roles, but suggesting that he produce and co-star with her in *Joseph [and her Brethren]*." At the same time, Kobal, like every other Hayworth biographer, notes that the actress *looked* for men to rely on, to guide her, to take charge of her career—and James Hill, her last husband, did exactly what Dick Haymes is accused of without the condemnation of historians or commentators. Hill also notes that her marriage to him and to Orson Welles reflected her tendency to marry father figures—or strong men upon whom she could lean. Because Dick Haymes's fortunes had fallen so swiftly in these years, the criticism of his trying to restart his career with Rita's help was ferocious; yet Frank Sinatra, who in the same period used everyone who might help him to secure the role of Maggio in *From Here to Eternity*, was admired by the press for his tenacity.

The biography by Joe Morella and Edward Z. Epstein, *Rita: The Life of Rita Hayworth*, appeared in 1983, and the authors thank the "many people" who have helped, adding, "In some instances names have not been revealed." Hayworth was still alive when the book was published; but, lacking any notes or sources, it is not persuasive, especially when the authors, before mentioning his name, refer to Dick Haymes as "the man certain people in the industry referred to as 'Mr. Evil.'" They reveal their bias clearly when they admit that Welles was unfaithful to Rita and that Aly Khan was neglectful and hurtful, but that the real villain was Dick Haymes, according to vague and undocumented sources.

James Hill never mentions Haymes in his *Rita Hayworth: A Memoir* (1983), but he adds important information about his former wife. He describes their heavy drinking and notes, "Rita had this glazed unseeing look as though I wasn't there. I had only seen a look like that once before. It was during the war, on a machine gunner carrying a Browning automatic who had just wiped out an entire pocket of the enemy." Hill was attempting to do

Dick Haymes. Historians accepted the version of events more favorable to Rita Hayworth—with Dick Haymes emerging as the villain of a drama that would play out for two years.

Any discussion of the relationship between Dick Haymes and Rita Hayworth must take into consideration the many biographies that have been written of her and the continued interest in her by historians of the golden age of Hollywood cinema. A dramatic presentation, "Rita Hayworth: Latin Love Goddess," at the Smithsonian National Portrait Gallery in 2001, marking the publication of a new volume of photographs of Hayworth, is a good example of the mythology that has grown over the years regarding the star and her numerous husbands. No one in the audience could emerge without citing Dick Haymes as the most unsympathetic of the men she married—the actor playing the role tried to convey the distasteful portrait of Haymes that emerged in the early 1950s. The sources for the drama were the authors of the biographies that trashed Haymes as well as the memoir by her last husband, James Hill, that should have raised questions about the negative view of Haymes that was presented as fact. Because Rita Hayworth was so famous and so treasured by moviegoers and film historians, the accuracy of biographers' statements about Haymes has never been questioned.

A number of sensational tabloids purported to give readers the "inside stories" of the lives of celebrities. Actually, the articles used hearsay and speculation to arrive at spurious conclusions that invariably tarred the subjects of their reports. When *Confidential* named Haymes "Mr. Evil," based upon a remark someone had made at a country club, other papers picked up the epithet, and it became part of the mythology of the Haymes-Hayworth relationship.

The first of the books devoted to Hayworth, John Kobal's *Rita Hayworth: The Time, the Place, and the Woman*, appeared in 1977. Kobal's source for his negative remarks about Haymes is a *Photoplay* magazine article published some years after the two had parted (he does not give the date). He quotes his source's judgment, "If there was one marriage that was predestined to failure before the ink was dry it was the marriage to singer Dick Haymes."

justice to Hayworth and to face his own responsibility for the failure of their marriage. His reminiscences are particularly helpful in reconstructing some of the problems in the Hayworth-Haymes union. One notable example is his recollection of the night that he and Rita, while drinking, played Russian roulette with a loaded pistol, writing down complaints each had with the other and then firing the gun. One of the shots actually hit a wall and neighbors called the police. There was little publicity about the incident, unlike the attention given to even the slightest gesture by Dick Haymes.

By far the most serious attack on Dick Haymes is by Barbara Leaming in *If This Was Happiness: A Biography of Rita Hayworth*, published in 1989. The author is generally authoritative: copious notes at the end refer to specifics in the text, and she does name her sources. But if we look closely, we realize that her documentation of the Haymes/Hayworth relationship is flawed. She relies on hearsay ("people" who told Rita's friend, June Allyson, about Dick's abuse) and David Marcus, a former attorney for Haymes to whom the singer owed money. Their attorney-client relationship was severed, and we do not know what kind of ill feeling remained with Marcus after the break. Her main source is Jonie Taps, the Columbia Pictures producer who was close to Harry Cohn, the probable instigator of the deportation action, and to Bob Schiffer, a close friend of Rita's. Leaming does not use even one source remotely friendly to Haymes and relies on gossip columnist Earl Wilson's remark, "Dick plainly did all the thinking and talking for her," to conclude that he was a conspiratorial, manipulative, and controlling husband.

Leaming describes Dick Haymes in such terms as "loathsome," "insidious," "a loser," "a man on the way down," "a deadbeat" (twice), "Mr. Evil" (several times), "a lowlife," "notoriously dissolute," "a notorious drunk," "cruel," "abusive," "paranoid," "despotic," a "Svengali." Dick "ranted" and "seethed" and subjected Rita to "persistent abuse" and humiliation. She credits his brilliant performance at a nightclub as the result of his being exhilarated "by all the personal attention he was getting." She uses documentation as sources for reporting on the deportation hearings and Rita's custody proceedings, but draws conclusions about their relationship from the statements filed by Rita and her attorney to obtain a divorce from Haymes. Such divorce statements are usually exaggerations—and, in many cases, concocted for the occasion.

In her dispute with Columbia Pictures, Rita admitted that Dick had been guiding her (as had all of her other husbands); and Leaming uses as negative evidence Judge's Benjamin Harrison's comment, "The testimony has Mr. Haymes woven throughout the whole picture, and I wish that attorneys for both sides would research the right of a husband to speak for his wife." The judge's remark seems to the biographer evidence of Dick Haymes as a Machiavellian despot, whereas the judge was simply responding to the claims of Hayworth and her attorney. When Leaming quotes James Hill's comment that Rita "put herself in a lover's hands and basically did what he wanted her to do," she fails to acknowledge that Dick Haymes simply assumed the role Rita expected of him.

Neither Leaming nor any of the other biographers who relied upon popular and frequently unreliable magazine pieces cited a long article in one of that genre, *Adult Psychology*. In "Rita Hayworth's Secret Life" (December/January 1955), after a lengthy examination of the star's problems, particularly her self-destructive behavior, the author concludes, "Willing, docile, eager to please, she would undoubtedly have been happy with any one of her husbands if he had paid enough attention to her. But it was Rita Hayworth they were interested in—an actress with a brilliant career. Dick Haymes is the first one to accept Margarita Cansino, the first one who has not tried to play Pygmalion to Rita's Galatea. He is the first one to love her just as she is."

Such pop psychology is as much public relations oriented as the negative pieces in the scandal sheets that relied on press agents, studio publicity releases, and gossip columnists. But the biographers often used the most lurid of the unreliable sources and ignored some of the positive assessments of Dick Haymes as a popular singer/movie star or as Rita's lover/husband. Unfortunately, Barbara Leaming's biography, which provides an excellent portrait of Rita Hayworth, has also become the definitive

portrait of Dick Haymes, the source for his depiction in the television biographies of Rita Hayworth and the staged enactment of her life at the
Smithsonian Portrait Gallery.

There is no doubt that following the interview at the Immigration
Office, the lives of both Dick and Rita would spin into a nightmarish,
chaotic whirl from which few individuals could emerge unscathed. For
Hollywood celebrities, the spotlight could not be dimmed, and in the following months their names would remain in the headlines.

Dick Haymes had many faults: although most of the singers and musicians with whom he worked spoke affectionately of his charm and particularly of his sense of humor, he could be cool and aloof toward those he
regarded as vulgar and uneducated; he was completely unreliable regarding
his financial obligations to his ex-wives and children; he could be abrupt
with interviewers when questioned about his problems. He found it difficult to draw close to people, but when he did make a good friend, his loyalty was unswerving, as Peter Marshall, Helen Forrest, and, later, Russ Jones
would assert. But his childish expectation that things would right themselves, his lifelong tendency to flee from problems rather than to face them
squarely, and, above all, his increasing dependency on alcohol would, in
the two years following his meeting with Rita Hayworth, bring him to one
of the lowest points in his personal and professional life.

These months of crisis for Dick Haymes would revolve around three
issues: deportation, exemption from the draft resulting in the epithet "draft
dodger," and attempts to collect money by the U.S. Internal Revenue
Service for past income tax as well as by lawyers for Joanne Dru and Nora
Eddington to collect child support and alimony. A constant issue for Rita
was the question of Yasmin's visits to her father.

After his interrogation with the Immigration Service, Dick was notified
that the bureau would withhold action for sixty days. Dick was understand-
ably distraught at the turn of events, and Rita's support was his lifeline during these turbulent months. After she completed filming on *Miss Sadie
Thompson*, the couple left for New York City in mid-July, where they tried to

enjoy themselves before facing the latest developments in the deportation crisis. Dick had also contracted with the Sands Hotel in Las Vegas for a singing engagement that would begin on August 12. On July 30, 1953, at the end of the sixty-day period, the Immigration Service tried to arrest Dick, but he and Rita had left for California before 5 PM. That day would also mark the arrival of Prince Aly Khan in New York, where his hope of seeing his daughter was dashed by Rita's flight. He had to return to Europe quickly after learning that his father, the Aga Khan, was seriously ill.

By early August, newspapers and magazines began to report the story of Dick and Rita after Dick's car was stopped on Sunset Boulevard by federal agents with an arrest warrant. A bold headline in the *Los Angeles Herald and Express* proclaimed, "Haymes Arrested and Ordered Deported." The *Los Angeles Times* reported that his relatives in Argentina were "elated at the hope of seeing the singer." His mother tried to help by telling the newspapers that she was, in fact, born in the United States but gave up her citizenship to marry a British businessman in Argentina. She repeated the story that she had brought her two sons to the United States. On August 8, Dick Haymes was reported to be going to Washington to talk directly to Senator McCarran, and on the same day another paper quoted the district manager of immigration to the effect that only an act of Congress could reverse the deportation decision. A two-page feature in the August 9, 1953, *Los Angeles Sunday News*, "Just When Haymes Discovered Rita," describes the past lives of both Dick and Rita, quoting one of her friends who insists that this crisis will bring the two closer together, for, she says, "When Rita's in love with a man, there's nothing she won't do for him." The article is slanted in Rita's favor, asking such questions as, "Did success go to his head?" and summarizing how much he owes his former wives.

Dick's opening in Las Vegas was very well received by the audience, which applauded his entrance. Rita was so distraught by their current problems that she was unable to be at the opening, and Dick flew to Los Angeles to check on her condition. She later joined him and remained in Las Vegas for the duration of his engagement. She affirmed her love for him and her determination that they marry. She refused to leave him when Columbia Pictures ordered her to return to Los Angeles for publicity pictures for her film.

Dick earned twenty-five thousand dollars from his engagement at the Sands, but that money could not nearly begin to meet his financial obligations. When his plane landed in Los Angeles, he was served a summons by attorneys for Joanne Dru. On the day of his hearing, he was served with Nora's divorce suit papers, and a process server was waiting with a bill for four hundred dollars from a department store!

By August 25, Senator McCarran, on the eve of the Haymes deportation hearing, made it plain that he fully backed the deportation order, that it would be carried out "no matter how great his talents are." McCarran's firm stand against Haymes was in part a response to several groups that had rallied to Haymes's support in an effort to challenge and discredit the controversial McCarran-Walter Act.

The questioning at the deportation hearing was very difficult for Dick. Aspects of his life that he had forgotten were exhumed, like his early and very brief marriage to Edythe Harper and the fact that his name was sometimes reported as "Ricardo" on old documents. He was accused of failing to provide his latest address and once again had to defend his draft deferment. That he had tried to enlist on two occasions following that deferment was considered irrelevant. On one occasion, he was asked by a prosecutor if he intended to marry Rita Hayworth. His attorneys, Robert A. Eaton and David J. Marcus, objected strongly to the question and their objections were sustained. Further, they argued that a trip to Hawaii did not constitute leaving the United States and, additionally, that Haymes filed the address notice on February 2, just after the deadline with the Immigration Service that had then accepted his explanation that he was unaware of the rule. After the court gave the case a continuance until September 28, he left for Nevada to wait for his divorce to become final. Nora insisted that her divorce be granted in California, but she would agree to allow Dick to marry in Nevada when his decree came through. On September 18, he was granted an interlocutory decree of divorce from Nora. The testimony, typical of many Nevada divorce suits, charged that he was cruel to her, insulted their guests, and drank too much. His suit charged Nora with mental cruelty for refusing to accompany him on tours. Nora signed a waiver allowing him to proceed with his marriage to Rita in return for eight thousand dollars and one hundred dollars per week in alimony. At the same time that Dick was trying to resolve his problems, Rita had received threats to Yasmin's life, and she was wrestling with her fears that if she sent the child for a visit to her father, he might not return her. She was also concerned that her child be raised Christian, not Muslim. Her path during this period was that of avoidance, and she and Aly Khan, although in contact by telephone, did not meet.

On September 24, 1953, Dick and Rita were married in the Gold Room of the Sands Hotel. The much-publicized wedding was attended by Rita's two daughters, a few close friends and business associates, and Jack Entratter, who produced the shows at the Sands. Rita announced to the press, "I want a wedding with no frills this time. . . . After all, I'm getting Dick Haymes and that's all that matters." The couple allowed photographers and reporters full access after the ceremony, in large measure to counter the negative publicity of the previous weeks.

Rita Hayworth looked beautiful and very happy on her wedding day, and Dick seemed overjoyed. The welcome they gave to the media was in stark contrast to the pair's avoidance of publicity during their courtship. Reflecting—and influencing—public opinion regarding the couple, a columnist for *Modern Screen* comments in its October issue, "For some reason, they felt it necessary to be so discreet that it became a kind of cloak-and-dagger performance. No one could understand why. . . . The plain, simple, appalling answer to their strange headline-making behavior is that they both occasionally have very poor judgment about their personal lives." After reviewing Haymes's personal history, including his draft deferment and his subsequent efforts to enlist, the author states, "He doesn't think matters through." However, he continues, "All of Haymes's former wives agree on one thing, that Haymes is a good and golden and honorable lover. He is a man of loyalty and fidelity." Clearly, the marriage had at least temporarily worked to his advantage, for the public perception, fed by such articles, was that Rita had at last found someone "to love her just as she is," with "unasking devotion." The article notes that the headlines have made Dick once again a valuable commodity on the entertainment circuit. It concludes that all Dick wants now is to pay his debts and to love Rita, clearly a public relations effort to counter negative criticism.

Adjacent to the last column of the *Modern Screen* article is Dick Haymes's, "My Side of the Story," written on August 25, 1953. For the first time since the newspapers began reporting his tribulations, he took this rare opportunity to offer his explanation for the difficulties in which he was currently enmeshed. Here, he devotes most of the column to his efforts to join the military, trying to deflate the "draft dodger" notoriety. He also notes that Richard Cody had given him permission to leave the country without any warning that he might be breaking a law. He says that he was arrested while on his way to consult an attorney and further lists the violations of his rights by the Immigration Service:

I was called an "excludable" although the department knew of my draft rejection. I was called an "excludable" after having been given permission to leave the country, and when I asked why I was given permission in the first place I was told, "Well, the officials can't know everything."

I was then told to prepare my defense or "get the Congress to pass a law that would give me citizenship within sixty days." I was given that word by the Immigration Department.

On the twenty-ninth day, I was called and told to call the Department the next day.

The very next day I was on my way to see a lawyer—a sacred privilege in America—when I was arrested. I did not get the sixty days I was promised by the Department to make legal arrangements. I got no explanations for their actions since then—only tight-lipped silence that keeps burrowing into my peace of mind with suspense and anxiety.

In a short time, I am to appear for a hearing on my case. But politicians' statements have deluded the public into pre-judging me as a criminal, a deliberate betrayer of the wonderful privilege of living in the U.S.

If, in the confusion of official hearings and through the screen of authority, these facts are not properly presented to the press and public or are distorted by the shadows of inference of deliberate violation of the laws of this great country, I will at least rest in the peace of having given my side of the story.

The statement was obviously composed by Dick, his lawyers, and Rita's public relations staff. It was very important for Dick that he present his position to the public, and this article would be among the very few that showed any sympathy for Dick Haymes as his troubles continued to escalate in the days and months following.

After spending their wedding night at the Sands, the couple flew to New York, as Dick was scheduled for a two-week engagement at the Latin Casino in Philadelphia; and Rita left with her two daughters for a large home in Greenwich, Connecticut, that had been rented for them by Dick's mother. Throughout the ordeal, Marguerite was a constant and supportive presence to both Dick and Rita.

On September 29, a meeting was held at attorney Robert Eaton's office for Dick's creditors, one of whom was Eaton. Dick owed a total of $180,000, and his lawyer presented a plan to place him on a strict budget rather than to declare bankruptcy. His debts were broken down into three groups: $55,000 in taxes, $900 to forty creditors, and the balance to creditors who were owed from $1,000 to, in one case, $30,000. His smallest debt was to a drugstore for $2.50. Just five days later, Eaton resigned as Dick's attorney, stating that the $5,000 he was owed did not play a part in his decision, but rather that "personal differences" led to his resignation. Dick issued a statement to the press that all he wanted to do was to work and pay his debts, but that if the U.S. Government attached his salary, he would not have sufficient funds to cover his travel and business expenses.

If he were allowed to continue to work, he continued, he could pay off the debt within a reasonable time. His salary was attached by the IRS, and Dick then cancelled the remainder of his engagement in Philadelphia, unable even to pay his pianist. His next tour, accompanied by Rita, took him to Alabama, Indiana, and Texas, but because he had arranged to be paid in advance, the IRS was unable to make its collection.

Dick and Rita knew that they had to take some action to prevent his future wages from being attached, so on October 15, Rita convened a news conference to report that she was "flat broke" and had to be supported by her husband. She told the reporters that she hoped a plan might be made whereby Dick could pay his income taxes on an installment plan. Of course, she was still receiving income from Columbia Pictures (she received a percentage of the income from *Miss Sadie Thompson* as well as a salary), but she spent it quickly on attorney fees and other necessary expenses.

Her public announcement did not stop the criticism now leveled at her husband on a daily basis. One columnist headlined, "Dick Haymes' Actions Will Cost Him Fans," and criticized him sharply for having cut short his engagement in Philadelphia. Further, Rita's admission of "poverty" was ridiculed, as readers were reminded that she had been married to one of the richest men in the world.

For Dick Haymes, it seemed there was nowhere to turn. He was distraught and the constant tension took a toll on him physically as well as emotionally. Scheduled for an appearance as guest of honor at a club in Pittsburgh where he was to start a singing engagement, he did not appear, having been admitted to a hospital on November 2 in New York with a severe case of hypertension. His lawyer, David Marcus, said that his client had been driven "to the edge of a breakdown" by the constant pressure of the previous weeks. Haymes had told him that his nerves were shot: "I don't know where to turn. I want to work. I'm trying to work, but they won't let me." He seemed to see no way out of his current predicament, and his inability to fulfill his singing contracts was the subject of severe criticism by the press.

His most recent deportation hearing on October 28 had been particularly trying, especially when he was asked if he had ever stated that he was a U.S. citizen. He stumbled in his reply, for in his application for Actors Equity he had to claim to be a citizen to be admitted to membership. When learning of his status as a non-citizen, Actors Equity gave him six weeks to answer questions about his misstatement; and if he failed to do so, the union would have no choice but to cancel his membership. On November 26, the union took formal action to cancel his membership. For Haymes, this latest blow was not serious, as he was not a stage actor. But he was disturbed that he had been placed on the singer's union's (AGFA) unfair list because he owed arranger Nelson Riddle more than nine hundred dollars for the Pittsburgh show which he had cancelled. He would be required in the future to post a bond with any club where he might be scheduled to perform.

He left the hospital for a brief trip to Connecticut to see his family and then returned for another week to rest in preparation for his next road trip. In the following few weeks, he would be either on the road or at the Madison Hotel in New York City. During this period, the newspapers and magazines followed the story avidly. Dick and Rita allowed photographers to take informal pictures of the apparently happy family, with Yasmin and Rebecca featured prominently. The focus was clearly on Rita Hayworth, with one headline promising "The Truth about the Loves of Rita Hayworth." The article compares her own life to that of one of the most famous women that she had played: "the loves of Rita Hayworth bear a close resemblance to the loves of Carmen . . . because they've always been tempestuous and always varied." Of her love for Dick Haymes, the author notes that all who witnessed their wedding ceremony were convinced of one thing: "both were tremendously sincere—and deeply in love." Another fan magazine found that "in Dick, Rita has found a man who has none of the characteristics of all her other husbands—a man who adores her, looks up to her, and wishes her nothing but well." This very sympathetic piece sees Dick as "confused, unsure and much maligned." And it goes on to chastise those who would cast aspersions on his character for his indebtedness, noting that he refused bankruptcy and that when he was refused enlistment, he toured the world in USO shows "because he felt it was his duty." The public relations staff for Rita used the fan magazines for a counter-offensive to the scandal sheets and the daily newspapers, where reporting on the couple was unvaryingly negative.

But the troubles would not lessen. After receiving a notice of eviction for nonpayment of rent from the owners of the Greenwich home, they made the necessary payment and agreed to move by February 15. But on February 1, 1954, Dick and Rita were faced with new and particularly sensational headlines.

A sheriff's deputy with a warrant for Dick's civil arrest knocked on the door of their room at the Madison Hotel. The warrant was for Joanne Dru's alimony claim of over thirty-three thousand dollars, and it was delivered at this time because she was concerned that if Dick were deported, she might never receive the money. Dick was so distraught at this latest assault that he refused to open the door, and their attorney, Bartley Crum, as well as Joanne's lawyer met in the hallway of the hotel just outside Dick and Rita's suite. A crowd of reporters had heard about the fracas and soon camped out in the crowded hallway with the attorneys, later describing for their readers the "siege" at the Madison Hotel.

After speaking to his attorney from behind his barred door, Dick finally admitted Bartley Crum. Neither Dick nor Rita had eaten, and eventually they allowed the room service waiter to enter. Crum and Joanne's attorney reached an agreement regarding Dick's future payments, and after twenty-four hours Dick and Rita emerged from the hotel where they remained in residence. But in Greenwich, a deputy sheriff arrived with a complaint from the owner, who feared that the couple would leave without making their last rent payment. They were also charged with damages to the premises amounting to four thousand dollars. A guard was placed in the living room of the house inhabited only by the baby sitter, Mrs. Chambers, and Rita's two daughters. After moving the family out of the house, Rita sent the girls to Mrs. Chambers's home in a lower-class neighborhood in White Plains, New York.

A man appeared at the door of that house on March 18, claiming that he was interested in renting it when Mrs. Chambers left (she was to accompany the family on their travels). She admitted him, not knowing that he was really a reporter for *Confidential* magazine who was interested in the shabby premises and the yard filled with garbage cans where Yasmin and Rebecca were playing. He returned the next day with a photographer whose pictures of the girls in their unpleasant environment would soon make new newspaper headlines for Rita—and add another dimension to her struggles with Aly Khan.

Dick had another deportation meeting on March 22. He arrived with Rita, in a mink coat, and her two children, who had moved into the Madison Hotel. Both Dick and Rita looked ravaged from the turmoil of the past few weeks. They seemed unprepared for the committee's verdict: Dick was to be deported. The Immigration and Naturalization Service held that Haymes was an alien ineligible for citizenship because he claimed that his birth in Argentina, a then neutral country, provided him with exemption from the wartime draft laws. Invoking the McCarran Act, the service decided that since he was ineligible for citizenship and had left the country, he could not return—and thus would be deported. Ironically, the publicity about the Hawaiian trip came at an embarrassing moment for President Eisenhower, who was supporting a bill currently before Congress that would give statehood to Hawaii. As one newspaper noted, "If the deportation order interprets the McCarran Act to mean that Hawaii is a foreign country because it is not part of the continental United States, then Congress will be in the position of conferring citizenship on people who clearly are not eligible for it." The ruling effectively nullified the depositions his lawyers had submitted from a doctor and an army sergeant in February to the effect that Dick had, in fact, been in the army for several days in 1944 while undergoing a physical examination that he subsequently failed because of hypertension.

Leaving the hearing, the couple looked stunned; and although they avoided reporters, a photographer caught the bewilderment on the faces of the children and the shock and dismay on the faces of Dick and Rita. But two days later, unshaven, wearing sunglasses, Dick flew to Washington, D.C., where he and Bartley Crum would seek help from Senator Langer of North Dakota, who was reportedly a good friend of Rita Hayworth. Rita spoke out to the press, implying that Hollywood pressure was responsible for Dick's plight. The Immigration Service quickly rejoined that any implication that it had acted to safeguard the interests of Columbia Pictures was unfounded, maintaining that its action was a routine procedure.

Rita asserted that she would leave the country with Dick if he were deported; the whole family arrived at the Rockefeller Center passport office, where Rita and her children renewed their passports. Columnist Leonard Lyons noted on April 5 that after two futile days of rushing around the capital and trying to speak to the right people, Haymes took Rita out to a nightclub where he interviewed them. Lyons reports, "[Haymes] wept, 'If I could change my bones, my flesh. . . . No, no second beginning. I know this land and love it. . . . When I leave I guess I'll just say America forgive me.'" Rita added, "Well, they're set to fry us and we're ready."

They could not foresee the new trouble that would await them in a short time. Leaving the children with Mrs. Chambers, they drove to Key West and to Miami for a vacation—in part seeking to avoid confronting Aly Khan, who was expected in New York to pursue his claim for Yasmin's visit. On April 21, the Westchester Society for the Prevention of Cruelty to Children, acting upon the complaint of a neighbor of Mrs. Chambers, arrived to investigate the conditions of her home and, particularly, what they viewed as neglect of the well-being of the children. Rita and Dick, driving back to New York, learned that Yasmin and Rebecca had been placed in protective custody and that a hearing would be held in a few days. The reporters were camped outside the house, and photographers snapped every angle of the premises. They took a photo of Rita and Dick, looking grim and drawn, leaving Mrs. Chambers's house with the children, whom they had rushed to claim as soon as they reached New York. All four checked into the Roger Smith Hotel in White Plains to await the hearing. Both Aly Khan and Orson Welles offered statements that Rita was a loving and caring mother, refuting any charges of neglect, but the court did not lift its order of protection for the children.

In the deportation case, there was some good news: Bartley Crum charged that Dick Haymes was "trapped" by the government when he was not told that a trip to Hawaii might endanger his residency in the United States. He offered an affidavit by Richard Cody, who was the immigration officer who had interviewed Haymes before the Hawaii trip and had said that he needed no additional documents to be admitted back in the country. Cody stated that his superior at the office called his attention to Haymes's possible excludability, but instructed him not to warn the singer about it. The Washington attorney for Haymes, Welburn Maycock, informed the court that thousands of similar warnings had been issued to persons leaving the country. "This was like officially lying to him," Maycock told the board. "He would never have gone had he known [the true situation]. . . . He got a dishonorable deal by the government of the U.S." The result was that the deportation order was suspended, and the case would be sent back to the Immigration Service for further hearings. The entrapment charge was widely reported, creating much-needed sympathy for the couple, and Rita and Dick greeted the deportation suspension with overwhelming relief. Attorney David Marcus said they were crying "tears of joy."

Beset by financial problems, and with Rita's tense negotiations with Columbia Pictures, the couple decided in late June to move to Nevada. They drove to Las Vegas, arriving at the Sands Hotel before the two girls, Marguerite (who was now escorting them), a tutor, and a nursemaid came in by train. They found a two-bedroom house in Crystal Bay in the mountains at Lake Tahoe, where Marguerite and the two girls would wait until Bartley Crum, David Marcus, and Welborn Maycock arrived in Las Vegas to make plans for the deportation hearing scheduled for June 26 in Los Angeles.

An article headlined "Dick Haymes Deluged by Subpoenas" aptly introduces the free-for-all that began his latest hearing. The reporter writes, "In a turbulent scene that rivaled wide-screen movie epics, the harried 36-year-old husband of actress Rita Hayworth was the target of subpoenas from his alimony-anxious ex-wife, Nora, the tax-hungry Bureau of Internal Revenue, and a creditor." With process servers on his heels, Dick and his attorneys reached the hearing room through a back stairway, but not quickly enough to avoid a server who threw a subpoena regarding alimony payments onto the table where Haymes was sitting. Soon another process server arrived and began to wrestle with the guards who tried to hold him back, declaring that he was a federal official. The guards released him and he handed Dick a subpoena ordering him to appear July 9 for an income tax accounting. Finally, the hearing proceeded, and the attorneys made a charge against Herman R. Landon, district director of the U.S. Immigration and Naturalization Service, for ordering an underling not to advise Dick Haymes that he faced deportation in making the trip to Hawaii a year earlier. But the charge against Landon was based on the testimony of Richard Cody, who was now accused by the government's attorney of suffering memory lapses because of a brain injury. Cody, who had suffered a wound in Tunisia in 1943 while serving with General Patton, denounced the "strictly smear tactics" now being used to discredit him. The government refused to drop the charges against Haymes and the hearing was adjourned. One further blow awaited him in Los Angeles—a summons to appear in court on July 2 to answer Joanne Dru's charges of nonpayment. Dick quickly returned to Nevada, aware that if he missed that court date, he would face arrest if he ever returned to Los Angeles. On July 29, his plea of entrapment was rejected, and his attorneys planned an appeal— even to the Supreme Court if necessary. Their troubles continued, for the following week the White Plains court extended its jurisdiction over Rita's two children after Aly Khan sought a court order to spend more time with his daughter. They later learned that the court's jurisdiction over the children would not end until December 24.

They had read Columbia Pictures' denial of charges by attorneys David Marcus and Bartley Crum, implicating Harry Cohn specifically, that the studio had instigated the deportation hearing. Crum replied that he believed proceedings were inspired from a "source or sources outside the government and Haymes was getting a raw deal." Crum stood by his comments regarding the studio's probable involvement.

Both Dick and Rita were, as might be expected from months of torment, worn out, depressed, and filled with anxiety. They needed to escape from the morbid curiosity and outright hostility that they faced daily from the same public that had once idolized them. Dick and Rita joined the girls at the small house in Crystal Bay, far from the celebrity rituals that had defined their lives for more than fifteen years. A July 1954 magazine story is headlined "Poor Richard Haymes," with a subtitle, "Money fame and the love of four beautiful women have failed to bring the handsome crooner peace of mind. He's still behind the eight-ball." The article examines Dick's career, concluding that he was naïve about the need to cultivate gossip columnists and disk jockeys, offending many in the industry whom he now needed at least for sympathy and moral support. The article is cynical about Dick's hospitalization, observing that the nightclub in Pittsburgh suspected "that his illness was more financial than medical." Other comments highly critical of Dick Haymes are exhumed, so that the final picture that emerges is decidedly unflattering. The newspaper articles and columns that focus primarily on Rita Hayworth are far more positive toward both her and Dick. Columnist Earl Wilson visited them in Lake Tahoe and persuaded a reluctant Dick to give him an interview. Dick was so disturbed by all the recent efforts to entrap him that he believed at first that the columnist had had his phone tapped. In the interview held at the Cal-Neva Lodge, Dick did most of the talking for both himself and Rita, in large measure because of her reluctance to speak to the press, her own anxieties over what might prove to be detrimental publicity, and her long reliance on a public-relations staff that normally spoke for her.

During the interview, Dick mentions Columbia Pictures' dislike of him—indirectly supporting the widespread belief that Harry Cohn had initially contacted the Immigration Service. Rita chimes in that her animosity toward the studio is based upon the roles they have been assigning her—"bad girl" parts that she believes are typecasting her. Wilson praises Dick's courage in returning to Los Angeles for a deportation hearing, knowing that he was subject to arrest for back alimony and child support in California. After reviewing the lives and loves of both Rita and Dick, Wilson wonders if their love can survive the pain and grief of recent events, and concludes that it is strong enough to withstand past and future assaults. For the women of America, Rita is a sympathetic figure, for they are saying, "What's she done wrong—except stick by the man she loves?" Another movie fan magazine is squarely on their side, again citing their love as the basis for sympathy: "The bottom of pretty nearly everything has dropped out for Rita and Dick. But they still have their love. And with that for a foundation, there are no heights to which they cannot ascend." Clearly, the saga of Rita Hayworth and Dick Haymes was the key story in the culture of celebrity of that era. But what of their lives during this year when they were awaiting so many decisions crucial to their future?

Dick's son Skip (Richard Jr.) spent the whole summer in Lake Tahoe, the only extended time he remembers spending with his father following his parents' divorce. (His younger sister, Pidge, remembers spending two weeks there.) Skip had first met Rita in a restaurant before his father and Rita were married. The child was very impressed with movie stars, and on the way home he learned who she was. The next day, when his father picked him up at home to drive him to school, he said, "Do you mean that was Rita Hayworth?" repeating his question several times, to which his father responded, "I've told you a thousand times, yes." Rita was a very nice person, he recalls, very quiet except when she drank, then becoming erratic. He remembers how isolated they were at Lake Tahoe, his father leaving the premises only to shop in Reno. They did not read the newspapers or listen to the news on the radio. Dick and Rita slept late, the result of nightly drinking until pre-dawn hours. Richard Jr. recalls how difficult it was for the children to adjust to the new sleeping hours, learning to remain in their room until 11 AM.

He remembers his father's sense of humor and his unabated pleasure in playing pranks and performing as a mimic. On one occasion, he was sitting on the porch looking at the trees when a red light appeared to dart from tree to tree. It kept coming closer and finally lunged at the children. It was Dick with a flashlight in his mouth, playing to a delighted young audience. His daughter, Pidge, recalls how much fun they all had in Lake Tahoe with Rita's two daughters. He and Rita, she recalls, were great in the daytime, Dick hard at work writing a screenplay, but at night they would fight and drink. She too remembers how funny and playful he could be, how he and Rita would tell them ghost stories. Pidge remembers that in these weeks in Lake Tahoe she came to know her father better than at any time until the last decade of his life.

Because of their strained finances and an uncertain future, Dick and Rita thought that they should open negotiations with Columbia Pictures regarding renewal of her contract as well as the sale to the studio of her film production company, Beckwith Productions, worth $700,000. The terms they worked out provided for a loan of $50,000 to Dick so that he might pay his most pressing obligations to his ex-wives (he was to repay the loan at $10,000 per year). The contract also provided that Dick be allowed access to the Columbia lot and that the studio help with his efforts to reverse the deportation ruling. Finally, it stipulated that Rita might shoot new films abroad if, indeed, her husband were deported. She would now make two films for the studio at a salary of $150,000 each. She also received an advance so that she might be able to meet current expenses. Columbia worried that Rita might back out of her film contract after receiving payment for Beckwith, so she had to deposit $100,000 in escrow as security for Columbia. And Dick was given an option by the studio for his services as a screenwriter. In the next few months, Rita also worked out a new agreement with her former husband, Aly Khan, which was signed after the court order in Westchester was suspended.

Leaving the girls in Nevada, Rita and Dick returned to Los Angeles, where planning was under way for her new film, *Joseph and His Brethren*. Dick had grown a beard and was hoping that he might be cast as Joseph. The film would be made by the couple's new company, Crystal Bay Productions.

A fan magazine headlined "Things Are Looking Up" described their idyllic time in Lake Tahoe and a future that once again seemed to promise the couple happiness. The article noted gossip items hinting at troubles in the marriage but concluded, "These are inevitable for stars in the spotlight."

Yet again, the plans that had seemed so promising were doomed to fail. Both Dick and Rita were drinking heavily and quarreling at home and in public. Unquestionably, Dick was closely guiding and monitoring her career, and Columbia Pictures finally ordered that he leave the premises. As a result, Rita did not return to work at the studio April 5 (shooting on the film was scheduled to begin by April 11), and Dick notified the director that Rita was ill; actually the two were dining at the Polo Lounge of the Beverly Hills Hotel. They remained there for hours, both noticeably drunk. The next day, Columbia ordered Rita to return to the studio within twenty-four hours. Rita instead replied that the contract was invalid as the production was not on schedule. Her lawyers demanded return of the escrow payment as well as her contractual fee for the film. Columbia responded with a lawsuit against Rita, and the legal battles continued.

One month before their lease in Nevada was over, the couple rented a beach house in Malibu. Dick had been booked by the Dunes Hotel in Las Vegas for two weeks, June 18–July 8, 1955. Their social life was certainly livelier than it had been in Nevada, but their drinking and quarreling escalated. Richard Jr. remembers one occasion when his father and Rita rented a sailboat and took him and Ian Bernard to Catalina Island. Humphrey Bogart was part of the group, sailing his own boat; he raced Dick back to Los Angeles. Richard Jr. recalls how congenial they all were and how Dick amused everyone with his imitation of Bogart, whom he nicknamed "Captain Bligh." In Malibu, he recalls, Rita was soft-spoken and very nice to him. One night, however, when she was quite drunk, she decided to have a talk with him, but soon she and Dick were caught up in one of their ferocious quarrels.

In November the Board of Immigration Appeals in Washington affirmed the deportation order, and David Marcus announced immediately that he would file a petition with the U.S. District Court in Washington to determine the constitutionality of the McCarran-Walter Act. The next months were marked by increasing tensions within the marriage, as the couple seemed unable to extricate themselves from the pattern of drinking and mutual verbal abuse. The following April, Dick was dealt another blow when his lawyer, David Marcus, asked to be relieved of representing him. As reported in Louella Parsons's column, Marcus charged Dick with not keeping appointments with him, but the most serious charge was that he had not been paid. "The only money Haymes has advanced is $114 and $400 for telephone calls and court costs."

Two months later, however, Dick and Rita received the news they had hoped and prayed for during the past two years. On May 31, 1955, U.S. District Judge Burnita S. Matthews, in Washington, D.C., ruled that Dick Haymes was "not deportable" as he had not reentered the United States from a foreign country. Hawaii, Judge Matthews ruled, was "a geographical part of the United States." Dick was speechless when he received the news while lunching in Beverly Hills, and he said, "[Rita] was kind of laughing, so excited she could hardly speak." Both said they were in a state of shock, but Dick quickly paid tribute to his wife: "Throughout this long ordeal, I've had my moments of extreme despondency. She has been my strength and my courage." Rita declared to a reporter that she was "the happiest woman in the world."

Yet the strains on their marriage would prove insurmountable. Rita, from her childhood, was emotionally reserved. She never really faced the anguish of her teen years and did not question why she looked for security in the men she married. Dick, too, from childhood, could not admit to the emotional neglect he suffered, and so the two were blind to their own needs and the needs of the other. And as their distress at their situation grew, they each sought solace in drink—resulting inevitably in outbursts of anger. Yet Ian Bernard, who was with them often in this period, recalls that he never saw Dick acting in a cruel or abusive manner to Rita.

On August 23, 1955, Dick opened a two-week engagement at the Cocoanut Grove in the Ambassador Hotel in Los Angeles, where the couple planned to stay during the engagement. Rita was at ringside as Dick entered to "a tidal wave of sentimental frenzy without parallel in supper clubs," according to a reporter at the scene. The club was filled to capacity, and Haymes was accorded the kind of reception normally reserved for heroes. Clearly, the public was on his side in the highly publicized deportation struggle as well as in his marital problems. After every song, he had to quell the applause which threatened to shake the palm trees loose. His nine songs took almost twenty minutes longer than usual. He dedicated "Come Rain or Come Shine" to Rita and then introduced her to the audience. He was touched by the response, repeating, "You're wonderful," to the audience and acknowledging that Ian Bernard, his piano accompanist and musical director, was "two-thirds of the show."

During intermissions and after each show, however, Dick and Rita resumed their quarrelling, and years later he would look back sadly on those days: "We tried—but we also were spending more and more time looking into the bottom of emptied bottles, brawling—often in public—and generally taking out our disappointments in life on each other. Tragic, but true. Our parting was as sudden as our meeting. I was singing at the Cocoanut Grove in Los Angeles and as the aftermath of an opening night drunken fight between the two of us, I came home and found that Rita had simply disappeared out of my life." Dick admitted years later, "We had a fight, I hit her—something I was never proud of—and she left." They fought every night, but it was after the Saturday night performance that he struck Rita. She left the Ambassador, drove back to Malibu to pick up her children, and left him forever. He found out when he finished the Sunday show and returned to their home.

Dick completed his engagement at the Cocoanut Grove, the audience clearly sympathetic when he sobbed while singing "Love Me or Leave Me" and was again moved to tears when he reprised his dedication of "Come Rain or Come Shine" to Rita. He spoke openly of their problems, but could not face the finality of her leaving. "I know she loves me and I love her," he said, and expressed his conviction that she would return. But he was clearly devastated by her departure. His son remembers his father taking him to a restaurant in Santa Monica and starting to cry about Rita. He was clearly getting drunk, and later at Malibu, his son recalls, "It was utterly grotesque." Dick poured beer into the bowl of the dog, Brutus, and soon both he and the animal passed out on the floor.

The damage that the marriage to Rita Hayworth wrought on Dick Haymes's personal and professional career was incalculable. Rita filed for divorce in Reno on November 4, and he filed his reply on November 30, routinely denying her charges of extreme mental cruelty. Neither party asked for financial consideration. The divorce was granted on December 12, but even before the final decree the publicity machines were attacking Dick Haymes. One headline from December screamed: "WHAT DICK DID TO RITA: THERE ARE SOME ACTS NO WOMAN—NOT EVEN A WOMAN IN LOVE CAN FORGIVE. THIS IS WHY RITA FLED FROM DICK HAYMES." The implication is that since she fled *after* their problems seemed to have been resolved, there is more to the story than the deportation/financial problems. The allegations that Dick "controlled" Rita began at Columbia Pictures, and there is little doubt that the new publicity emanated from its public relations department. The article concluded that Dick brought Rita a "long history of heartache." The most sensational magazines continued their attacks on him for years: a "Crazy, Mixed-up Crooner" or "This Month's Candidate for 'In the Pit': The Guy They Love to Leave" or, in a story about Rita, he was simply "Poor Richard" who "belted the bottle and his bride."

It is ironic that Dick would be blamed for Rita's troubles for years to come when shortly after their divorce she once again placed her personal and professional life in the hands of a man she had just met. Egyptian-born producer Raymond Hakim wanted Rita to star in a film about the life of Isadora Duncan. Hakim was entrusted by Rita with getting her released from her Columbia Pictures contract. Leaving her children with Aly Khan (she had traveled to France some weeks earlier for Yasmin's reunion with her father), she and Hakim sailed for New York on December 13, the day after her final divorce decree from Dick Haymes. As in the past, she left legal matters unfinished when she sailed, failing even to inform her attorney of her plans.

Critics of Dick Haymes then and now have found it simpler to blame him for this latest unsuccessful marriage than to explore the possibility that, as in many divorces, it is difficult to place blame solely on one person. Both brought serious problems into their relationship, and he was vilified and she was victimized in the press. As the foregoing account demonstrates, the responsibility rested on both Dick and Rita, but ultimately, and particularly damning for his career, all of the blame for the collapse of their marriage was placed on him. For Dick, the future was still clouded by the need to resolve his financial problems and to restart his faltering career. He looked to the nightclub scene and, like Frank Sinatra, who was making some of his finest albums in this period, to the recording studio, where he hoped to join the ranks of legendary singers of the era. He knew it wouldn't be easy, but he was determined to reclaim at least some part of his early success.

CHAPTER 6

The Late 1950s

Triumph and Despair

Rita Hayworth's departure affected Dick Haymes deeply, and he fought to overcome the pain and insecurity that drinking could not assuage. Yet scarcely two weeks after the divorce became final, he would meet with his friend and musical arranger Ian Bernard to record what many believe to be among the best romantic ballad albums ever recorded by any artist, *Rain or Shine*, to be followed within a year by the equally impressive *Moondreams*. Through his agent at MCA, Capitol Records had signed Dick to a two-album contract and wanted Nelson Riddle, the noted accompanist for Frank Sinatra, to arrange and conduct. Another possibility was a noted figure in the music industry, Billy May. But Dick instead chose Bernard because he "wanted strings" in the arrangements. He knew that he wanted an accompaniment that was strong yet would not overpower his delivery. Bernard believes that Dick's selecting him was "generous and brave," as Bernard was just starting out in the business and Dick badly needed a successful recording after a two-year hiatus.

The two had just concluded a very popular engagement, the lavish Magic Carpet Revue at the Dunes in Las Vegas; and, as Ian Bernard recalls, Dick was so impressed with his arrangements for those performances that he asked Bernard if he could do the same for his Capitol sides, using even more strings in the orchestra. Bernard says that he will never forget how Dick went to bat for him with Capitol—a courageous act considering how much Dick's future depended on the new recordings. For Bernard, it was a challenge, and he remembers wondering what sound would come out of the orchestra when he gave the downbeat. One of the notable musicians was the first violin—Felix Slatkin (father of noted conductor Leonard Slatkin)—who at the time was the conductor for the Hollywood Bowl orchestra. Some of the fine arrangements were by Johnny Mandel.

Reminiscing about these recordings some years later, Dick said they were probably "a culmination of a lot of things being projected through me; when you sing a song, you don't sing it just with your throat and your head. It was probably a lot of things that were coming through—like Sinatra's *Wee Small Hours*—vocally he has been better, but the truth, the feeling was there. It could very well be that I felt the career was slipping out of my fingers. When I sang 'The More I See You' I could have been thinking of the peak of my career when I was working with Betty [Grable], walking around like the kingpin of Twentieth Century–Fox."

A few years earlier, Dick had expressed his opinion of the contemporary craze in popular singing, the bellowing styles, over-produced records, multiple recording methods, pseudo folk tunes, and gimmicky songs with ludicrous lyrics. He told a reporter,

I can't tell you why the public's interest has left intelligent standards for sensationalism, but I can tell you one thing that's keeping it that way. The music publishers, record companies, and everybody between the two are telling one another their best sales are to be made by riding the crest of flash-in-the-pan artists and material.

About the only good result of this are the efforts of the established singers, who've gotten fed up, to go back and revive the good tunes. By now the split is well defined—either you're a guy that's known for stunts or you sing almost nothing but vintage material.

He bemoaned the young singers looking for the "fast buck," unaware that they have been seduced by the promise of instant popularity and big money. The money goes quickly, as he knew; and for Dick Haymes, what he sang was inseparable from his personal values. "A person's life span is an awfully brief bit of time and, I guess, I'm past my halfway point. Call it integrity, aesthetics, conscientious objection, or whatever you will, but I refuse to turn to something I don't believe in." Such remarks did not endear him to the leaders of the music industry; but to his credit, he did continue to record music—old and new—that he admired. In an interview for *Downbeat* in January 1956, Leonard Feather asked him to judge some new recordings. He liked recordings by Buddy Rich, Frankie Laine, Harry James, and Mel Tormé, but was highly critical of Elvis Presley: "It's very sick. It's a shame to massacre a pretty song like 'Blue Moon.'" His highest praise went to Frank Sinatra's Capitol album, *You Make Me Feel So Young*, in his view, a perfect album.

Dick and Ian Bernard met at the Racquet Club in Palm Springs to discuss the recordings. Ian remembers that he suggested many of the songs for what they both agreed would be a romantic album. The standards on *Rain or Shine* include songs Haymes had recorded earlier in his career, "It Might as Well Be Spring," "The More I See You," "Where or When," "Little White Lies," and the title song, "Come Rain or Come Shine." The follow-up album, *Moondreams*, is equally if not more impressive, with extraordinarily moving renditions of "Skylark," "What's New?" "When I Fall in Love," and an unusually slow-paced, almost tragic rendition of the Jerome Kern–Dorothy Fields classic, "The Way You Look Tonight." Haymes is never pretentious, and his phrasing is always impeccable. Ian Bernard remembers that it was Dick's decision to record that song at a particularly slow tempo, which brought out its darker dimensions. It is unlike the song made popular many years earlier by Fred Astaire, who sang it with cool sophistication and a more swinging tempo.

The differences between the songs as they were recorded earlier and in these albums are striking. Haymes's sensitivity to the lyrics is so profound that listeners often feel that they are hearing familiar songs for the first time. Will Friedwald notes that on the Decca recordings Haymes "came off as assured and even-tempered; here, he's just a little bit trembly and mussed up, exactly the mood that Ian Bernard's offbeat stylized scores require." Friedwald rates *Moondreams* as equal to Sinatra's much-praised and similar album, *Close to You*, for "unsettling introspection." Another critic felt that no other artist had approached the songs on the album with such "tender love, deep understanding, and romantic caress." And the same critic described Ian Bernard's orchestra as "coolly inspired, a perfect backup to the vocals, never overstated, always swinging, lush in strings when appropriate, and setting off with each song in a different instrumental mood." Perhaps British radio host Dave Gelly, looking back at Dick's career, best expressed the quality of these recordings:

> *Moondreams* and *Rain or Shine* caught that wonderful voice when it reached its precarious maturity. There is something new: a melting tenderness that's only hinted at in earlier recordings. It shows itself in a slight feathery haze—the hint of a whisper at the edge of a tone that he manipulates to devastating effect. He pauses before a note and lets it slide downwards with a tiny shudder, on the brink of an unspeakable passion. He concentrates on slow ballads, but when he chose to move the tempo up a little, he could bring out a very attractive light swing. He doesn't dig into the rhythm or wind up the pressure in the last chorus like Sinatra. If anything, Dick Haymes's approach is more like Crosby's, floating along with the beat. In the 1950s, the best work of singers is *Rain or Shine* and *Wee Small Hours*, in the same year. The styles may be different, but in sheer quality, they're just about equal.

There is, indeed, an emotional gulf between Dick Haymes as a singer in the 1940s and in the mid to late 1950s, with a maturity, a depth of feeling, a sense of tragic fatalism that few singers ever convey. We have seen that these albums were recorded when Dick's personal life was filled with anguish; and as one critic has observed, the scars of life were beginning to show in his voice—to advantage. Dick always said that his best acting was in his singing, and there is no doubt that these two albums are among the richest, most profound expressions of sorrow, loss, and romantic yearning that have ever been released. Most music critics believe that Haymes here outclassed every other ballad singer, and some believe that he equaled or surpassed Sinatra.

Frank Sinatra had been recording at Capitol since 1953, working with Riddle and Billy May. The first albums helped establish Sinatra's new swinging personality, and in 1954 he was chosen the top male singer by *Billboard*. His film career, following the Academy Award for Best Supporting Actor in *From Here to Eternity* in 1953, was equally successful; he starred in the romantic comedy *The Tender Trap*, an adaptation of the Broadway musical *Guys and Dolls*, and the dark drama *The Man with the Golden Arm*, all in 1955. He was also a regular performer on television, with an outstanding star turn in a musical version of *Our Town* (1955). But like Dick Haymes. his marriage to a beautiful movie star, Ava Gardner, had broken up, and he, too, was distraught. In five sessions in February and March 1955, Sinatra and Riddle recorded *In the Wee Small Hours*, regarded by critics as perhaps his most moving and vocally perfect album. The listener shares the longing and quiet desperation in each of the sixteen songs. Dick's two Capitol albums convey similar emotional depths, but Sinatra's recordings have become standards of popular music whereas Dick's were forgotten until they were re-released and rediscovered in the 1970s. The CD *The Capitol Years*, which includes both albums, is unavailable today, but a number of the selections appear on *The Best of Dick Haymes* and *Easy to Listen To*, neither selling remotely close to the volume of the Sinatra albums.

Dick was well aware of Sinatra's popularity, but he never expressed resentment or envy. Indeed, he never spoke of Sinatra except in passing; and according to Ian Bernard, he did not listen to Sinatra during the period when he was recording for Capitol. Bernard sees no similarity between the two as singers and notes that Dick's singing behind the beat on these albums (typical of Sinatra) occurred because he was so relaxed and having a good time. Dick was well prepared when he entered the recording studio and was sober on all of the six recording sessions for the two albums. Bernard admits to being a hard taskmaster, and he and Dick worked well together. Only on one track, the concluding song on *Moondreams*, "When I Fall in Love," did he seem to be slightly hung over—and it is reflected on his coming in a little late on the beat.

Dick Haymes and Ian Bernard were on very good terms for almost nine years, and Bernard remembers that Dick always paid him on time—remarkable for someone with a history of financial delinquency. Somehow, Dick Haymes knew that in Ian Bernard he had found an artist who shared his goals and would enable him to reach a level of perfection to which he had always aspired.

There is no question that the Capitol recordings could have resurrected Dick's waning career, but because so much had changed in popular music tastes, the general public that was now enamored of Elvis Presley and rock and roll ignored them. Recording companies were not eager to sign ballad singers, apart from Sinatra, and Dick Haymes was not offered another contract by Capitol, although he recorded a few sides with Bernard and with Billy May and his orchestra in 1956. No, for Dick Haymes, the new recordings could simply open the doors to much better club engagements and to guest appearances on television and radio variety shows, but they would not restore his past star status.

In 1956, Dick Haymes was back in New York City, where he teamed with Cy Coleman (who would become famous for the scores of such Broadway musicals as *Sweet Charity* and *City of Angels*) and his trio of drums, bass, and bongo drums, with Coleman on the piano. They opened at the Versailles club, and Gene Knight, in the New York *Journal American*, described it as a "highlight of the winter season"; Dick "delivered like the real pro he is. . . . Very good was the way Haymes sang 'Two Different Worlds,' 'Our Love Is Here to Stay' and 'Rain or Shine.' When Dick whispers these songs, there's no sweeter voice in the supper clubs. And when he hits the high notes, they're round, full and on pitch. . . . [H]ere is a real good singer. Best, I think, was his 'Hollywood Love,' the words of which had a special meaning for Dick and those who know his colorful career." His appearance at the Versailles was greeted by sustained applause, a clear indication that he was on the road back.

Cy Coleman liked Dick and remembered that they were good friends. He believed that Dick had the best range of any singer; and in the remarkable "On a Slow Boat to China," where Dick takes a bass low note at the very end, Coleman remembered that it was Dick's idea—increasing the jazz effect on the recording. Coleman believed that Haymes just adapted to his jazz trio and could do jazz singing as well as any of his contemporaries. Dick asked Coleman to record with him; and, as with Bernard, he was sober during the sessions, even though he was drinking heavily during this period. Their recordings, which included several numbers with Maury Laws's orchestra, are distinctive in that the tempo is much faster than in Haymes's standard recordings, and he reveals how skilled he is as a jazz singer. Unfortunately, these recording came at a time in his career when it was difficult to re-establish his persona in popular music, as Sinatra had done some years earlier; although, in a recording he would make a few years later, he would again demonstrate the same skill with a jazz beat.

He recorded two songs in 1958 with Marion Evans conducting and arranging. Evans, who liked Dick very much, remembers an amusing story that circulated widely among musicians who were by now aware of Dick's naiveté and his inability to handle financial matters. The musicians' union contracts stipulated that performers would have to pay additional fees if a recorded arrangement was to be used in movies or in nightclubs. After one of their sessions in the RCA studios, where they were recording for Sunbeam, Dick took the music with him, planning to use it in a Las Vegas nightclub. In the taxi taking them to their respective homes, Evans said to Dick, "I know that you are going to Las Vegas tomorrow for a rehearsal. I have to tell you something. You'll have a rude shock if I don't tell you that a chemist manufactured a twenty-four-hour ink, and you'll be rehearsing in Las Vegas and all the notes will disappear off the page." Dick replied, "You're kidding! I never heard of such a thing." Evans replied, "My friend said nobody wants to pay him for the additional category to be used [the night-club venue]." Dick asked, "What can I do?" to which Evans replied, "Well, fortunately, he had the same chemist do a fix-it and put it in an aerosol can, and if he sprays the sheets of music anytime up to twenty-four hours, the notes will never disappear." Dick then said, "Can you take the music and spray it?" Evans said, "You'll have to pay." Dick said that he would give Evans a check, but Evans said that the musician would acccpt only cash. "Give me the music, and I'll get it sprayed; it will take a few hours to dry. In the meantime, if you can find the cash, I'll call you in a couple of hours after I spray it, and give it back to you." Evans remembers that he went home and watched TV until Dick called telling him he had the cash. Evans then gave him the music. The anecdote is certainly amusing, but it is also sad, in that Dick's childlike acceptance of the far-fetched story reveals how much he had become accustomed to employing foolish financial trickery even in his professional life.

Apart from one or two appearances on variety shows, notably on *Stage Show* with Tommy and Jimmy Dorsey in October 1955, Dick had made no appearances on television during the years when he was with Rita and was fighting his legal battles. In 1956, he again served as host on the Tommy and Jimmy Dorsey *Stage Show* in May 1956. The program featured a tribute to Irving Berlin, and it would prove to be one of Dick's most successful appearances on television.

From his first entrance, there is a striking similarity between him and Sinatra: the relaxed, swinging delivery, the expressive hand movements that emphasize a song's meaning, the use of the full body to convey nuances of a song's lyrics. Haymes opens with a rhythmic rendition of "Isn't This a Lovely Day?" and then dons his glasses to introduce singer Roberta Sherwood. Later, he sings the title song from his new album, "Rain or Shine." The dark background emphasizes his face, hands, and movements, particularly in a close-up, high-angle shot, as he looks up and we see him apparently *thinking* the words. It is doubly moving to see him in a dramatic performance of a song from one of the best albums he ever made, *Rain or Shine*. Haymes is a polished and gracious host, and his voice and style are impeccable.

Also in 1956, he became a frequent guest on other television shows: the *Ernie Kovacs Show* in July 1956; the *NBC Bandstand* on several occasions (as "Mr. Music"), with the Johnny Guarnieri Trio from August through October 1956; on *The Jackie Gleason Show*; and *The Tonight Show* with Jack Parr in 1957. On one occasion in the same year, he was featured in a television drama, *The Lord Don't Play Favorites*, on NBC. These appearances served to keep him in the public eye and to help with his expenses, but a firm career in television eluded him.

Some years earlier (in 1952), he had starred with actress Diana Lynn in the Ford Theater's drama, *National Honeymoon*. The story was a forerunner of two recent films, *The Truman Show* and *Ed TV*, using television itself as a phenomenon shaping lives of ordinary people. Here, the gimmick was the newlywed couple appearing on TV immediately after their wedding, revealing how they met, their first kiss, the wedding proposal, their plans for the future—all on national television and rewarded by lavish gifts and a honeymoon night in a deluxe hotel. It is a morality tale that excoriates the materialism of a culture that exploits young people for the amusement of millions of people—and interestingly, it is an early example of the current "reality" television programs. A bride has arranged for a television appearance for herself and her groom without telling the young man, whose sense of privacy and wholesome values are offended by the public display. Haymes is the groom, bringing genuine feeling to the story: the plight of the bride, who is overcome with guilt at arranging the TV appearance, and her new husband, who is humiliated by the vulgarity of the show and the very public airing of private, treasured moments of his courtship.

Haymes acts with conviction, and because the drama features flashbacks of mostly comic key moments in the courtship, and then focuses on the current moral crisis, Haymes has the opportunity to display a wider range of acting skills than in a musical program. He captures the shifts in mood— anger, disgust, despair, and finally happiness. It is a slight drama, torn between a serious message and a comic form, but it was a fine vehicle for Dick Haymes, who looks like a matinee idol and gives a measured, thoroughly convincing performance. It seemed in 1952 that in the next years television drama would become an important medium for his talents, but that was not to be. His personal dramas would become insistent, and after a brief role in a Roger Moore "Saint" drama in 1965 (filmed in England), Haymes's television career was as a singer until the 1970s, when he returned to drama, but only in brief supporting parts. *National Honeymoon* is important in the Haymes canon as an indication of his unfulfilled potential as a dramatic actor.

After his two fine recordings that did not achieve large sales in a world that was reeling with Elvis Presley and his imitators, Dick was playing nightclubs around the country. As always, he had a female companion, now Kitty Kelly Tanenbaum (her former husband was a furrier in Los Angeles), who joined him in heavy drinking soirees. Al Lerner remembers that he heard Dick would be opening at the Latin Quarter in New York City with singer Kay Starr, and so he phoned Dick to wish him well. Lerner had been suing him for a month, but Dick was very friendly, saying, "That's got nothing to do with you and me." We were like brothers, Lerner recalls, and Dick wanted me to hear his new album, which Lerner didn't much care for ("too breathy," he feels). They were both drunk, and they fought over Lerner's remarks. Kitty intervened, telling Dick that he always respected Al Lerner's opinion, at which point Dick shouted, "Who's talking to you?" and almost struck her. Al wrestled Dick to the floor until they were both bloody and Dick told him to leave. Al left, taking Kitty with him. This was not the Dick Haymes that Al Lerner knew in the 1940s—"a very docile guy" whose only vice was borrowing money. Lerner saw Dick's temper only when he was drunk and believes that Dick's anger at some of the women he knew reflected his resentment of his mother.

In February 1957, newspapers reported that Dick Haymes and a girl were booked for drunken driving in Miami, where he was appearing at a club. Two policemen, investigating loud music coming from a parking lot, found Haymes and a girl "enjoying a pre-dawn tango." Nearby was a sports car stranded on a pile of rocks, with music blaring from the radio. The couple was booked on charges of being drunk, and each was released on a twenty-five-dollar bond. According to the arresting officer, Haymes was so drunk that he should not have been dancing, for he could barely stand up. They both claimed that because they were unable to dislodge the car, they decided to dance. Kitty said that she was driving, as Dick did not have a driver's license. The car was traced to Red Rand, owner of radio station WINZ, who confirmed that it was his and that Dick was his houseguest. Kitty was identified as a secretary in a Miami Beach theatrical booking agency. Dick admitted years later that he was going downhill: "Self-pity was taking over where self-respect had once reigned supreme. I was losing total objectivity in my work and when that happens you eventually topple."

Dick was living in a one-bedroom apartment at 1040 Park Avenue in 1957, and his son, Richard, having problems in Los Angeles, decided to move in with his father. He remembers that his father was concerned about him but remained distant. Dick bought his son a set of drums, but was not at all interested in hearing Richard Jr. play them. He remembers attending a private school and seeing little of his father, who was usually in bed, nursing a hangover. He slept on a couch in the living room. He quickly became bored and spent a good deal of time with his grandmother (nicknamed "Tootie"), who lived in a penthouse on East Sixty-fourth Street.

In 1955, Marguerite Haymes had revealed to the press that she had been married since 1943 to Fred Waters, her former student, who was four years younger than Dick. This marriage did not last, and her two sons had once again to cope with their mother's penchant for self-promotion, as the newspapers carried pictures of Marguerite holding up photos of her young husband. Yet she would prove a devoted grandmother to Richard Jr., who remembers her with great fondness. Bob Haymes, he recalls, went into therapy to deal with his feelings about his mother, and ultimately concluded that she did the best she could but was a "flake." Dick never did explore his anger toward his mother; indeed, until his last years, he avoided confronting the emotions that were increasingly leading to his self-destruction.

Marguerite had always craved luxury, and her penthouse in New York City was breathtaking, featuring a huge terrace with water fountains. She had several poodles and birds, and the furnishings were lavish. For Richard Jr., her apartment was a much-needed refuge from the adolescent turmoil he was experiencing. He was having a difficult time at school, fending off bullies and deciding that he just couldn't bear it any longer. Dick showed up at the school in a limousine but did not take his son out of the school. Richard Jr. was trying very hard to succeed academically but was afraid to face spring exams. He packed up his belongings and showed up at his father's door. He did not want to tell his father that he was fearful of being put back a year. He went to California for his spring break, and when he returned he decided not to go back to the boarding school. His father, drinking, shouted at him, "How could you let me down?" But the two never spoke of Richard Jr.'s school experience again.

The young man saw a book on the table next to his father's bed. It was *Song of God* by Sir Edward Arnold. "I asked what it was," he recalls. "He told me about his experiences in California and how he met Yoganawa, the head of the Self-Realization Fellowship, and how he could leave his body." To the young boy, it was very exciting, for he was fearful and depressed, terrified of death. He went to his grandmother's and told her of the new joy he was experiencing. Maybe, he thought, there's something that transcends death. Tootie had a meditation group that he began to meet with weekly. She had a Ouija board; she and her guests sat around and tried to make contact with the dead. On one occasion, she said she had spoken to Carole Landis, the actress who had killed herself years earlier. "Carole visits me all the time," she told her grandson. His relationship with her was always positive: she praised his musical ability and told him he was destined for greatness. He was always happy with her.

Dick was constantly on the road, often with Kitty accompanying him; but, according to his son, Kitty knew that she was just a companion and that he would leave her if he fell in love with someone. In 1958, he met a lovely and talented young singer/actress, Fran Jeffries, and Dick Haymes, for the fifth time, would go to the altar with a new bride.

At the time that Dick and Fran met, he was touring the country performing in nightclubs to decidedly mixed audience responses. One fan remembers Dick performing at the Boulevard, a club in Queens, New York. He recalls that the audience was very rude, noisy, and inattentive. The master of ceremonies said to the audience, "Let's see if we can get Dick to come out for an encore," but someone in the audience could see him waving his hand to the MC, expressing his unwillingness and his distaste for them. As the fan left the club, Dick was sitting at the bar, completely alone, "hunched over a drink. There was not another soul in the bar. Dick was the picture of absolute despair and dejection."

Another fan remembers the opening of a club in New Jersey that featured on weekends only all the swinging big bands that were still trying to survive as well as small jazz groups like those of George Shearing and Erroll Garner. The club was far different from the elegant venues to which Dick had become accustomed during his successful years. Admission was five dollars, which included two drinks. The club was a converted restaurant with an embossed tin-covered low ceiling and an uncarpeted wood floor that resulted in poor acoustics. Plain wooden chairs and small tables were the only furnishings, but the musicians more than compensated for the setting.

The fan, John Wira, remembers arriving early on a Saturday night and sitting at the small oval bar near the entrance. The club began to fill, and there were an unusual number of women in the audience. Dick Haymes was scheduled for a nine o'clock appearance, but by nine thirty he had not appeared and the audience was growing restless. Finally, Dick entered through the front door and walked directly to the stage. According to Wira, he looked pale, with sunken eyes and hair tinged with gray. He remembers thinking that it was not the same Dick Haymes he remembered from movies and television.

Backed by a trio, he began singing songs that were familiar to his audience, and although in good voice, he performed mechanically. Instead of the normal forty minutes, he sang for only twenty; and saying, "I'll be back," he walked out of the club through the front door. The audience was shocked, and after an hour passed, the crowd became restless and people were beginning to leave. Then Dick returned, sang a few more songs, including a few bars of "The Nearness of You," remarking that he did sound a little like singer Bob Manning, then sang a few more songs, and again left the club quickly. Wira remembers, "Dick Haymes didn't endear himself to many fans in the audience that night but maybe he had the same thoughts as I had, 'What am I doing in a dump such as this?'"

Dick was booked into Room 365, a club in San Francisco where a talented young singer, Fran Jeffries, was also appearing. She knew he was the star of the show, but he was clearly impressed with her performance and they soon became friendly. Before the run ended, he asked her to do some duets with him, and they were so successful that the initial one-week booking was extended to a month. A few months later, Dick phoned Fran and asked her to appear with him in Phoenix and Hawaii. They were both represented by the William Morris Agency, and their bookings came in quickly.

They were married in Arlington, Virginia, in November 1958, and their daughter, Stephanie, was born on July 22, 1959. Fran Jeffries (born Frances Makris), of Greek-French ancestry, was a tall, graceful, dark-haired twenty-one-year-old when they met. She was from California, where her father, a barber, ran a restaurant, the Porthole. She had an active childhood, starting to work at the age of thirteen, folding boxes and then selling dresses. She taught dancing at Arthur Murray's and tried radio and movies, working as an extra. She had had a brief marriage to a pianist, Ed Blasco, whom she credited with helping her musical career.

Fran and Dick had a highly successful act that was produced by Dick Williams, who had done the same for Steve Lawrence and Eydie Gormé. Fran says that she and Dick were the second "Steve and Eydie," and from the reviews that followed their appearances, there is no doubt that they were among the top club performers and an outstanding team on the circuit. They played the major cities, returning to Florida three times a year, playing in the big hotels like the Fontainebleau, at which their successful headline act debuted. Frank Sinatra had recently played at the hotel, and Dick was particularly nervous about following Sinatra's dazzling performance. Fran unquestionably bolstered Dick's confidence, and very quickly the old Haymes emerged. Their act consisted of solos by Dick and Fran and then duets for the remainder of the show. They were held over in Florida for several weeks after their debut. Dick was thrilled to hear the cheers of the audiences at the Copa and the other leading clubs, and he thanked Fran publicly for her support and for her talent and vivacity. When he appeared without her at the Crescendo Club in Los Angeles, his first appearance in that city in several years, he was accompanied by Ian Bernard on a bill with Stan Kenton's band. A local reviewer praised his voice, his "likable personality," and great arrangements by Bernard, but noted that turnout was scanty for Haymes's bow. He needed Fran Jeffries, as praise for their joint appearances indicated.

After many appearances by Dick and Fran throughout the country, the reviewers were once again ecstatic in their praise of Dick Haymes. After a lengthy recapitulation of Dick's troubled past, the *New York Daily News* critic describes Dick and Fran's appearance at the Roundtable, wondering, "Who is doing most for whom in the act." Dick's voice, he observed, "is more flexible and he has authority and style." In *Cue Magazine*, the critic had seen the pair in the Empire Room of the Waldorf and at the Roundtable: "Now here they are again, in the same season, and I find I've got to reach for some of my rarely employed superlatives. They have been clever enough to improve. The rumor may have reached you that Mrs. Haymes (Fran Jeffries, that is) is one of the most attractive women yet to appear— in real life, let alone on a supper club floor. What's more, she is singing better, with more assurance, than she did a few months back. . . . Go see the Haymeses. I'm sure you'll enjoy them as much as I do." Other critics echoed the superlatives, praising the new boyishness of Haymes and the dazzling

beauty and talent of his wife. In 1961, the pair broke all previous atten-
dance records at the Empire Room of the Waldorf.

Dick's old friend Earl Wilson wrote a sympathetic account of Dick's
past troubles and a future that once again seemed promising. Dick mused
about the past, revealing his reluctance to live in California. "All my close
friends are dead. Ty Power, Bogart, John Hodiak, Flynn," he said, and he
expressed interest in moving perhaps to Florida or the Virgin Islands. He did
recapitulate his past financial woes, when, despite his enormous income, he
fell so deeply into debt: "I had a personal manager getting 30%, an agent
getting 10% and a business manager getting 5%. I figured I was paying
those people, so I'd do what they said." In that era, mismanagement of stars
was not uncommon. Doris Day lost a fortune to the mismanagement of her
husband, Marty Melcher, and Debbie Reynolds's wealthy husband, Harry
Karl, gambled away her money.

Flattering headlines led the movie magazines to take notice of the
new singing team. Once again, Dick attributed his resurgence to his latest
marriage. "Until I met Fran I was dead physically, spiritually, and career-
wise. Then started the long hard climb back from the dead." (We might easily substitute Nora, Rita, and later Wendy, as the familiar pattern emerged
once again.)

Because his debtors were so insistent, and with new responsibilities
as father of Stephanie, Dick reluctantly decided to declare bankruptcy as
the first stage of what he believed would be his road back to financial stability. On March 18, 1960, he filed the necessary papers, showing assets of
$5,493 and liabilities of $522,242. He still owed the United States government $40,000 in back taxes.

Dick's recording career was also revived, as Marty Krofft, a young producer, arranged for Dick to make an album for the Warwick label, which
also produced an album for Fran. The album, *Richard the Lion-Hearted: Dick
Haymes, That Is!* was arranged and conducted by Ralph Burns. Burns had
worked in Charlie Barnet's band, but by 1944 he was working with Woody
Herman as the band's pianist and chief arranger. Later, he did arrangements

for Peggy Lee, Tony Bennett, Johnny Mathis, and Ray Charles, notably on Charles's legendary "Georgia on My Mind." He would go on to win two Academy Awards for scoring the Bob Fosse films *Cabaret* and *All That Jazz*. Burns's jazz background provided a different sound for Dick's new recording. Indeed, the first number, "Pick Yourself Up," might be regarded as the singer's statement about his life and the future that now looked so promising. Although some ballads are included on the twelve-song album, there is no mistaking the jazz arrangements and the upbeat tempo, very different from the Ian Bernard ballad classics. His phrasing and timing are as precise as ever; but, unquestionably, Dick was trying to set a new course for his career, much as Sinatra had done so brilliantly several years earlier with *Swing Easy* and *Songs for Swingin' Lovers*.

The album was meant to complement Dick's new singing career with Fran, to signify a new persona and, at the same time, to reinforce his reputation as one of the great singers of the era. The album received good reviews, but Dick in later years complained that the band was too loud and overpowering. He felt that the backings were without feeling and that, despite his reputation, Burns was a much-overrated arranger.

Some time after they began appearing together, Dick and Fran attended a show by Bobby Darin at the Copacobana. After Darin concluded, he introduced Dick to the audience, and Steve Blauner, Darin's manager, reports that he had never seen such a warm and prolonged ovation, longer than that given for the legendary Judy Garland. Blauner met Dick that night and asked if he could manage him, for he believed that the country was ready for another comeback of a screen and music legend. So Dick left the William Morris agency, as did Fran, and Blauner booked them into the Copa for the summer and for appearances in Florida, Puerto Rico, and the Flamingo in Las Vegas. Blauner later heard their act at a charity performance attended by Dick's friends, Richard Quine and Blake Edwards, and remembers that the audience response was overwhelming. Blauner remembers that he had told Dick, "If you drink and it gets in the way, I'll quit." One night Dick was drunk, and Blauner informed his client he would no longer

represent him. Dick never owed him money during their six-month business relationship, but after he announced the end of his work as manager,
Dick left him with a bill for an airline ticket.

Dick and Fran made a number of appearances on television, notably
on the *Ed Sullivan Show* and on Hugh Hefner's *Playboy Penthouse*. On one of
the latter shows (they appeared on two *Penthouse* shows), Hefner introduces
the program, noting that Dick Haymes is obviously "two drinks ahead of us."
That may have been the case, but the only evidence of inebriation is his
relaxation, his clear enjoyment of the experience, the sense that he is having
fun. "The More I See You," his first song, delivered while seated, has an
improvisatory quality; when, for example, he sings, "Can you imagine," he
strings out the last word, forcing the audience to wait expectantly for the
next, and repeats the pattern at the very end, very cleverly, making the last
full-throated word, "try," follow a long pause after a casual "won't" ("My
heart won't try").

His rapport with the orchestra is warm and appreciative, and he
accompanies them on drums from his seat during Fran Jeffries's song, "No
Moon at All." In a delightful swinging duet, "Let's Take a Walk Around the
Block," Haymes is the consummate polished entertainer, very much like
Sinatra in these years, as he takes little dance steps to punctuate the rhythm
and swings his shoulders and arms in consonance with the music. Although
Jeffries is a fine entertainer, she is not quite as relaxed as Haymes.

On the *Ed Sullivan Show* on April 23, 1961, each sings a solo with the
other against a cold, geometric expressionistic set that tends to distance the
performers from the audience. As Haymes watches in the background,
Jeffries sings "I've Got a Lot of Living to Do" with a Las Vegas–style belting
delivery. She is clearly a very skilled performer, very young, with charm
and great beauty, but as yet lacking the distinctive voice or delivery that
would make her competitive with such singers of the era as Connie
Francis. Dick Haymes's rendition of "You Are Too Beautiful" is vintage
Haymes, smooth yet heartfelt, acted as much as sung, as his eyes fill with
longing as he shrugs his shoulders and with a rueful half-smile concludes,

"I'm such a fool for beauty." The obligatory closing duet is a mélange of lines from familiar tunes, very brief, delivered with almost forced energy, probably successful as the finale of a nightclub appearance, but less so under the scrutiny of a television camera.

Looking back at those years, Fran recalls how much she loved Dick. "It wasn't hard to love him. He treated me well, and was a very cultured man. He loved to sail, swim, play tennis. Dick was very well read, charming, handsome, a beautiful man, but with many problems." She remembers him telling his mother, "You left me in the school," and feels that he should have sought help from a psychoanalyst to resolve his childhood anger. She also feels that had there been a Betty Ford Clinic available, he might have been helped with his alcohol problem, which plagued him save for one year in New York City when the two performed at the best venues: the Plaza, the Waldorf, the Copacabana, the latter three or four times. Then he had a beer, saying, "One won't hurt," but it led him to resume drinking. When she told him that she had been asked to do an appearance in a Jule Styne production on the Ed Sullivan television show, he became angry and, now drunk, "got physical with [her]."

According to Fran, their daughter, Stephanie, feels that he was not a good father and that he did not make an effort to stay in touch with her or with his other children. But Dick was always too busy touring and trying to earn enough money to meet current expenses to do more than see his children at intervals. And his efforts to make a comeback with Fran were taking a severe toll on his nervous system, thus intensifying his reliance on alcohol.

Richard Jr. remembers when Fran moved into the apartment where he was living with his father. They rarely spoke, he recalls; and when Fran became pregnant, they were planning to find a larger apartment. They did find one, on York Avenue, but Richard Jr. did not want to be part of the new family. He told his father that he wanted to return to California, which he feels was a bad blow to his father's ego. Dick was out of town when his son told him of his decision over the telephone, and when he returned to New York, while drinking, he physically attacked his son, wrestling him to the ground. As a result, Dick needed to walk with a cane for a time, and Fran blamed Richard Jr. Dick accused Joanne of enticing their son to return to California; but, as in the past, he never sat down and discussed the matter with his son or tried to help the boy deal with his conflicted emotions. When Dick and Fran were on the road, Richard Jr., deciding that he wanted to leave, sold his drums and bought a ticket for California. He would not see his father again for almost two decades.

But Marguerite Haymes was a supportive presence in her grandson's life. She took him on a trip to the Virgin Islands and was never too busy to teach him to sing. But as he recalls, although she was the most constant and reliable female figure in his formative years, she too was a damaged person, and he never found the parental support he needed from childhood.

Meanwhile, Fran's career was going well—and without Dick. She was booked on Perry Como's show and Dick was furious, and she returned to the Ed Sullivan show alone. She had done the *Pink Panther* film, and many opportunities awaited her. Dick was drinking heavily and had grown increasingly dependent on Fran. She remembers, "I felt that it wasn't going anywhere after a couple of years. I had a deal to do another movie. I told him to do the musical *Pajama Game*, which lasted a few months out of town, but he missed me and came back." His drinking continued, and Fran says she was concerned that his anger toward her would affect their child. After his outburst when she announced that she was doing the Sullivan show, she called Marty Krofft and said, "I'm afraid for my child and me." She and Dick appeared together at the Copacobana in New York on February 12, 1962, but shortly afterward she left for Los Angeles to prepare for a film to be directed by Richard Quine, who was a good friend of Dick (he directed *Cruisin' Down the River*). She married Quine after her divorce from Dick became final in 1965. She describes him as in many ways similar to Dick, "very generous, talented, but had a weak side too—drank and got depressed." After their divorce, Quine married one of Fran's friends and, ultimately, committed suicide. Fran and Dick would remain friendly throughout his life, and Dick's daughter, Pidge, speaks of her fondly.

Years later Dick would recall how much he needed a woman in his life when he met Fran. His memories are different from hers—but in any divorce, each of the parties has a personal perspective at variance from that of the other. As Dick recalls,

> The only way I can explain her is that I fell in love with her voice first and then went through an ego trip because I decided we would get married and I would put together an act—for the two of us. I dressed her, rehearsed her and even got an act written for us. As a result she became a sensational performer. I was so proud because I felt I was doing something productive again—something more than just going through the paces. We were making the big comeback together. We were, until our marriage began to crumble. Fran started listening more to her girl friends and not enough to the people concerned with her career—and a happy marriage.

Dick said that he had introduced her to Blake Edwards, who signed her to the original *Pink Panther*, which was shooting in Rome. When she left for Europe, he had remained in New York with Stephanie, where he recalled doing a musical show. He believed that Fran's newfound fame was overcoming her judgment, for when he and Stephanie joined her in Rome he remembered being confronted immediately with the revelation that she was involved in a new romance with Peter Sellers. "How much of the gossip was true and how much was simply fancied isn't important. The problem was that I couldn't handle anymore humiliation in my life." Others remember how angry he was when he burst onto the set, accusing Fran of infidelity. He says that he sent Fran to Hollywood, where his friend Quine would take her under his protective wing. "What happened was, she divorced me and married him." Dick did not remain angry with Quine, especially as Quine's marriage to Fran did not last.

Looking back, Dick saw his marriage to Fran as a Band-Aid for his problems. Another marriage built on great expectations met the same fate as those with Joanne, Nora, and Rita. But now, he was almost forty-five years old, and there seemed to be no place that he could call home. "By the early sixties," he admitted, "I was a desperate alcoholic. I had been forced into bankruptcy with half a million dollars in debts and no assets. More importantly my love affair with America had dwindled down to a one-sided nightmare with no hope of any reconciliation."

In November of 1962, he was arrested for drunk driving in Los Angeles and failed the sobriety test. Free on bail, he skipped his court date but had his attorney enter a guilty plea, as that would normally result in being released on probation. "In an effort to escape my abysmal circumstances I fled to England in hopes of finding something to make my life worthwhile again." But his dream of personal and professional renewal would have to wait, for his immediate future would be filled with ever deeper despair and unceasing humiliation.

CHAPTER 7

A New Start in England in the 1960s

When Dick Haymes left for England in early October of 1963, he was once again hopeful that he could rekindle his career and solve some of the financial problems that had plagued him for over a decade. His mental state was probably as close to despair as it would ever be: he was unable to control his drinking, his personal relationships had all soured, his bookings were disappointing, and, like many others, he believed that a move to another locale would itself signify a new beginning. He later realized that his problems accompanied him: "I had run away from my beloved country but I couldn't hide from Dick Haymes."

A show business agent, Michael Sullivan, remembers that a small-time talent promoter in London called him to arrange bookings for Dick. Sullivan met with him at the Piccadilly and recalls that Haymes was unshaven and looked "a mess." He arranged for Dick to go to Paris, where he met Dick Emery, a popular comedian who knew of Dick's background and was eager for him to appear on the Dick Emery TV show broadcast on the BBC TV network. Before the scheduled program, Haymes appeared twice on a minor TV show, *Juke Box Jury*.

The appearance for Emery was scheduled for October 27, and Dick's rehearsal in the afternoon was excellent. But in between the rehearsal and the show, which was broadcast live, he had had several drinks and was unable to mask his slight inebriation from the audience. The reviews were not kind, and Dick effectively was banned by BBC television productions, as the government-operated station strictly enforced standards of behavior among its performers. Once again, Dick recognized his mistake after the fact: "It was getting to be the same old story. I'd already blown a television show in London for showing up drunk. I'd had a great rehearsal in the afternoon but by show time I was out of it. Somebody said they should have filmed the rehearsal. Word had gotten around fast and the BBC is death on anybody showing up drunk. That would take some undoing."

Ken Barnes interviewed Dick in his dressing room before the afternoon rehearsal. Dick greeted him warmly, and Barnes noted that his tall, slim figure still suggested the youthful performer of twenty years earlier. "A trifle eccentric, he chews gum and smokes a pipe at the same time. But it was the dark glasses he wore which intrigued me most about his appearance, plus the fact that he needed a shave—this was indeed a far cry from the young man who serenaded Betty Grable." Barnes felt that Dick Haymes was a shamefully neglected singer and hoped that his interview would offer some insight into his personality. After inquiring about Haymes's plans for working in England, he turned inevitably to the subject of Frank Sinatra. Dick was generally very positive in his discussion of Sinatra, but then Barnes asked him, Why, of the three biggest singers of the 1940s, are Crosby and Sinatra still household names, "but you seem to have been the most unfortunate member of this trio. Can you explain that?" Dick was clearly angered by Barnes's question, replying, "I don't know what you mean by 'unfortunate.' That's a pathetic word and I hardly think it applies to me. It would be true to say that I have never been a good businessman. Things could have been a lot different for me if I'd been as bright as Frank, but I was never that kind of planner. No, I don't think I've been unfortunate. Impractical maybe."

The interview continued with a discussion of music, and when asked about his latest album, *Richard the Lion-Hearted,* Dick spoke forthrightly of his disappointment in Ralph Burns's arrangements. "I know Ralph's got a big reputation and a lot of people will be gunning me for saying this. In my opinion Ralph is one of the most over-rated arrangers in the business. His backings for me were far too heavy and without one ounce of feeling. It was the worst album I ever made." Barnes noted that not everything Haymes said that day was derogatory, for he said that he could listen to Sinatra any time: "Anything with his name on it is good enough for me." The comparison with Sinatra would continue in this and in other interviews, and for Dick it undoubtedly would become a painful subject, although he would on most occasions handle the Sinatra comparisons gracefully. One exception was on Russell Davies's BBC Radio show in late 1963. After the inevitable questions about Sinatra, Dick said bluntly, "He's a grasping, overly ambitious, *talented* idiot. . . . He's so talented that he doesn't realize he doesn't have to go through all this *shtick*." Here, Dick was clearly referring to Sinatra's Rat Pack antics that he felt detracted from his singing. Dick was always devoted to his craft and was proud of his refusal to be diverted by popular trends that demanded that performers play up to their audiences with the latest tricks and fads.

Dick was not diplomatic when speaking of other singers and musicians; rather, he was direct and unabashed in his praise or criticism. In the Barnes interview, he singled out Bing Crosby, Mel Tormé, and Tony Bennett for praise; but of Andy Williams, he said, "I used to like Andy until about a year ago when he started recording with baby sounds and echo chambers. It seems like he has completely deteriorated. Personally, I would never make a record of THAT kind." When Barnes asked him if such an attitude might obviate his chances of commercial success, he replied with a half-smile, "I've been down that path once before . . . and it's the wrong path."

The Ken Barnes interview is a perfect illustration of Dick Haymes's self-destructive impulses, his awareness of those impulses, and his unwillingness to counter them so that he might find acceptance in the circles where the power of those who controlled his career resided. Barnes remembers that when Dick arrived in England, not one of the newspapers, including the musical press, announced the fact. Barnes attributes that neglect to the current fanatical obsession with the Beatles, but he believes that even had Haymes's arrival been noted, the emphasis by the press would have been on his turbulent private life. Barnes doubts if anyone under thirty has ever heard Haymes and recalls sadly that he was a top seller on both sides of the Atlantic, noting that the Haymes version of "You'll Never Know" completely outsold Sinatra's. He asks, "How could such a professional performer slip so far?"

Despite the poor reception for his television appearance with Dick Emery, Haymes became part of the touring Dick Emery Show. One reviewer praised him for "uncompromisingly singing the standards of popular music," adding, "Haymes should be required viewing for contemporary pop stars who have a record in the Top Ten before they have learnt how to walk on stage." Haymes shows why, according to the reviewer, in the forties "he was—with Crosby, Sinatra and Como—one of the Big Four of crooning."

He continued to make appearances in clubs in northern and north-western England, like La Dolce Vita in Newcastle. Reviewer Bert Warner praised his performance lavishly, noting that he made the lyrics of "Our Love Is Here to Stay" sound like "sheer poetry." He made his first radio appearance in England in September 1964 on the *Joe Loss Pop Show* for BBC Radio and was applauded by the musicians backing him.

Yet Skip E. Lowe, a well-known master of ceremonies and television host in California, was in England working with Dick during this period. In his solo appearances in the north of England, Lowe said that Dick would come on stage drunk, was paid poorly, was miserable, unhappy, and seemed to want to be alone. He was totally broke and blamed Hollywood for his plight, bitterly commenting on Harry Cohn and Rita Hayworth. He performed in Manchester and in Leeds in a "Working-Man's Club," and his performances were frequently poor. Lowe commented on how sad it was to see a great movie star so low, and one of the legendary singers come on stage only to repeat lines of songs. Backstage, Lowe reported, Dick would sometimes hit the wall after a performance.

A friend and former business associate, Vern Howard, who was in London in 1963, was instrumental in Dick's meeting the woman who would become his sixth wife. When Dick was married to Fran Jeffries, Howard had hired Dick to sing at his new club in Allentown, Pennsylvania. Howard remembers that there was trouble with a service union at the club and that Dick, despite a threat from the union's attorney, showed his loyalty to Howard by sitting out the first performance and showing up for the second when the employees decided to leave. He remembers that when the attorney told Dick he would be in "big trouble" if he did not go on as scheduled, Dick responded, "Counselor, you don't know what big trouble is. I know what big trouble is." Howard, knowing the crowd would assume that Dick had missed the first show because of inebriation, went up to the microphone and said, "I just want you people to know this delay had nothing to do with Dick, other than the fact that he was standing by me." Dick appreciated Howard's supporting him publicly and absolving him from blame—a rare occurrence in recent years. Dick was paid one thousand dollars in cash for two days, a good sum for him at that period. After that experience, he and Howard became good friends.

In London, Dick was living very modestly—in a kind of garret. Howard offered to help manage his finances, and Dick immediately took an advance from his friend. As far as money was concerned, he remembers that Dick had no conscience but was extremely bright and would admit to all of his mistakes—both financial and personal.

Howard was seeing a young woman who was a close friend of a young British model, Wendy Smith. On November 21, 1963, Howard's friend introduced Dick and Wendy as the four lunched together, and it was clear from the outset that their attraction was mutual. Wendy Smith was a popular young woman who had appeared in one film and worked as a model. Director Michael Winner (noted for his films with Charles Bronson) remembered the "bizarre British film" he made in the 1960s, *Some Like It Cool*.

Winner says, "In those days the film censor suddenly allowed nudity on the screen, so a lot of totally daft nudist 'documentaries' were made—and took a fortune! Wendy was one of my nudes. She played a lot of volleyball. I never heard from her again." (Years later, Wendy would write to Winner requesting a tape of the film, but the negative was lost.) Twenty years younger than Dick, she said she did not know of his background when they met—simply that he was charming and attentive. She was thrilled to learn that Dick Haymes was the star of *State Fair*, a film she remembered from her childhood. At their first meeting, she remembered that they all became drunk. "I fell asleep," she said, "and when I woke up Dick was crooning songs to me in a bar in Mayfair." Dick was drinking excessively, sometimes offering Wendy vodka for breakfast.

Dick's career took another sad turn when he accepted an engagement in Sydney, Australia, for January 1964. He left Wendy in London and opened at a nightclub, where he was clearly under the influence, so much so that he repeated one line from a popular ballad, "What Kind of Fool Am I," sixteen times. The club owner fired him for unprofessional conduct and took him to court in an effort to stop him from singing anywhere else. Haymes's excuse was that he had been treated with penicillin for a viral infection, but it was obvious to the audience that he was drunk. In court, a judge said that Haymes "was very much under the influence of liquor" when he appeared at the club on January 16, but he dismissed an application by the club for an injunction restraining the singer from appearing at the Coogee Bay Hotel, in a suburb of Sydney. He earned enough there to pay his return fare to England.

In London he was met by Wendy, who from this point would devote herself to Dick—both to his career and to his health. Years later, Dick would marvel at her love during perhaps the lowest period of his life. Although Wendy would later maintain that she didn't know that Dick was drinking when they dated (she said she thought he was meditating), she was so involved with him—as her anecdotes about their first and subsequent dates illustrate—that clearly she knew of his weaknesses from the start. Her devotion during those years was clearly a major factor in Dick's ability to perform, and he needed her support badly. "I fell in love with her—naturally. But my loving someone had never been enough. I was Dick Haymes and my loving had always been as much 'wanting' as anything else—and always 'getting.' Wendy was different. She met me at a time when I could not have been less presentable to a woman as a good security risk even as a room-mate, much less as a husband and father who would provide a good life and home for his family."

Wendy moved into a flat in Knightsbridge with Dick and accompanied him on his tours of nightclubs in England. He appeared in Liverpool and Birmingham (with Dick Emery, with whom he also appeared in Torquay and Brighton in the south of England) and later toured with a popular British comedian, Tony Hancock. In 1964, actor/director Roger Moore cast him in an episode that aired in January 1965, "The Contract," for his popular television series, *The Saint*.

While shooting "The Contract," Dick was reunited with a friend from Hollywood, actor Bob Hutton, who was living in London with his wife, Romy (short for Rosemary). Bob was a co-guest on the show with Dick, and the two couples became friendly. Russ Jones, a graphic artist, met Dick and the Huttons at the King's Head, a pub in Shepperton Square, not far from where Dick was living before the move to Knightsbridge. Russ would become a close friend of Dick both in England and in his last years in California.

Romy remembers that a group of former Hollywood stars formed a kind of "old-boys club/old-girls club" in England, where they met informally for drinks and dinner and to reminisce about the old days and comment, often acidly, on the new wave of stars and their films. When the old Hollywood crowd gathered, they constantly reminisced about their golden years, and Romy recalls vividly those occasions. "When you were royalty by the time you were in your early twenties and you thought it would go on forever and it came to a short stop and nothing else in your life had ever lived up to an experience that you had when you were that young, there is nothing left but underlying bitterness and sadness. They were all sad. You could guarantee that whenever any two of them met, within forty-five seconds one of them would say, 'It's not like it was in the old days.' Life was never ever the same for them and they couldn't be compensated." Roger Moore loved the old Hollywood people and often featured them in episodes of *The Saint*.

In January 1965 Fran Jeffries was granted a divorce from Dick in Los Angeles, and that month Dick and Wendy flew to Mexico to get married. Wendy had given birth to a daughter, Beverly Smith, some years earlier. As she pursued her career as a model, appearing on television and in a film, her daughter was raised by her family. Wendy recalled her decision to marry Dick: "I had to stop the merry-go-round, going with three or four men. I had been around. I had been engaged before, at eighteen, but broke it up." After the wedding, the couple returned to London, where Dick was booked for a club, the Cool Elephant, where Paul McCartney, at the height of his fame as a Beatle, lavished praise on Dick Haymes and remarked of his appearance, "It can't be true. It must be his son." The couple then left for Dublin, for Dick wanted to become an Irish citizen. "I've lived there on and off for years and have finally decided to settle there. . . . We have a place just outside Dublin." His troubles over citizenship had plagued him ever since the debacle with the U.S. State Department, and he wanted definitive citizenship of a country to which he might feel some allegiance. His mother's ancestors were Irish, and the process was therefore not difficult. His application was granted fairly quickly, and by December 15, 1965, he could state unequivocally that he was a citizen of Ireland.

He and Wendy lived in a basement flat in Dublin's Rathmine district, but they soon learned, to their surprise, that Dick's final divorce decree would not become effective until March 1966. Wendy was now pregnant, and they wanted their marriage to be legal, so they were officially married on March 18 at the Kensington Registry Office in London. Their reception was held at the Irish Club in Belgravia, where Lady Moynihan, Prince Faisal, songwriter Hal Shaper, and actor Terry-Thomas were among the guests. Shaper and drummer Pete Bray were the joint best men. A very pregnant Wendy and Dick honeymooned briefly in France and Italy. Their first child, Sean Patrick Haymes, was born on May 19, 1966.

It might seem odd that Dick and Wendy could attract such wealthy celebrities to their wedding, and equally odd that they could afford a honeymoon in France and Italy, given their shaky financial status. But in those years, it was possible to vacation abroad for relatively little, and Dick and Wendy always lived up to every penny Dick earned. Vern Howard and others who knew him during that period remember how he could dine and dress well and yet ignore bills for daily living expenses (like rent and telephone). Despite all of his troubles in these years, Dick still retained his celebrity status, particularly among those who remembered his extraordinary success as a singer and, however briefly, as a movie star in the days of the studio system.

Dick continued to accept singing engagements throughout the United Kingdom, opening to uneven reviews. He said on several occasions that he had stopped drinking—which was true for long periods—but as with any alcoholic, just one drink would invariably lead to the resumption of old habits. A British radio host, Chris Ellis, remembered, "I went to see his act with a view to recording him and was so saddened that I left without meeting him." Dick was forced to travel for appearances in clubs that were inconvenient for the new resident of Ireland, as, for example, in Johannesburg, South Africa, where he played at the Civic Center with the popular pianist Russ Conway. Wendy and baby Sean accompanied him on that tour, and although his appearance was well received, it could not re-energize his career.

Dick and Wendy returned from Ireland and moved to a home beside the Thames in Mortlake. Dick appeared on the *Tony Hancock* television show and the *Mike and Bernie Winters Show*, and in 1968 he made a recording that many regard as one of his finest, Hal Shaper's ballad, "Far from the Madding Crowd." On March 16, 1968, Wendy gave birth to daughter, Samantha; and after some weeks, the family moved once again, to Weybridge in Surrey.

Despite his efforts, which in retrospect might be regarded as heroic, his income for 1968 and 1969 was only 125 British pounds.

Dick and Wendy resumed their friendship with Bob and Romy Hutton when they returned from Ireland. Romy remembers that they were "wonderful people. The only thing that mattered to Wendy was Dick and her children, in that order. They existed in a sort of bubble." The two couples had dinner together on the Haymeses' first night out after the birth of Samantha. Dick told the Huttons that he was writing a song about Wendy. They were still living in the Mortlake apartment, which they said was very damp. Wendy had decorated it beautifully and was often very tired in the evening after cooking dinner. Romy recalls, "She adored him; she had no existence without him. She seemed to live only for and through him and seemed to be in a fugue state when he wasn't there." Both Dick and Wendy were very health conscious, she remembers, eating vegetarian meals and avoiding alcohol except on two occasions that Romy recalls clearly. Dick and Bob Hutton, both alcoholics and both avoiding alcohol for many months, somehow consumed a few drinks one night. Dick became drunk and announced to Wendy, "Let's go and buy a Rolls Royce"—a wish that might have been realized twenty years earlier.

Always prone to coughs and colds, Dick had to be hospitalized for tuberculosis in one lung; and when he was released, Wendy was admitted to the hospital for the same disease. Both recovered, but Dick's lung was permanently damaged. Remarkably, it had no effect on the quality of his voice.

Soon thereafter, Alan Dell, a producer and radio host, invited Dick for an interview on his *Be My Guest* program that would result in his first major recording date since he had left the United States. Dick's interview with Alan Dell was broadcast on March 17, 1968, on BBC 2 Radio. Dell asked the usual questions about Dick Haymes's childhood and rise to fame. By now, Dick had adopted the mythology of the fan magazines, telling Dell that his parents were "passing through" Argentina and that he went to a university, Loyola. Dell quickly asked him about his rivalry with Frank Sinatra, to which he replied, "We got along very well; we're still very good friends." Actually, Dick had had very little contact with Sinatra for the past two decades. By the end of the interview, he had conveyed the impression that he was in demand in Las Vegas, and he mentioned a new film project he would be working on with Dick Quine.

Alan Dell was a great admirer of Dick Haymes, and he arranged for Dick to record a new album, *Then and Now*. The recording was a labor of love for Dell, and when Dick was hospitalized for tuberculosis while the album was being recorded, Alan drove Wendy to and from the hospital to visit him. Dick managed to complete the recordings after leaving the hospital. Although a reviewer found occasional signs of vocal strain, he praised several songs as showing "all the old ballad mastery, the warmth and the sincerity: the gentle bossa nova. . . . It is encouraging that he manages to recreate the magic of the earlier era with no sense of anti-climax." The reviewer then comments sympathetically on Dick's life: "Dick Haymes is now resident in Ireland and, from what one reads in the national press, is still having troubled times. For my part, I hope he manages to come through them and somehow achieve a measure of personal contentment. He has surely earned his place in the front rank of popular singers and deserves some kind of recompense for his past achievements and the pleasure that his records have given to a great many people."

The modest comeback Dick Haymes would achieve later in the 1970s was the result of his *Then and Now* album, as his friends and his brother, Bob, distributed it in the United States. Many had forgotten him, and the album was a reminder that Haymes was still alive, still singing, and that the magic of his voice endured. But there was little distribution of *Then and Now* by the album's producer, Mercury Records, and it ultimately became a collector's item, thus far not released as a CD. Dick was not drinking during this period and, as always, was thoroughly professional at the recording sessions, according to Max Harris, who arranged the music and conducted the band. One of the songs on the album, "Just Another Sunset," was composed by Dick, who with his friend Dick Quine wrote the lyrics as well. In the *Gramophone*, reviewer William Gilman, after the inevitable recapitulation of

Haymes's career, concluded that he was singing as well and professionally as ever and that the album would rank with the best of any era "in terms of tasteful, competent talent."

After the release of the album, Dick still had to perform, and he continued to accept engagements in second- and third-rate venues in order to support his new family. One of these clubs, near Manchester, gave him top billing; and for six nights he sang to an audience of no more than twenty, only half of whom appreciated his efforts. The building, according to someone who attended one of the performances, was "complete with corrugated iron roof that rattled away at about ten thousand decibels every time it rained." Some of the places were decidedly better, like the Brighton Palace Pier Theatre, where he appeared on July 25, 1970, to a small but appreciative audience shortly after he had completed his recording dates. Critic John Marley quotes Haymes: " 'You have no idea what that kind of applause means,' he told his somewhat sparse but wildly enthusiastic audience. 'What can I say?' " Perhaps the saddest aspect of these appearances was Dick's gratitude for any kind of recognition of his status as a former star. Marley said that despite Dick's "silver locks which may be growing a little thin, . . . a once a week show at the end of an English seaside pier may be a bit different from the glamour of the days when he sang with Tommy Dorsey and was a Hollywood film idol. . . . He is still very much a master of his particular brand of vocal gymnastics."

On July 9, Dick had substituted for the Irish singing star, Josef Locke, as the special guest in the Al Read show at the Central Pier in Blackpool. When interviewed by the local press, Dick compared the venue: "It has a Las Vegas atmosphere in an English kind of way. I will be entertaining my audience with today songs like "My Way" and with songs of yesteryear like "It Might as Well Be Spring." Dick was asked to return after other scheduled appearances, to fill out the engagement for the ailing Locke, and he agreed. The show would last for several months.

Dick Haymes's most important concert of this period was held on July 24, at the Fairfield Halls, Croydon. Alan Dell was there, serving as the master of ceremonies. The roster of songs was composed largely of standards from Haymes's past successes, but he added such new favorites as "Raindrops Keep Falling on My Head" and the song that Sinatra made into a personal anthem, "My Way." The critics were enthusiastic, Ken Barnes remarking, "Haymes has still got it. As a ballad singer, he rivals Sinatra." Barnes continued to express reservations about Dick as a swinging singer, but said, "There's no denying that Haymes is one of the all time greats of popular singing." But critic Laurie Henshaw expressed the poignancy of the occasion when she opened her interview with Haymes before his appearance in Fairfield Hall: "From Hollywood stardom to the Palace Pier, Brighton, is quite a step, but that's where Dick Haymes has wound up some 30 years since the balmy days when he was the pin-up balladeer who took over from Frank Sinatra in the Tommy Dorsey band. Now eight million dollars and several wives later, Dick Haymes this Sunday starts a series of concerts at Brighton." Undoubtedly, part of Dick Haymes's appeal during these years was the curiosity of a public that wanted to see how the former star had weathered so many years of adversity and, unlike other former Hollywood legends, continued to court an audience.

Bob Monkhouse, a musician, recalls seeing Dick at one of his appearances in a variety show with the British radio personality Clive Dunn:

> I visited the Bristol theatre on the Monday Evening and was quite surprised to note that the Handsome Dick Haymes of *The Shocking Miss Pilgrim Days* was not surrendering to age and wore no make-up on stage.
>
> Backstage, Clive introduced me to Dick and I began to understand why he was content to go on unmade-up and with his grey hair in mild disarray. He hadn't the least vestige of vanity. When I mentioned this he said, "Bob, I'm not like you and Clive. I was never a vaudevillian. Oh, I was in on the tail end of vaudeville, just a few dates, but I was always too easygoing about the way I look, I guess. Besides, the sound I make is all people come for. I don't think they care what they see. I don't.

A few months earlier, when Dick was invited for a rare television appearance (on *The Golden Shot*, ATV), he looked, according to Monkhouse, "very tired and dejected. The young women in the ATV make-up department in Birmingham were excited to see him and they took special care with his appearance, cutting his overgrown grey hair and restoring his rather florid face almost to his former Hollywood look. A dresser cleaned and pressed his wrinkled suit while Dick sat around in his underwear and by the time he stepped onto the studio floor he looked terrific." After the broadcast, once again Dick expressed his gratitude and wonder: "It's a real glamorous show and I've really been treated like I'm still somebody." Such comments reveal clearly how deeply the events of the past years continued to trouble him, and how low his self-esteem had fallen. But he had not relinquished his old habits from his glory days. After he had received a successful review or encountered an enthusiastic audience, he would take whatever money he had and treat a small group of friends to lavish dinners, often leaving his musicians unpaid.

But his reception by audiences and critics was now often tepid, at times distinctly negative. A newspaper review by Barry Shinfield comparing him to a new folk rock group is illustrative of the familiar pattern of what was now a decidedly uneven career: "He stood woodenly at the same microphone for most of the evening. . . . There was no genuine rapport between artist and audience, just a string of mannerisms in hackneyed pretence of rapport." But the main criticism of his act was that it was too plodding and predictable. "The performance lacked sparkle; it was slow and perfunctory, laboured and lifeless. That is not to condemn this genre of singing; in the hands of Sinatra the songs would have been delivered, one felt, with more emotion and with more dynamism." The inevitable comparison with Sinatra was particularly painful to Dick at this point in his career. Yet John Gibson, a reviewer in Edinburgh, praised Dick's performance at the Salutation Hotel in Perth. He clearly felt the depths to which the one-time star had been reduced: "A tingling performance by a singer who shouldn't be working in the wilderness to audiences of a couple of hundred and the rattle of pint glasses. Ludicrous when you think of it. All Britain should be seeing him on television." Dick Haymes knew, despite the availability of club and concert performances, that he had to rekindle his career, if not through singing, then as a screenwriter or director/producer—goals he had long sought.

Richard Quine was working on a film in Spain, *A Talent for Loving*; and in early 1971, despite bookings in Scotland and other locations in and near the United Kingdom, Dick decided to move his family to Madrid, where he might try to write a screenplay and work with Quine on his projected film. Wendy remembers that in Spain she was able to hire a caretaker for the children, allowing her to accompany Dick regularly on his club and concert appearances. Despite the far more affordable cost of living in Spain, Dick and Wendy did not curtail their expenses and even joined a club where Dick could play tennis.

Dick traveled between London and Madrid on several occasions. He was very happy in Spain, as he revealed in a letter to a former manager, Peter Elliott: "To answer your question on how things are for me in Spain, briefly, every single thing is working out the way I want it to, & that is fact. In simpler terms, I am delighted with my life & the way my career is developing & progressing in all areas! *'My cup runneth over.'* " In May, he received a notice from the London bankruptcy court, but he delayed his appearance there for an additional month. In the second week of July he appeared in court, where he was scolded by the judge for his tardiness. He admitted to the court that extravagant living accounted for the fact that he had no money and was again in debt. He conceded his tangible assets were $1,920 and his debts were $38,400. But he told the court that he was writing a script and had the potential for future earnings that would more than cover the debt. The bankruptcy receiver declared harshly that Haymes was "living in the past and in the clouds." Dick replied, "I don't think I have been willfully dishonest."

He returned to Madrid by July 19, and soon his spirits would be lifted by an unexpected offer: he was called by a representative of the National

Broadcasting Company who had seen him perform at a club in Shepperton some months earlier, listened to his new album, and made him an offer to appear in a television special. London Management, a talent agency, signed him and advanced ten thousand pounds, in anticipation of his appearance in the United States on the Tennessee Ernie Ford television show, *The Fabulous Fordies*, a salute to the golden era of Hollywood musicals.

Dick and Wendy were overjoyed. The American representative of his new management was James Fitzgerald, then married to screen star Jane Powell. Dick and Wendy booked a flight to the United States in early September and were soon followed by Sean and Samantha, who were supervised by airline personnel. The couple stayed temporarily with the Fitzgeralds and then found a small apartment for the family. Rehearsals for the special began in late September, and Dick could not have been happier: he would once again sing "The More I See You" to Betty Grable, and for the first time in ten years an American audience now numbering in the millions would welcome the return of the former "King of the Jukeboxes" and Twentieth Century–Fox musical star. Dick was home again to a warm reception, "the opposite of [his] departure from America when [he] had sneaked away to oblivion." Could there be a second act in the life of Dick Haymes? The next years would answer the question that had obsessed him and those who had never forgotten and would always treasure his golden years.

CHAPTER 8

Dick Haymes Comes Home

Searching for the Second Act

When Dick returned to the United States, he began rehearsals at NBC for the Ford show. He had not seen his children, Joanna (Pidge), Richard, and Nugent, in years. Pidge had recently purchased piece of antique English furniture and in one drawer found a British newspaper with an article that carried a photograph of Dick Haymes and a headline announcing his imminent death from tuberculosis. Shortly after her discovery, she received a telephone call from her uncle, Peter Marshall, who said, gently, "Poo-face, I have this man here [at the NBC studio] who really wants to talk to you—your father." Dick clearly felt that re-establishing contact with his children was his first priority. He told Pidge that he wanted to see her. She called her therapist, who advised her to talk with her father; so, accompanied by her husband, she went to meet her father. Pidge had felt his absence keenly, and she admits that she was jealous of Sean and Samantha—his current

194

family. She recalls that as she and Dick walked toward each other from opposite ends of a corridor, they both began to laugh: they looked exactly alike, she recalls, and the childhood bond was quickly restored. For the rest of Dick's life, they would remain close.

His first words at their meeting in the late fall of 1971 were immensely moving. He said, "You know, Pidge, I've made a lot of mistakes in my life. I've hurt my children. I regret that. You're too old to sit on my lap and be my baby girl, but you can be my friend. We can love and respect each other." Pidge became close to him very quickly, and at first Wendy was very warm and welcoming. Soon after the reunion, Pidge recalls that Wendy became jealous of the time Dick was spending with his oldest daughter, for the two enjoyed their time together, especially when they built systems with Heathkits (do-it-yourself electronic kits for amateur radios, broadcast radio receivers, television, audio, and other electronic equipment) that they purchased together.

Dick's return to the United States led to appearances on the *David Frost Show* (syndicated) and the *Johnny Carson Show* on NBC—even before his appearance on the Ernie Ford special, scheduled for airing on February 29, 1972.

The Tennessee Ernie Ford *Fabulous Fordies* show was a slice of unabashed nostalgia for the World War II years. Undoubtedly, the contemporary crisis in Vietnam made many in the audience long for the days when the country was united against a common enemy—without the steady protests that were eroding support for the controversial conflict that was spreading from Vietnam to Cambodia. Ford's nostalgia seems heavy-handed today, primarily because of its deep sincerity. Popular culture in the past thirty years has become sharply satirical, and glimpses of past performances on television or in films are now often laced with ironic commentary, as in the recent film *A Mighty Wind* (2003), a humorous riff on the folksingers of the 1960s and 1970s.

The Ford show features Haymes, Maureen O'Hara, Frank Gorshin—a master at impersonation—and Betty Grable, making a rare public appearance.

After Gorshin's imitations of stars of the 1940s and '50s, like Kirk Douglas and Burt Lancaster, Betty Grable sings "Forty-Five Minutes from Broadway" in an unexpectedly deep voice, her face distinctly heavier and her dance steps carefully measured.

Maureen O'Hara displays a fine voice and extraordinary charm in several songs, but the most dramatic moment of the evening follows when Ford introduces Dick Haymes, "one young man with perhaps the easiest singing style of them all, in his first television appearance in this country in ten years." Haymes is not on stage, as the other performers have been, but enters from the rear of the orchestra and walks down the aisle surrounded by an audience whose cheers and clapping continue until he starts to sing "It Might as Well Be Spring." His face looks worn, particularly around his eyes, he is wearing a new hairpiece (he is all gray now), but his movements are graceful and unexpectedly youthful. He uses his hands for dramatic emphasis more than he had in the past, and his enthusiasm is contagious. The audience continues to clap as he climbs onto the stage. He then sings a stunning up-beat medley: "On a Slow Boat to China," "All of Me," and "Always," as though he wished to remind critics that he could swing as well as Sinatra.

When Betty Grable joins him onstage, he reprises the song from *Billy Rose's Diamond Horseshoe* that had become one of his greatest hits, "The More I See You," and perhaps the highlight of his and Grable's costarring films. She looks very moved as he sings to her (she pretends to sing with him, but just moves her lips), and then places her hand on his shoulder and kisses him—brushing away a tear. (The two also appear together at the Academy Awards ceremony on April 10, 1972, again evoking huge applause from a nostalgic audience as they announce the awards for best musical scoring.) She is clearly surprised by the emotional reception and holds Haymes's arm as they walk toward center stage. Again, she seems to contain her tears. Betty Grable would pass away from lung cancer on July 2, 1973. Her appearance with Dick Haymes on the Ford show would be her last public performance, and there is an unmistakable sadness in her demeanor, in marked contrast to Dick's vitality. It is apparent that she is comfortable with him and that they share a mutual affection.

Following the Ford show, Dick Haymes had good reason to be optimistic about his future in American show business. He was booked for two weeks beginning the last week in April at the Cocoanut Grove at the Ambassador Hotel in Los Angeles. Backed by Les Brown and his band, with arrangements by Dick Grove and Alan Copeland, who also conducted for Haymes, and musical director and pianist Don Trennor, his opening was a triumph. The audience (including such celebrities as Steve Lawrence and Eydie Gormé, Ann Miller, Jane Powell, Phil Harris, Margaret O'Brien, Martha Raye, Peter Marshall, Dick Quine, and Roddy McDowall) rewarded his performance with two standing ovations and tumultuous cheers. He sang his old hits from *State Fair*, then added a simulation of his old *Club 15* radio show, with Patty Andrews surprising everyone by doing a bit that recalled her appearances on that show. Dick then sang his most memorable hits: "Little White Lies," "Stella by Starlight," "Mamselle," and "The Very Thought of You," among others, and then launched into a humorous yet touching self-parody of his life, including the many marriages, the roller-coaster career, and a frank and honest appraisal of his own limitations and aspirations. He thanked everyone who had helped him, from Jim Fitzgerald, who produced the show, to his wife, Wendy, for her enduring support.

The reviews were more than he could have hoped for; the *Hollywood Reporter* described his "triumph," noting, "Physically and musically, Haymes revealed himself virtually untouched by time and adversity." The *Los Angeles Examiner* noted his "caressing voice with a strong suaveness in his presentation. . . . He was smooth, perceptive and captivating, excelling on slow moody tunes but handling the uptempo offerings with adeptness." *Billboard*, *Daily Variety*, and the *Los Angeles Times* echoed the other reviewers, the latter adding, "He has returned to headline status." He was asked for interviews by the local press, and for the first time in decades there was no criticism of his personal or professional life, and he affirmed his delight at being back in the United States: "It's like coming home. This is where it all is." Frank Sinatra had recently announced his retirement from show business; and in a warm telegram, Sammy Davis Jr. praised the show, adding, "With Frank retiring, it's a good feeling to know that there are still some of us left and *cookin'*." He urged Dick to record the album—and it was issued very quickly by a small company, Daybreak. John Gibson, who had written so movingly about his sad days touring in the United Kingdom, announced "Dick Haymes at the Cocoanut Grove" as heralding "quality week among male vocalists," noting that "the old magic's still there."

The family had been living in a modest apartment but soon was able to move to a small home in the Malibu Hills. Dick's older son, Richard Jr., who had not seen his father in many years, went to visit him there in response to Dick's attempt to telephone him. His son describes himself as a "hippie" in the 1970s, and when he presented himself at the door, his father was out of town and Wendy was distinctly averse to having the scruffy young man stay with them. Richard left, and it would be several years before he and his father would reunite—largely as a result of the efforts of Anna Poole, a member of the original Dick Haymes Associates and later a family friend.

Dick had asked Pidge if Sean and Samantha might stay with her while he was rehearsing for the Cocoanut Grove. The children remained with her for a month, and Pidge became resentful of her new role as baby-sitter: "I realized that they were as disposable as the other children he had." She faults Wendy, who did not make an effort to take the children back, seemingly unaware or unconcerned about the extra work demanded of her—particularly as Pidge had two young children of her own. Wendy clearly enjoyed being with Dick when he was performing at clubs and hotels, sharing the life of a celebrity, especially after the bleak years they had endured in England. Romy (Rosemary) Hutton Starrett remembers that when she called Wendy after she and Bob Hutton arrived in New York from England, Wendy was excited about her new house, their new Mustang automobile, and the expensive sound system they had installed. Romy says that she and Bob Hutton never went to California because of her conversation with Wendy, for "Hollywood did this to her in less than a year."

Alan Copeland remembers rehearsing for the Cocoanut Grove show. He had reunited with Dick after reading in *Variety* that the Haymes family was returning from Spain. Copeland had called James Fitzgerald and offered to do the arrangements at no fee after having seen the *Tennessee Ernie Ford Show.* They reunited in Fitzgerald's office, and Copeland began to work with Dick at his own home and at the Haymes place in Malibu. "We became like a little family," he recalls, and they often sat and listened to classical music. Copeland would prepare the arrangements for Dick's appearances on the road, but they would not work closely again until 1974, long after the euphoria of the Cocoanut Grove had faded.

Dick was scheduled for another important opening, in New York City at the Maisonette in the prestigious St. Regis Hotel. He was again hailed, now by the New York reviewers, like Tom McMorrow of the *New York Daily News,* who praised the singer for refusing to alter his appearance and relying solely on his artistry. "Dick Haymes is back, and brilliant. He is strictly himself, shunning the cosmetician's art: the hair is silver and the voice is gold. You won't see him strain or struggle, because he climbed that mountain before he got to New York this week, in an astonishing and exciting comeback from boozy bankruptcy." McMorrow quotes the London bankruptcy referee who had accused Haymes of "living in the past." But he then continues, "He isn't singing as he did in the past: he's just a little bit better. . . . He doesn't try to sing sexy: he just is." *Variety,* too, praised his performance and then compared his career to Sinatra's: "Their career ran virtually parallel for a time. . . . The difference is that Sinatra today has retired with a fortune stowed away, while Haymes has to start over again on the path to financial security." And columnist Earl Wilson, who had reported on Dick's troubles in the 1950s, headlined his report on the Maisonette show, "He's Still in Action." The influential musician George Shearing, whose quintet had played at the same club just before Dick's opening, wrote in *Crescendo,* "I happen to be a guy who feels that when Dick Haymes is at his best there are few singers around who can touch him. He was singing better than ever that opening night in New York and I was delighted. He's been away from the musical scene far too long."

The critics were clearly responsive to Dick Haymes as a representative of the golden days of popular music—before Elvis Presley, the Beatles, and new rock groups essentially pushed aside the songs and the singers from the past. Older audiences in particular were repelled by the new sounds and performers and enjoyed the nostalgia evoked by the few remaining singers from another era: Tony Bennett, Steve Lawrence and Eydie Gormé, Vic Damone, and the longtime idol Bing Crosby, who, in addition to television appearances, would a few years later launch a new stage show featuring his new family along with Rosemary Clooney and the Joe Bushkin band. Earl Wilson quoted Dick's remark as he came on stage, "Bring back the '40s," before his medley of hit songs from the past. Wilson's concluding remark is indicative of the prevailing attitude of audiences toward the newcomers who had taken center stage: "Haymes made his comeback to NY without pelvic movements or tight pants."

Gene Lees, a writer specializing in popular music, was asked by a friend of Dick to write an article about Dick's comeback for *High Fidelity* magazine. Lees was uncomfortable in the role of helper to someone who had once been at the top of his profession. Years later Lees remembered his own reluctance to conduct the interview: "It cost me nothing to give him some space in a magazine. But I disliked the fact that he needed the help. I am not one of those who take pleasure in seeing the mighty fallen, and Dick Haymes had been a very big star. He was also a very great singer, which is another thing. I have had uncountable conversations with singers about singers, and Dick Haymes' name would be on the most-admired list of almost every one of them."

Lees found Dick calm and philosophical and looking extremely fit, and the two simply had a quiet conversation about the past and the present. "I saw not a trace of bitterness in the man. If there was any in him, he was concealing it. Correction: he was unable entirely to conceal his feeling about his mother, which came out in a muted way." Dick assured Lees that his mother had taught him nothing. He told Lees that he no longer drank and blamed nobody but himself for his troubled past. When Lees left, he reflected that he wanted Dick's comeback to succeed. "I wanted him to make it. . . . I wanted it not only because his glorious deep baritone had warmed the American 1940s but because I like him as a person."

In 1973, Wendy presented Dick with a Kahlil Gibran diary containing excerpts from *The Prophet* and other selections from the Indian mystic's popular writings. For the next five years, Dick would write as frequently as he could in his diary, alternating between fervent prayer filled with deep spiritual yearning and pragmatic business decisions that might ensure that he would once again become a star in Hollywood, either as an actor or, as he hoped as the years went by, as a producer, director, and, above all, writer. Wendy's inscriptions at the beginning of each year are loving and supportive, and Dick clearly valued the diaries as tangible evidence of his search for a higher power that might offer guidance and comfort. At the same time, the diary provided an outlet for the expression of his deepest fears and his anxieties about the future.

Dick's diary entries consistently indicate his deep love for Wendy and his devotion to Sean and Samantha. But early in January, he expressed his dissatisfaction with Jim Fitzgerald as his personal manager and decided to let him go. He spent an evening with Sammy Davis Jr. and his wife to explain his decision, telling them that Fitzgerald had ignored Wendy and that he couldn't forget the slight to her. He decided to forego a personal manager and just rely on his management agency, CMA. His spirits were high, and he was particularly excited about the new home in Malibu. His primary vow for the new year was to settle with the Internal Revenue Service. By the end of the month, he declared, "I must make every move count, for I must reach super-stardom & I must do it *now*! When I say I, I mean God & I."

Once again, he went on tour, to Flint, Michigan, where an audience of six hundred did not fill a two-thousand-seat auditorium, and to Cleveland, where the audience at the Music Hall was "perfect." On returning to Los Angeles, he declared his overwhelming love for Wendy and was delighted that she would accompany him for his next performance in Houston. They would travel first class, for Dick, happy in his new acclaim, believed, "That's the way it shall be from now on regarding everything." Wendy returned home from Houston and Dick went to Toronto, where he was displeased with the audience ("These people mean to be nice but don't quite know how") but had an excellent television interview.

But his financial troubles would never end. He gave his attorney, Joe Wolf, eleven hundred dollars as an act of good faith, realizing that it did not begin to compensate him for past work. He hired Don Gregory to do his public relations work, an abrupt departure from his decision to avoid a personal manager—for Gregory would serve in that capacity for months.

Joe Delaney, a columnist for the *Las Vegas Sun*, wrote a long feature on Dick Haymes and his family for the Sunday, September 2, 1973, edition, with new photographs of the happy family in their Malibu home. Dick would be opening in the Congo Room of the Sahara Hotel with Rowan and Martin headlining a ten-day stand, and Delaney clearly wanted to help Dick on his road back to stardom. Delaney refers to Haymes's new and crucial battle: "only this time the cards will be stacked in his favor." He reports that he is now "a healthy, sober, completely at peace Dick Haymes whose rather hectic first five decades left his marvelous baritone vocal instrument virtually as good as new." After a survey of Haymes's history, including his many marriages and financial troubles, he quotes the singer as having given up alcohol forever: "I realized that I never really enjoyed drinking in the first place."

After the Sahara opening, Delaney praised the Rowan and Martin comedy team and asserted that the real beneficiary of their brilliant performance, "a deserving one," was "master balladeer, Dick Haymes, . . . Sinatra's chief rival in the 40's, now in his 50's, [who] looks like he is only in his late 30's; time and travail have left his marvelous vocal instrument virtually intact."

Dick believed that his future was now assured, assuming that his appearance on the Henry Mancini television show was "the beginning of much television for [him]." Although his role in Rock Hudson's detective television series, *McMillan and Wife*, is little more than a cameo (he appears for just one minute at the beginning as a business tycoon whose life is

being threatened, and he is running away from his attackers), he is credited as "Special Guest Star." He regarded the show as just the first step
toward the renaissance of his acting career.

He was extremely happy in these months: he called their home "our
Ashram" and happily reported that his brother, Bob, in a rare visit, "flipped"
at the library in the house. In March, Pidge brought her two children to
Samantha's birthday party, and Sean presided over the younger children.
During this happy period, all too rare in recent years, Dick wrote frequently
of his personal responsibility for his earlier errors, for his habits and "thought
patterns." The diary ends at Christmas 1973, as Dick described the family's
celebration: "Samantha shouts with joy that can only come with the secure
knowledge of being surrounded by love & knowing that this house, this
'Ashram,' is her home and castle."

Dick clearly realized that, despite recent successes in Las Vegas and
other cities, he would have to find another show-business venue for his talents. He had long wanted to be a writer and was working on a script based
on the life of John Rossi, a friend who had started a youth foundation that
aided troubled young people. In his diary for 1974, he made several commitments that reveal not only his current state of mind, but also his habitual
inability to accept the reality of his situation. He vowed:

1. to write continuously until I am a good professional writer,
2. to constantly act in film, constantly progressing to better parts, until I
   have my own film series,
3. to manifest the right recording situation, stay abreast of the times so
   that the records sell, thereby, to become box-office,
4. to manifest the right headlining situation in the main rooms of Las
   Vegas, Reno & Tahoe
5. to become financially solvent
6. to build a creative productive empire, for God, Wendy, myself & the
   children
7. to constantly seek Cosmic Consciousness.

After a New Year's Eve show at Harrah's in Reno, he returned to Los Angeles, spending time with his children, enjoying meeting them after school, and becoming caught up in the daily life of the family. He had an upcoming performance scheduled for Puerto Rico, stopping briefly to give a show at a resort in the Poconos. He was offered another cameo in the *McCloud* television show, which he was prepared to accept, hoping that it would lead to bigger roles in the future. But he was always looking to regain his fame as a movie star. "Somehow I must convince my agents and Don [Gregory] that films take priority. I may be involved in radio which will bring a steady income while I re-establish myself in films and records. I know it is coming." Even after preparing for what would be a successful show in the Poconos, he wrote, "I shall do a good show tomorrow night, but I belong in films."

His mind was constantly on his home and family, and he was very upset when he learned that Sean had been bitten by a friend's dog. He was most disturbed that he was not there to offer support and comfort to his wife and son. His longing for them was so acute that when he was offered a major role in a touring company of the stage musical *No, No, Nanette*, he realized that he could not accept it unless Wendy accompanied him—and that would be virtually impossible given the need for someone trustworthy to care for the children and the Ashram.

As in the past decades, the primary problem was financial. He reported meeting the local tax man, who took 10 percent of his gross pay of forty-five hundred dollars. He saw film work, which required only a commission to his agent, as the only solution, but he overlooked the taxes he would have to pay. His debt to the Internal Revenue Service would, in fact, never be fully paid.

Other tempting projects attracted him: making a pilot for Jack Webb's production company, working with Jackie Mason in a Catskills resort for a fee of twenty-five thousand dollars, joining his old friend Larry Shayne in trying to sell him to a record company, even taking over Playboy Records, selling his script on Rossi and starring in the production, and working in a western television show with Clu Gulager. His difficult schedule and constant worry led to a series of flu-like illnesses. His "feeling of dislike for [him]self" revealed a deep depression that seemed closely linked to his physical ailments. His eight-day engagement in Miami required two shows a night, but his voice was fine and he enjoyed entertaining "elderly people who are beautiful." But he rejected an offer to sing on a cruise ship, knowing that doing so would place him in a lower show-business category.

The Miami shows paid sixty-four hundred dollars, leading him to declare that he would not accept any more "gigs" like that. But once again, he was ready to dismiss his personal manager, Don Gregory, and needed some pay-off money. It is never quite clear why Dick Haymes parted from every manager with whom he had worked, leaving some of them bitter at what they considered his ingratitude. The common thread, however, in his frequent severance of ties with managers, agents, and attorneys over the years was financial. Several months later, he saw Fitzgerald in Las Vegas and reported, "Got a lot of static from poor Jim Fitzgerald, he's a bitter man, but that's his problem."

Dick continued to make appearances on television interview shows, with Mike Douglas and Merv Griffin, with whom he would appear several times in the next few years. He finished another television drama, *Betrayal*, starring Amanda Blake, where he plays a judge. Although he is announced as one of the stars, he is on camera for no more than five or six minutes of this one-hour show. He looks his age and, again, he is given no opportunity to do more than walk affably through the role. Clearly, he was cast for his name, not his ability.

Once again his family was looking for a new home, a recurrent pattern in his ongoing financial saga. His bid on a Malibu home was rejected, so he began to look for a "perfect house" with a lease option (so that he need not come up with cash for a down payment). Another bid for a Woodland Hills house was rejected, even though a friend, Errol Gillis, offered to lend him eight thousand dollars, and his lawyer, Joe Wolf, volunteered to be a guarantor. They lost that bid when the price was raised, found and lost another, and finally found one in Encino.

He and Alan Copeland left for Dayton, where he would earn thirty-eight hundred dollars for five shows in three days. When he returned, he noted that the loan was approved for the house and that his "Rossi" script was under consideration at Universal Studios. His partner in that project, Herm Saunders, had advised him, he wrote, that "it is mandatory to make the important 'social scene'. My name, it seems, opens all doors so, we shall do same. I feel once 'Rossi' is on the floor, we will get into 'features' for theatres slowly."

In June, he and Alan worked on his upcoming Las Vegas show, and he kept making television appearances, again with Merv Griffin, with Bobby Gentry, an appearance (for three hundred dollars) on *Name That Tune*, and at a testimonial to Mary Tyler Moore. Dick had appeared earlier in the year at a similar event honoring Stevie Wonder, noting that it was important that he be seen at as many star-studded shows as possible.

Also in June, his daughter Stephanie came for a visit. Dick wrote, "She was a joy to have with us and Samantha worships her older sister." Later that year, Fran Jeffries would try to obtain child support from him, and although he would not be able to give her what she needed, he felt she had "a right to ask for help for Steph." The following year, he accepted the court decision as a fair verdict and expressed sympathy for Fran and her own problems.

In late June, the script for *Rossi* was rejected by ABC, the network to which he had submitted it after Universal expressed no interest in the project. He planned to submit it to other networks, but started on a new script, *Alter Ego*, a thinly veiled account of his own life in show business, that he would complete in 1977 as *Reprise*.

Clearly concerned by recurring bouts of flu-like illnesses, he stopped smoking and duly noted his progress or his failure to keep to his vow. He also purchased a new hairpiece that he would wear on his upcoming tour to Puerto Rico, with a stop in Great Gorge, New Jersey, and his scheduled opening in Las Vegas in the fall. But before he left Los Angeles, he wrote in his diary, "I dismissed Alan Copeland—needless to go into why but it's been coming a long time." Alan had prepared charts for Dick for a currently popular song, "The Way We Were," that became a new, much-praised standard in his repertory. According to Copeland, Dick started to drink in 1974, and they lost touch for several years until Dick called to ask his former accompanist/arranger to work with him on his new show in Akron. "We talked a lot," Copeland recalls. "We had a lot in common—classical music we both loved. This was a few years later; he was writing a screenplay. It was not the euphoria of the Cocoanut Grove."

Joy Holden, who, with Debby Keener, became Dick's back-up singer during the next year when he was on tour, remembers how content he seemed in those days and how fondly, without bitterness, he remembered the early years of his success. Harry James would come by after a performance, and they would reminisce about the big band era and Dick's early success in the days when he would take his friends on his plane to go to dinner at some new restaurant. He never said anything negative about anyone, she remembers. Dick was a stickler for getting everything right, so they would rehearse at his home—the new house in Encino—for eight hours prior to a show. Above all, Joy Holden remembers, Dick seemed proud of his two children and of his family life.

Concluding his eastern tour before the Las Vegas opening, Dick made an appearance in St. Paul. He was still doing his old act, and he could not work up any enthusiasm for his Midwest performance. "I'm so sick and tired of people who live in the past," he wrote. "I have compassion but firmly believe it's the kiss of death." Again, he contracted a flu-like illness, called a doctor who prescribed antibiotics, and canceled the remainder of his Minneapolis engagement. Local singer Andy Roberts recalls meeting Haymes after the show and talking with the singer in his hotel room about his Hollywood years. Dick was friendly and helpful to the veteran performer. When Roberts saw him before he left St. Paul, "he was bundled up in his robe not feeling good at all, we shook hands and I said, 'Dick, the next time I see you, I hope you have a million bucks in your back pocket.'" Dick felt well, however, the minute he arrived in Los Angeles and spotted Wendy at the airport.

Frank Sinatra, who had quickly rescinded his retirement, had a television special from Madison Square Garden, and Dick watched from his living room. "Saw the Sinatra Special. Not impressed but the fans loved him; mostly old fans & Hollywood devotees. I'll do my own thing." Dick knew that the nostalgia craze would fade and thought that his talent would place him in the top rung of entertainers. He was clearly unable to face the reality of his age, his status, and the changed face of the entertainment world—both in music and in films and television. The following year, he would have another occasion to view Sinatra on television, at the tumultuous 1975 Academy Awards presentation. Bert Schneider, producer of the award-winning documentary *Hearts and Minds*, an antiwar film about Vietnam, read a telegram from the Vietnamese people of the Viet Cong delegation to the Paris peace talks, as the country was preparing for liberation. The telegram thanked the American people for their help in achieving peace. Bob Hope, a host for the show, was furious and insisted that a statement be read to the effect that the Academy Awards are nonpolitical. Bob Hope wrote the statement and gave it to Sinatra, who delivered it to a mixture of boos and cheers. (Shirley MacLaine would scream at him offstage, "Why did you do that!? You said you were speaking on behalf of the Academy. Well, I'm a member of the Academy and you didn't ask me.") Dick Haymes wrote in his diary, "I saw Sinatra on the Awards tonight & had to admire his guts but, I'm taking over; he's had his run & since I'm better, it's my turn. I'm being guided." He never mentioned the Vietnam War or the political turmoil that was roiling Hollywood, but kept his focus on his own long-awaited comeback.

The *Los Angeles Herald-Examiner* announced his return to Las Vegas and mentioned that Haymes was "talking a direct sale to the screen or TV of his life story—and what a life it has been." Again, readers are treated to a list of Haymes's past difficulties to prepare audiences for his ongoing comeback.

Dick and Wendy checked into the MGM Grand Hotel in Las Vegas, where he opened to a full house, appearing in three shows a night, receiving standing ovations at each show. The possibilities for his future again seemed bright, and such popular show-business figures as comedians Rich Little and Don Rickles expressed interest in working with him, and Alan Bregman offered to start a new publicity campaign. He and Wendy had some disagreements, quarreling and quickly reconciling. During his month-long engagement, she spent weekends with him, enjoying the celebrity culture that once again seemed to welcome her husband. Dick was disturbed by their disagreements and was clear about his view of her role in their marriage. "Wendy must get over her fears and insecurities. She *must* learn that ours is a partnership & her job is our home & beautiful children & mine is succeeding at my career. It's all so simple." It was not so simple to Wendy, who was a talented artist and aspired to a career of her own. But Dick had experienced competition from all of his previous wives and was unwilling to see this marriage succumb to the pressures of competing careers.

Clearly buoyed by his success, Dick sent his mother a check for one hundred dollars, noting, "I must help this helpless old lady in some way in this coming year." Marguerite was living in Nevada in the kind of austerity she had never imagined could overtake her.

On Christmas Eve, his daughter, Pidge, her husband, and their children joined Dick and his family for his "best Christmas." Then he was off to Scottsdale for a six-night engagement at the Safari Hotel, plagued once again by a head cold.

Frustrated by his inability to secure a recording contract, Dick decided to cut six sides privately, in the hope of attracting backing from a major label. Two of the sides were released by Crescendo. In a June 16, 1975 letter to Roger Dooner, who directs the U.S. branch of the Dick Haymes Society, he mentioned the recordings: "Glad you like the 'Single,' it comes from a record date that I set up myself, produced, mixed down, and paid for myself. We recorded six songs on the date and I own the Master, I only loaned it to Crescendo to press the two sides you heard. It became a thing with me, I just *had* to get into a Studio! Anyway, some of the record stations are playing the record, which can only do us good. By the way, I did not sign with Crescendo, as I am in the middle of negotiating a deal with Mike Maitland, President of M.C.A. Universal Records, a deal which I am sure will come to fruition shortly. I am doing all of my own business these days."

Shortly after that session, Dick was asked to record with the Air Force Band—the "Airmen of Note"—for the U.S. Recruiting Service. The recordings were broadcast in the form of public service programs in a series entitled *Serenade in Blue*. Dick was introduced by Charles Hughes, who represented the U.S. Air Force. In an interview conducted by Paul Anthony, Dick stresses that he is happy to sing contemporary songs so that he will not be locked into musical memorabilia. He mentions all of the entertainment projects he is working on with Herman Saunders (who is a former musician), a producer in Jack Webb's company: a feature film, a television *Movie of the Week* (ninety minutes, with a spin-off for a dramatic series). After singing two songs with fine Alan Copeland arrangements, he concludes the performance with a medley with the Airmen of Note. The interviewer thanks him, commenting, "Let's hope that it will not be too long before someone tempts Dick into a recording studio again—to cut a *commercial* album." *Modern Screen* sent a reporter to the recording session and wrote a sympathetic article, "Catching up with Dick Haymes." The writer was "astonished" not only by how well he sounded, but also by how well he looked. "He sang with a vigor that made me wonder how anyone who had been in show business for more than 30 years, with numerous ups and downs, could still have such forcefulness."

After the session, Dick and his son Sean, who had accompanied him to the studio, went into a deserted room for the interview, in which Dick openly acknowledges his past mistakes (a pattern he would repeat in virtually every interview) and then admits in public the truth that he could never admit to himself, that he became a superstar when he was too young and that he felt he didn't really deserve it. "I sensed that I was living a false existence, and out of that came over-indulgence." He admits to his alcohol problem, his lavish lifestyle that resulted in losing millions of dollars, his own role in the failure of four marriages, his laziness in not taking care of his finances, and his troubles during his marriage to Rita Hayworth. He expresses his deep love for Wendy and his happiness that she gave up her career for him. The article ends on a decidedly optimistic note: he is in "constant demand" for appearances at the big casinos in Las Vegas and Tahoe; he's "frequently" cast in segments of TV series; and he and Saunders have their own production company at Universal. He mentions the Rossi film (which had already been rejected), but expresses confidence in his ability to capture a new, young audience. The reporter, who was observing Sean throughout the interview, was moved to comment, "It's obvious he adores Dick. He told me proudly that he intends to be a singer like his dad, and that Dick is going to teach him how and what to sing."

Although Dick would relish the attention he received from the radio show and the interview, he would again be forced to go on the road to earn enough money to support his family. Apart from living in somewhat less expensive homes, the family did not economize. (Later that year, he and Wendy found a new boat they planned to purchase and were excited that Wendy would have the opportunity to do the interior decorating.)

After a week in Brooklyn singing to a small but enthusiastic audience, he returned to a headline appearance at the Thunderbird in Las Vegas. It would be, he believed, a stepping-stone to his own show at Caesar's Palace. In his diary, he repeatedly writes, "I am a super-star!"—probably to convince himself that the glow following a warm reception might last forever. He was signed for a cameo in a deplorable film that attempted to be a satirical comedy, *Won Ton Ton, the Dog Who Saved Hollywood* (inspired by the old *Rin Tin Tin* films), with walk-ons by everyone—and anyone—who had achieved fame in the movie business, including Edgar Bergen, Milton Berle, Joan Blondell, Cyd Charisse, Alice Faye, George Jessel, Dorothy Lamour, Peter Lawford, Victor Mature, Dennis Morgan, and Rudy Vallee. Sadly, Dick Haymes's very brief appearance would be his last in a Hollywood film.

Early in the year, Dick's health once again began to suffer, not only from the frequent head colds and flu-like illnesses requiring antibiotics, but also from hives that broke out on several occasions and were treated by cortisone.

He had to cancel several engagements, in one case forced to remain in bed for two weeks. He admitted in his diary that he had been drinking and was drawn by Wendy's interest in astrology to find a path he might follow to restore him to his former glory. As though in response to his wishes, he rejoiced whenever a check would arrive "in the nick of time to carry us."

On one occasion, he admitted to having neglected Wendy's need for the "love and romance that every woman needs" and having "hurt her very deeply." As his business deals continued to fall through (rejection by United Artists records), he believed all of his debts would be paid if he and Harry James teamed up together for an act that would play in Las Vegas, and then in films. And he experienced new financial problems, having placed his friends Errol Gillis and Joe Wolf in an embarrassing financial position: the mortgage payments that he had difficult in meeting affected Gillis and Wolf, who loaned him funds and served as mortgage guarantors.

Bill Loeb, his current public-relations manager, had promised to advance him funds for mortgage payments and bills, but the money never came through. He wrote, "Tomorrow I shall find $2000 somewhere, somehow." Through some slight-of-hand, he did manage to secure a bank loan, but was soon required to appear in court for a child-support hearing. "It doesn't worry me," he wrote; "all I have to do is pay the arrears." He released Bill Loeb's firm, noting that he felt "bad but Loeb didn't help." He quickly signed with a new manager, who was able to secure an advance on future per- formances. He renewed his green card after meeting with his lawyer, Joe Wolf, to go over the past three and one-half years of expenses and income for the IRS and immigration. After briefly entertaining the idea of having his mother move in with his family, he and Wendy prepared for a visit from her daughter, Beverly Smith.

In late September, he appeared at the Copacobana, which had relo- cated to Brooklyn, New York, to uniformly warm reviews. Celebrities were picked up in Manhattan and deposited at the club, normally a nightspot for locals. His two-week engagement brought three standing ovations each night, and he was happy that on one occasion his mother was in the audience.

While in New York, Dick attended a banquet for Lord Mountbatten and was very pleased that Cary Grant "graciously gave me his phone number." So buoyed was he by the Copacobana success that he once again felt his future was assured: "When I am solvent I shall begin to amass a fortune & that is not difficult."

Another appearance, this time in Warren, Michigan, near Detroit, was a setback. "I don't like what I'm doing in being forced to play mediocre clubs in cities that can ill afford to come out at night," he wrote of the disappointingly small audience.

As the year drew to an end, he enjoyed another Christmas with his family—including Wendy's daughter Beverly—and vowed once again to stop performing and, instead, move into production "of all sorts." His saddest thoughts were for his children, who had suffered from his "lack of compassion. What about the original recipients of my neglect? My children—now grown; have they forgiven me? Do they love me? or are they even interested? Dear Lord, a part of me took so long to grow up, with the other part to always remain a child." He seemed particularly saddened, yet resigned, about his failure to resume his role of father to Stephanie: "Take the father of a daughter who went away for some years leaving his young daughter with her mother. Upon his return, he contacted his daughter & expected all to be the same, but of course, as he had ignored her, she now ignores him. Sad, but true."

In 1976, Dick made diary entries only from January through March 21 and from May 31 through July 4. The second half of the year was one of his busiest since he returned to the United States, for it saw him not only touring in a new nostalgic vaudeville show, but also recording for a prestigious radio program that would return him to a recording studio and result in his first new album since Alan Dell sponsored *Then and Now* in England in 1969.

In January, Dick met Andy Maree, a business manager for many important Hollywood stars. He thought Maree would help him "to climb the mountain of achievement, the first step to abundant wealth & challenge in the money game." At the same time, he acknowledged that he was constantly fighting depression, even considering the possibility that medicine prescribed for hives might have affected him psychologically. He appeared to accept the limitations that his age was imposing: "I now realize that the 'performing' days of this life experience are coming to a close and I am about to start a new life, the goal of which is not yet clear to me." Sadly, he would never be sufficiently independent financially so that he might give up performing.

Dick and Wendy were quarreling again, according to Dick, because she thought he had not been a good provider; but Wendy would say later that he was abusive to her when he was drinking. Certainly, in his diary, he expresses his deep concern about the well-being of his children, Sean and Samantha, and, despite the tensions, repeatedly declares his love for Wendy, finding excuses for her arguments with him. "How can I remain angry? All that was said was said with love."

By the end of February, he had been ill once again, but more upsetting to him was his sense that he was psychologically and emotionally collapsing, repeatedly remarking on his depression and his fears. Nevertheless, he made a few television appearances and started to explore merchandising possibilities for television game shows. He was also interested in becoming involved in the production of Chevy Chase's new film, *Fletch*, but was unable to become part of the team. But he was approached by Roy Radin, a very young and ambitious theatrical producer who was interested in staging vaudeville revival shows, appealing to the nostalgia craze that would continue throughout the decade. Radin may be remembered as one of those working with producer Robert Evans on *The Cotton Club* in the early 1980s. Radin was brutally murdered in 1983, and his death was immediately linked to the production of the film. But in the 1970s, he created a show that toured cities and towns that normally did not have access to name performers. Radin became Dick's manager and advertised the first tour in *Variety* in March. The tour included a four-day booking ending on the Fourth of July at the Tamiment Resort and Country Club in Pennsylvania. On the bill with Dick were Milton Berle, Godfrey Cambridge, Pat Suzuki, the Ink Spots, the Harmonica Rascals, and George Jessel, who served as toastmaster.

Dick was proud of his work on the tour but was extremely lonely, yearning desperately for Wendy and the children. His handwriting was noticeably looser, less controlled; it seems clear that he had been drinking before writing in his diary. He disliked his first experience with a theater in the round and was exhausted after spending eleven hours in a bus, as they reached "the wilds of Wheeling, West Virginia," for a five-day engagement.

Dick's luck would change for the better after he returned home and received a call from an old friend, Alec Wilder. Wilder was a composer of classical music, popular music, and jazz. He had close relationships with the leading figures in the world of music, including Frank Sinatra, Mabel Mercer, Peggy Lee, and Tony Bennett. He composed songs for opera singer Eileen Farrell, chamber music for the New York Woodwind and New York Brass Quintets, and concert music for small groups and large orchestras. He won many awards and was nominated for a National Book Award for co-writing the definitive *American Popular Song—The Great Innovators, 1900–1950*. Among his own compositions are such standards as "It's So Peaceful in the Country," "I'll Be Around," and "While We're Young."

Wilder first met Dick Haymes when he was in the control room during one of Dick's recording sessions with Harry James many years earlier. They became close friends but lost contact when Dick moved to England. Wilder had read of Dick's performance at the St. Regis and attended one of the shows. He was again impressed with Dick's winning personality and with his singing that seemed to him even better than he remembered. When the Public Broadcasting System asked him to produce a fifty-six-show series of programs devoted to American popular song (the series would win a Peabody Award), Wilder phoned Dick Haymes and asked him to appear on one of the shows. (Coincidentally, Roger Dooner had written to the producers recommending that Dick Haymes be selected for a program in the series, and his letter was acknowledged by Dick Phipps, the producer.) The singers were selected for their identification with particular types of songs. Bobby Short sang Cole Porter and Teddi King sang Rodgers and Hart. Dick sang popular ballads, focusing on George

Gershwin and Harry Warren, among others, but including some of Wilder's songs as well. Dick was delighted and joined Wilder, Phipps, and Loonis McGlohan, who worked with Dick as arranger and leader of the trio that backed him up.

The group met at Phipps's home in Lexington, South Carolina, just a few days before Dick was to appear in another Radin show in Roanoke, Virginia. He recorded twenty-six songs in two days. McGlohan had asked Dick to come a day earlier to have a preliminary rehearsal at his home, which was near Lexington. Dick insisted on staying in a hotel, and McGlohan went up to his room to escort him to dinner. He noticed that Dick had his dressing gown laid out carefully on his bed, as if he could just slip into it effortlessly. "It struck me as a person holding onto the last remnant of that stage of stardom where you had someone—a valet—doing everything for you. I've never seen anyone else do that," McGlohan remarked. He said that Dick was not drinking, save for a glass of wine at dinner.

At dinner, they chatted and he asked Dick about his childhood. He learned that Dick still felt the hurt at his mother's having left him and his brother at school for the Christmas season. He said that was the worst Christmas of his life—and he recalled other aspects of a childhood that McGlohan saw as profoundly unhappy. After the session with Wilder, McGlohan and Dick remained in contact; and the next year, with the support of the Dick Haymes Society, they would work on his last recordings.

Dick felt that the Wilder experience was thrilling. He was interviewed by "Tee" Dooley, a member of the Dick Haymes Society—then known as "Friends of Haymes"—after the November 1 show at the Roanoke Civic Center (where Donald O'Connor was a special guest star). Dick exulted in the success of the recording session and in the rapport among the three, he, Wilder, and McGlohan. "I was very, very proud of what happened and the reason I was. Alec . . . got teary a couple of times and I couldn't look at him, because I started to get a lump in my throat too, because we were just vibrating beauty around the whole thing, and they were very nice people. It was a great joy." Dick admired Wilder for his uncompromising dedication to everything he did, even to having lived at the Algonquin Hotel in New York City for forty years, when at times he was unable to pay the bill.

The program was broadcast on PBS on January 1, 1977, and Dick's session was praised by reviewers and musicians. The result was the issuance of an album, *For You, For Me, For Evermore*, by Audiophile Records, that included twenty of the songs recorded for the program.

Dick returned home to prepare for his Labor Day weekend appearances at the Aladdin Hotel in Las Vegas, where he would be backed by the Les Brown band, with Count Basie and his orchestra on the same bill. He spent the rest of the year writing and making appearances both locally and on brief tours to other states.

By the holiday season his financial troubles had not lessened. He tried out for a part in a film, *The Other Side of Midnight*, but was not hired. To buoy their spirits, Dick and Wendy drove to San Diego for New Year's Eve, staying in a fine hotel and trying to forget their problems. Dick's diary reflects his despair: "I would like to 'like me' again"; and in it he admits that whatever has happened is his own fault, recognizing, as he had so frequently in the past, "I am a child who never grew up and develop[ed]." It is particularly sad that Dick Haymes could recognize his faults, the errors he had made in the past and was still making, and his childish refusal to make the kind of life-altering changes that he realized were necessary to his survival.

One decision that seemed to indicate that he recognized the need to act to relieve his financial difficulties was to sell his house in Encino and get rid of his debt to Joe Wolf. He and Wendy owned the furniture, and so he felt that the expense of moving to a new home would be lessened considerably. He stated, "Oxnard? We shall see. I'll buy what I can pay for, & no more, until I can pay more." He and Wendy had a serious argument about the prospective move, and she left briefly with the children. "I am alone—I don't know if Wendy wishes to come back or find another life. I love her, so whatever she chooses I shall accept. I think the fault lies with me—not all— but some." He then wrote, "Disregard the above—will rent house in Oxnard until I can afford to buy." He constantly sought relief in meditation, noting that it helped him to stop drinking. "It's just a habit that I don't need." Like many alcoholics, he felt that he could control his problem and never sought the help of Alcoholics Anonymous.

As possible recording deals and business enterprises fell through, he once again blamed his agents for their refusal to acknowledge that singing was no longer for him (despite the reality that his only work was as a singer), and he looked to film as his only recourse.

Dick and Wendy found a suitable house in Oxnard, and he was happy with his home, his boat, and his family. Wendy had her first art show, sold two paintings, and secured a consignment for a third. Dick was delighted at her success, noting that "she deserves it." The pleasure in their house and the possibility of achieving financial stability, unrealistic as it would prove, led to Dick's vow to go on the wagon for a while (after having one drink at a house party to celebrate Washington's birthday). He would adhere to his vows for a few days, begin drinking, and then once again vow abstinence.

He noted that he felt he should end his association with Roy Radin, for Radin was busy with other enterprises. But Dick was soon engaged to perform in Lake Tahoe, one of the better milieus, and he and Wendy decided to buy a new boat, *The Buccaneer*. He was happy with his performance in Tahoe and noted that he had experienced a "day of sobriety." But in April he was reminded of his lack of control by a most unlikely critic, his son Sean. "I am a bit sad, for I was told by my son to stop drinking so much. I shall cut down a good bit for what happened is not good."

Wendy opened another showing of her artwork at the end of May, attended by many friends, including Andy Maree and Dick's friend from his years in England, Russ Jones. Again, Wendy sold three paintings, and the event would be described in a forthcoming edition of the local magazine devoted to boating and recreation in the area, *The Islander*. Headlined "Dick Haymes—Mandalay Bay's 'Star' Resident," the article repeated the old, almost mythological story of Dick's background, concluding with a description of the family today. They owned a twenty-five-foot Buccaneer sloop berthed at their home in Mandalay Bay; and, although they were happy there, they were looking for a beach property. The article quoted Dick: "We want a monstrosity of a house on the water that nobody else wants, which we are willing to recondition ourselves. A five-bedroom place where I can have all my goodies with plenty of wall space for Wendy's paintings." The article concluded with a description of Dick's career: "in high gear again, with TV guest spots, Las Vegas, and other top nightclub engagements, and occasional motion pictures. He's piloting himself into writing and producing for films and television." But as his diary entries reveal, Dick was still insecure, depressed, uncertain of his future, and fighting to control his alcohol addiction.

His primarily endeavor for the next months would be the completion of his screenplay, *Reprise*. He found strong support in Russ Jones, who read his work carefully, even suggesting new characters. (Later, Dick, although he would always treasure Russ, would feel that his good friend was not sufficiently critical.) Although he was writing productively, he had not stopped drinking, and he was stopped by police on a highway and ticketed for driving under the influence, with a court date scheduled for September.

On August 5, his *Reprise* script was registered by the Writer's Guild of America. Written with the obvious intention of playing the major role himself, Dick constructed a strong screenplay, sharp and absorbing in the first half, but becoming melodramatic and disappointing at the end. The plot is really composed of two stories, the first part devoted to an aging singing star, Steve Britt, who finds new strength and personal success after his discovery and training of an aspiring young singer, Tony Carr. The second part of the screenplay introduces a beautiful girl, a jealous, ugly man, and a kidnapping and concludes with the murder of the young singer. Whereas the first part reflects the authenticity of the writer's feelings, the second half tries to tailor the material to the supposed needs of a mass-market audience. The script uses the names of individuals with whom Dick Haymes had worked or those well known in the music industry, like Quincy Jones and Herb Alpert.

There are lines in the script that clearly reflect Dick Haymes's decline, like the bartender's remark to young Tony, who is looking for Steve Britt: "Yeah. He'll be around, . . . if he can crawl outta the bottle." Young Tony recalls Steve's past, essentially that of the young Dick Haymes: "It's just that, to them [Tony's parents], you were the *biggest* star! Goin' overseas to entertain the 'boys,' and all those movies you made. . . . And they played your records all the time . . . and talked about you." Dick Haymes was a genuinely gifted writer who might have succeeded at screenwriting had he not been forced several times a year to resume tours that would cover the family's daily expenses.

During the family's months in Oxnard, Dick enjoyed taking Sean and, on occasion, Samantha sailing—and he dreamed of a larger boat that he hoped to buy. He and Wendy did go out to search for a new boat, and they found one for which they planned to make an offer of nine thousand dollars in cash. They obviously could not afford to purchase a new boat, because he never mentions the matter again.

In September, Russ Jones accompanied Dick to a television studio to rehearse a new interview show with Merv Griffin, a salute to Harry James featuring Dick Haymes and Helen Forrest, which would reunite three of the greatest figures from the big band era. Dick was delighted to see James and Helen Forrest again and sang two numbers with the band—effectively erasing the passing years. He, James, and Forrest reminisced about the old days, but Dick recognized that the show was simply another foray into nostalgia. His recent appearance as one of the "also starring" cast on another *McMillan* show had lasted no longer than two to three minutes.

At his court appearance for drunk driving, Dick was happy that the sentence was so light: a fine and two years probation. Although he wrote in his diary that he was happy that Wendy had made a birthday party for him and for Nugent, he worried about finding four thousand dollars to pay for the children's school. He toyed with the idea of moving to Oregon but always returned to the problem of finding cash to clear up his debts. "I have owed too many too long," he wrote. They were thinking of paying off the lease on their

Oxnard home and moving to one on Hollywood Boulevard, paying on a month-to-month basis, so that they could buy the camper they felt they needed. But as he noted in October, "My present cash flow amounts to zero."

Luckily, Roy Radin phoned and offered Dick over a month of one-night performances beginning in early November. He gladly accepted Radin's offer, for the engagement would meet his immediate needs—and then, once again, he started dreaming of his future, with his screenplay accepted and with him playing the leading role: "I should become very much in demand again." He wanted to learn "how to earn the way other people seem to be able to." He noted, for the first time, that he was no longer young, and again wished for something to come along so that he would no longer have to go out on the road.

His morale was boosted by a phone call from a business friend, Larry Penzell, who informed him that his own financial source, Lewis Eisner, was very interested in financing one million dollars or more in *Reprise*. Dick was particularly excited because the interest was based on only the first draft of the script. He decided that the family must move to Malibu, that he would find escrow money for the move from pre-production funds—even though he has not received a formal commitment from Eisner.

On the road trip, Dick was notably despondent—once again very lonely, longing for his wife and family and finding solace in drink. He had a battle with Roy Radin—never the easiest person to deal with—but found the audience reception in Erie, Pennsylvania, comforting. He was again part of Radin's vaudeville show, with Donald O'Connor and several second-rung comedians. But the trip was exhausting, much like the old days when he toured with the big bands. He reported that he spent eight and one-half hours "on the bloody bus"; and in the next few diary entries, his writing was less controlled, as he noted, "I am living day to day in a sort of limbo" and "I hate what I'm doing but it pays the bills." He made only one entry a day in his diary, e.g., "Sang well" or "Trying to keep my sanity."

The last day of the tour in the second week of December was in Honolulu, and he felt blessed on his return. "I rest," he wrote, and then, "getting better." Determined to escape the grueling grind of future tours, he decided to go "on the dry for a few days" to work on his screenplay. He could not really accept that his career as a performer was almost at an end, and he would be deeply moved by the praise that his final recording efforts would evoke in the next two years by the most knowledgeable critics of contemporary music. And he would soon face the most difficult challenge of his personal life; perhaps through his deep faith and spirituality he would finally find the wisdom that had eluded him for so long.

CHAPTER 9

The Long Goodbye

Once again, Dick and Wendy had decided to move; they could not afford their "dream house" in Santa Monica and finally decided on a more modest home in Malibu. Dick was genuinely exhausted and reluctant to go on the road again, but he knew that his only assured income would be from engagements in cities and towns across the country. By March, he embarked on a tour that ended in St. Petersburg, Florida. He first stopped at the Statler-Hilton in New York to record a program that would be broadcast on PBS: *The Big Band Bash*. The hotel was formerly the famous Hotel Pennsylvania, where the Dorsey brothers and Glenn Miller were popular figures in the glory days of the big band era. The Terrace Room, where they performed, was partially rearranged to suggest the old Café Rouge. Filmed in two installments (the first had been at Frank Dailey's Meadowbrook, famous from the swing era), the show was broadcast in March on many PBS outlets. It featured Count Basie, Woody Herman and Maynard Ferguson, a tribute to Tommy Dorsey by the Pied Pipers and Johnny Desmond, then Dick and Helen Forrest singing some of their hit duets, a segment devoted to Sammy Kaye, with Don Cornell, the Pied Pipers, and Fran Warren, and two additional segments featuring jazz greats Dizzy Gillespie, Anita O'Day, Earl Hines, Joe Venuti, and Teddy Wilson. The program was popular with viewers, and in the 1980s it was revived on Public Broadcasting with Merv Griffin introducing surviving legends of the big band era: Bea Wain, Herb Jeffries, Helen

O'Connell, and Bob Eberly. Griffin inserted a clip of the Dick Haymes/Helen Forrest segment from 1978, saying of Dick, "Many think that he was the best of the big-band singers."

In this segment, Haymes sings a medley from *State Fair* in a voice seemingly untouched by time, except for its deepening, which results in richer tones. A close-up shows his tired eyes and a slightly double chin, but when he sings he is the charismatic performer of forty years earlier, lingering unexpectedly over some notes, gliding from one word directly into the next—as in "It Might as Well Be Spring," when without taking a new breath he slides from one note to the next line of the lyric. It is a new delivery, emphasizing the wistful longing that is the underlying emotion of the song. When he sings, "Still I feel so gay in a melancholy way," he closes his eyes as if in reverie, but returns to an upbeat mood with "Hey—might as well be spring," delivered with a half-smile. As Haymes moves brilliantly between sadness and hope, we wait expectantly to see how he will end the number. And he doesn't disappoint us, for he waits many seconds to intone the last word, "spring," in a full-throated baritone. As if in response to the implied sadness of that longing, he virtually hurls the ending at us in denial of that sadness. The song becomes an affirmation of possibility, delivered in a deep, resonant voice that itself is testimony to life and love. Helen Forrest then joins him for a seemingly unrehearsed, utterly charming duet, all the more appealing in the genuine affection they share and their clear enjoyment of each other.

After recording the PBS television special, he toured in a new nostalgia show, *The Fabulous Forties*, stopping in New Jersey and other states along the eastern seaboard before concluding in Florida. After a big band medley conducted by Warren Covington, using famous arrangements by Harry James, Glenn Miller, Artie Shaw, and others, the singers made their appearances, beginning with the Pied Pipers, then Helen Forrest, and, finally, the performer the audience was excitedly awaiting, Dick Haymes. He sang a *State Fair* medley and ten additional songs as part of an autobiographical sketch in song that he had first performed in 1972 at the Cocoanut Grove. He added the recent "The Way We Were" and two songs that he had sung on Alec Wilder's radio program. Once again, Dick would receive standing ovations for every performance. Helen Forrest remembered the tour fondly and praised his endurance: "It was wonderful to be with him again and he was much the same as he'd been before. But like all of us he no longer was young. He'd lost some of his spirit, some of his confidence. Such tours were tough for him. He wasn't well. But he wanted to perform. Sometimes he sang well, sometimes he didn't. He always was nervous singing, he'd lose his strength, and he'd become inconsistent. But at his best he was still the best." And she added, "He was on the wagon." She thought that it hurt him "not to have endured better, not to have remained a star, not to have been a bigger star longer. I think it hurt him a little to be touring with a nostalgia show, playing a lot of small towns. Well, that's the way it is."

Dick wrote in his diary while in Florida that his performances were going well, some better than others, but the audience loved it. Yet the ovations did not really satisfy him: "What is it? I feel that I am sucking on the blood of bloodless old people for money! I don't like myself, though they seem to love me! I feel that the time has come when I can no longer mentally handle any more tours. I must re-arrange my life so that I am able to live the way I wish to & survive to the fullest & enjoy the rest of this life experience!" Written in the third week of March, that would be the final entry in Dick's diary.

Tee Dooley, who had interviewed Dick in Roanoke, was determined that Dick should make a new album, and the members of the Haymes Society came up with the money to produce it. They sent him one thousand dollars to cover his expenses and to show him that they were, indeed, serious about the endeavor. Dooley remembers, "When I called Dick, since he had heard so many promises in his life and career, he really didn't take me seriously. In fact, he said, 'What is the song and dance about recording me?' I assured him we were serious and we were soliciting money to make the project happen, and he seemed impressed but still wondering how we could pull it off." Dooley, Roger Dooner, and the British representative and co-founder of the society, Maurice Dunn, had compiled a list of songs previously unrecorded by Dick; and together, they chose those that would appear on the new album. The recording session was set for May 24, 1978, with rehearsals scheduled for the preceding day. Loonis McGlohan would again arrange and accompany Dick, accompanied by bass player Rusty Gilder and Jim Lackey, the drummer.

In addition to the notable classic songs, like "Last Night When We Were Young," "As Time Goes By," "I'm Glad There Is You," and "While We're Young," Dick included his brother's popular standard, "That's All," joking, "As this is my brother's song, I'd better do a good job on it, or he'll give me hell!" And he sang "I Love You Samantha," dedicating it to his young daughter. The following night, Tee, Loonis, and Dick went back to the hotel and listened to the house band. They spoke of the session, and Dick said that he hoped that he was worthy of the honor of having him record the album. "Thank you," Dooley remembers him saying, "for giving me the opportunity to create a few moments of beauty."

Loonis McGlohan remembers that on the night of the recording session, while they were having dinner at his home, a friend called him and said that he had fifty invited guests for a banquet to be held at the local hotel the following night and asked Loonis if he might perform with his musicians. He went back to the dinner table and said that he would have to perform the following night, to which Dick replied, "Do you have a singer?" Loonis told him that they had no money for a singer, and Dick offered to sing as a favor.

The audience at the hotel was awestruck to see Dick Haymes at center stage. He sang for fifty minutes, and Loonis felt a kind of paralysis in the room. After the last song, a man at ringside said, "You know, that young fellow sounds a lot like Dick Haymes." Dick received his by now customary standing ovation from the appreciative audience.

Loonis McGlohan remembers feeling that Dick was still trying to hold onto those golden days—like the robe he had so carefully placed on his bed. He did not play the role of the star, even though he certainly wished he might once again experience the heady excitement of those early years. McGlohan remembers that one evening he had a houseguest who was in her nineties with a daughter in her seventies, and Dick was gentle and polite. "Other people would have ignored them," he said.

Dick was completely sober throughout the recording sessions, and although he indulged in some wine with dinner, he was always the consummate professional. He was deeply grateful, saying that he didn't know of any better expression of love than what the members of the Haymes Society had done in producing this album for him.

Dick was happy to return to his Malibu home. He made a local appearance at an imitation-Vegas night club in Encino, owned and named by Dick Van Dyke's brother, Jerry. Dick sang so brilliantly that a member of the audience (a former county enumerator) decided to return for the closing performance the following Sunday. When he entered the club, he held the door for a "gentleman in his forties who was escorting a little girl of about nine." He realized that this little girl who was seated high on a platform backdrop to one of the dining/drinking booths was Dick's daughter. Dick sang "I Love You, Samantha," and he noticed that father and daughter were gazing fondly at each other. The audience gave him a huge ovation, for he was singing, the observer noted, "at the very peak of his powers." After concluding a particularly moving rendition of Antonio Carlos Jobim's song, "Wave," the observer recalled, "Serenading a diverse audience of young and old (mostly old, I must admit), and singing to his friends and business associates but also (and most importantly) to his daughter, Samantha, Dick Haymes made his presence felt while his audiences responded with their own waves: a wave of 'love.'" He performed at the Playboy Club in Los Angeles in July and, after signing with a new management agency in August, left California for Springfield, Massachusetts, where he would start a new tour.

But his life would take a turn that he did not expect: Wendy had inscribed "I love and adore you" in Dick's diary for 1978, but she had already begun to contemplate leaving her husband. When they had dinner at Andy Maree's home one night, she said, "He had sparks for me. . . . I heard he liked me." Maree would be the person she would call when she finally decided to end her marriage, and he would arrange for a house for Wendy and the children. According to Russ Jones, who saw quite a lot of Dick during these years, Dick knew about Wendy and Andy but said nothing, assuming it was a temporary infatuation on both sides. But Wendy was worried about their future, particularly their unsettled finances, and she and Dick quarreled often. She was disappointed, too, that she no longer enjoyed the celebrity life she had always sought. She would later say that Dick was consistently physically abusive to her, but Russ Jones was at their home one evening when they were arguing. He stood outside until they had finished, and when Wendy said to him, "He beat me!" Russ confronted her, telling her that he heard the whole argument and that her accusation was completely untrue. But after their separation, Wendy was unrelenting in her denigration of Dick Haymes as an abusive husband and father.

Their daughter, Samantha, who remained with her mother after the separation, says that her father could be abusive, but she felt that as a child "life was great," except for the constant upheavals caused by their frequent moves. Samantha does not remember him as an affectionate father and says that he hit her across the head with his ring turned around so that it would hurt her. Samantha believes that Dick tried to make himself into a good family man, "which he wasn't." Despite her negative comments about her father, Samantha says, "I adore him," perhaps reflecting the confusion of a nine-year-old child watching her parents' marriage collapse.

Sean, however, who elected to move into his father's apartment in Marina del Ray, feels that Dick was a good father. He believes that every talented person drinks and that his father "cleaned up his act" by not drinking or smoking in his last years. Sean feels that Dick always loved Wendy and that the breakup of his marriage was very hard for his father to bear. Sean remembers how supportive Russ Jones was. "He came to stay with us. He was a cartoonist for Marvel comics and a talented writer, and he was honest. I trusted and liked him." Sean was twelve when his parents separated, and he felt caught in the middle: "My mother tried to push me against my father, and my father against my mother." In the next year, Samantha and Sean would grow closer to the parent with whom each lived. And in Samantha's case, Andy Maree would begin to play the role of father (he would later adopt her, and she would take his name). According to Pidge, Dick's older daughter, Andy Maree told Sean, "Go live with your father. He's not paying any support," so Sean said, "Fine," and from the time Andy dropped him at Dick's, he had a wonderful time living with his father. Wendy invited Pidge to dinner after the separation, and his daughter remembers, "She trashed my dad so badly I never saw her again."

On September 29, 1978, Wendy went to court to request support from Dick. She asked for monthly payments of eight hundred dollars for the children and seventeen hundred dollars for herself. Clearly, Dick could not meet her demands, but he did not speak harshly of her, except for a brief comment that she was a "black widow." Russ Jones remembers the only negative remark that he heard Dick make about Wendy, "No matter what her resume says, she was a hair stylist and that was it." But Wendy continued to speak harshly of Dick to everyone, even accepting the worst allegations about his relationship with Rita Hayworth. Dick's friends and family could not understand her anger, which persisted long after his death. Russ never saw Dick raise a hand to anybody. "I'd heard stories about the old days, but not the Dick I knew." Dick seemed to Russ to be a devoted father and a calm, philosophical man who never defamed anyone or engaged in self-pity. If anyone asked him, "What happened to your career?" he'd simply say, "I blew it."

When the London *Daily Express* reported the Haymeses' plans to divorce, they interviewed Wendy's parents, who lived in Bideford, Devon. Beatrice Smith said that she hadn't seen Wendy since Sean was six months old, and never saw Samantha. She was clearly bitter about her daughter's neglect of her parents: "We were not surprised by the news—I would never be surprised at anything Wendy did. She's a bit of a sensationalist. We couldn't really care less. Wendy has never bothered to keep in touch—we never get any letters and we don't even get a Christmas card from her."

Dick was feeling upbeat about a recent review in *Stereo Review* of the recording that Audiophile had made from the Alec Wilder radio program,

For You, For Me, For Evermore. Peter Reilly praised him warmly, advising lovers of popular music to listen to Haymes, for "if he's new to you, all the better; you're in for a pleasurable surprise. If you remember him, I'll bet you don't remember him sounding *this* good."

He appeared with Helen Forrest at Jerry Van Dyke's club in Encino on January 17, 1979, and he was clearly nervous and unsettled, receiving a tepid review from the *Los Angeles Times* critic, who noticed his nervousness, resulting in a "somewhat dry" rendition of the standards from *State Fair*. The old Dick Haymes style, he wrote, "appeared only intermittently" in the more recent "The Way We Were" and in the Gershwin standard, "Our Love Is Here to Stay." Despite his ruddy complexion and his gray hair, the reviewer wrote, "he retains that mien of ingenuousness remembered from earlier times."

Dick was living with Russ and his son Sean in Marina del Rey, enjoying sailing and writing, always trying to find new business enterprises. At a party at Van Dyke's club, he met a young woman, Dianne de La Vega, who shared his devotion to Yogananda and the Self-Realization Fellowship. Dianne was a "consulting psychologist," and she was adept at using her techniques for relaxation to form a curious bond with Dick. She believed that she was "the tonic he needed," that she understood his moods, and that she helped him to stop drinking and smoking. But according to Russ, she would eventually take advantage of him, even to the point of having him hire her daughter to answer his mail. He would break off their relationship after several months.

After his death, she tried to communicate with his spirit, for she believed that they were soul mates, destined to spend eternity together. She was even put into a trance to communicate with his spirit. When interviewed for a book, aptly titled *Soul Mates*, she recounted the story of her love for Dick; she told the author that when she was "regressed," she asked Dick why he had broken off their relationship, and he replied that he was trying to spare her from future grief and suffering.

Although he was not touring in the spring of 1979, he was elated when Peter Reilly's review of his second album with Loonis McGlohan was reviewed. Reilly was even more enthusiastic of this album, *As Time Goes By*, than the earlier one, describing it as "incredible" in the level of achievement by someone whose career has had so many "zigs and zags." Reilly bemoaned the contemporary music scene and hailed Dick Haymes for upholding a tradition in American music that had lasted for over forty years, a "golden age" of pop music, "as civilized and sophisticated as anything ever produced by any Western country." During those years, it was probably "the most popular and universally identifiable American cultural export." Reilly praised individual songs with precision and care, revealing his range of knowledge and his appreciation of Haymes's artistry. He compared his renditions to those of other popular performers, like Judy Garland and Frank Sinatra, concluding that "the austere, elegant lyrics" of the Harold Arlen ballad " 'Last Night When We Were Young' are sung with such unpretentiously intense, deep feeling and gently wistful regret that they will knock you off your roller skates."

Dick was elated when Roger Dooner sent him the review. In his letter to Dooner, he says, "It is probably the best critique I have ever had in my professional life." He expresses his deep gratitude to the Dick Haymes Society and says that everything in his life is going well and that his plans are coming to fruition.

Other reviewers were equally impressed by the latest—and last—album Dick Haymes would record. In Canada, the *St. Catherine's Standard* in Ontario called it a "revelation, . . . the ultimate in popular balladry by a baritone. . . . The performance combines glistening mastery with a graceful style projected by a voice no other popular singer can match." Doug Ramsey, in *Radio Free Jazz*, praising Dick's low-note entry on "But Beautiful," wrote, "For years, I thought Crosby's version couldn't be surpassed. Haymes has surpassed it." Ken Barnes, writing from England, after a glowing review in which he recalls fondly the vintage Sinatra recording of one of the songs on the album, "Last Night When We Were Young," concludes, "It's for sure that I wouldn't care to back the contemporary Sinatra's chances against this thrilling Haymes performance."

Barnes and other commentators over the years consistently compared Dick Haymes and Frank Sinatra. Dick never expressed any dislike of such comparisons, but Sinatra clearly resented his earlier rival—despite his own megastar status. Singer Garry Stevens admired Dick Haymes, and one evening when he and Sinatra, who was his close friend, were dining, he asked Sinatra to accompany him to a club where Haymes was performing. Sinatra exploded in anger at the suggestion, telling Stevens that he disliked Haymes and would never go to see him. Since the two had never fought, Sinatra's response was undoubtedly an expression of his resentment at Haymes's recent successes. For years, Don Rickles, the comedian and a close friend of Sinatra, would tease him about Dick Haymes, indicating the competitive hostility he knew Sinatra harbored for Haymes.

The admiring reviews stirred interest in record distributors, and Tee Dooley, Maurice Dunn, and Roger Dooner, determined to keep Dick Haymes in the public eye, pursued every possibility of securing wider distribution for the album. Yet despite their efforts, the record companies they approached did not want to take on the task of national distribution. Some years later, Harriet Wasser, a publicist for Bobby Darin and a longtime admirer of Dick Haymes, wrote to *Billboard*, reminding readers that since Applause Records just reissued standards by Keely Smith, Harry James, and others, "perhaps some smart executive will go to the vaults and pick up on two of the best albums Dick Haymes ever recorded," Capitol Records' *Moondreams* and *Rain or Shine*.

In July, Dick was invited to appear on the Hugh Downs television show for an interview about his life, his career, and, primarily, his philosophy. First he sang one of his classic numbers; his face was unlined, but his eyes looked very tired. He talked to Downs about living many lives, speaking about his spiritual life and how it had helped him cope with the many problems he had faced over the years. The "immediacy of materiality is not that important," he said, adding that he "went through a bad hassle and chose to do something about it." He described the spiritual foundation of his life—not formal religion or church-going, but rather part of the church of all religions.

Downs was very impressed with Dick's apparent ability to surmount his difficulties and invited him back on the show in August. After a fine rendition of "The Way We Were," he sat down to converse with his host.

Downs said, "You sound exactly the same," and then asked him about the wisdom he had acquired over the years. Dick responded that going abroad worked for him, but that the United States was his home. He told Downs that he had conquered his drinking problem and had survived many marriages and breakups; and when Downs asked him how he had escaped the disaster that had destroyed so many others, he replied, "You make choices, skid row or survival—and get help from introspection and faith. I had a series of turning points, but remained interested in music, art, living. I think very young." He concluded, "The past is a good thing to reminisce about, but one shouldn't live in the past. I don't mind being alone. I have many interests, writing, studying. I'm a very curious person." The audience applauded his statements, and there little doubt that Dick had carefully prepared his remarks for a group of television viewers that would prove responsive to his upbeat message. Hugh Downs makes it clear that Dick Haymes is a survivor who has conquered his demons and is looking forward to a secure future.

Dick believed that these appearances would serve as public relations forums that would help him to reclaim his star status. Tee Dooley sent Hugh Downs the new album, and Downs's secretary replied, thanking him, yet informing him that Dick Haymes was not booked for another appearance on the program, "but we appreciate receiving the information you sent and will keep it for future reference." Dooley sent an album to critic Charles Champlin of the *Los Angeles Times* and tried to arrange a tour for Dick in Belgium and Holland. The response from the Belgium contact said, "A new record hit, and a good deal of help by the record company, might render his situation more commercial." Dave Dexter of *Billboard* appreciated receiving the new recording the following year, but wrote to Dooley that the DJs don't play Haymes "because he's a non-rocker." They don't play any of the former singing stars except Sinatra. The efforts by Dooley and Roger

Dooner to resuscitate Dick's career all failed, for no matter how much praise he received, the world of popular music had changed; and by the next decade, almost all of the radio stations that played the old standards would change their formats.

Dick, Harry James, and other alumni of the big band era would begin to tour in a new concert, "The Big Broadcast of 1944," devoted to the sounds of radio in the 1940s. Don Wilson, who had been Jack Benny's announcer, would reprise his role, Dick and Helen Forrest would sing; and in the three years that the show would tour, such stars as Dennis Day, Hildegarde, Gordon MacRae, and a new version of the old Ink Spots would join the show. The show received attention in the newspapers when it played at the Westbury Music Fair. Leo Seligson of *Newsday* remarked on the nostalgia quotient of the evening: "The years have added a look of distinction to a number of the entertainers. You could take Forrest for a senator from Montana. Dick Haymes, silver-gray now but boyish grin unimpaired, might be a visiting judge. The touch of incongruity adds spice as the performers sing with their still-young voices the songs of their youth."

Bob Sixsmith, who attended the closing performance, described the efforts of Anna Poole, who had spent a day preparing enormous Italian casseroles to feed the cast during intermission. Later, Sixsmith spoke privately to Helen Forrest and Dick, who spoke lovingly of his two children and confidently of his future plans.

For several months, Dick and Fran Jeffries were seeing each other again, and they talked of resuming their relationship, but they could not resolve their differences. Dick expected to continue the tour, and he was preparing for an interview on the *Dick Cavett Show*, but in October, after seeing a doctor about his health, he learned that he had lung cancer. He called his daughter Pidge and told her, "I have the big C," but she remembers that he sounded very positive. He would have to undergo chemotherapy treatments but expected to make a full recovery. He told the *Hollywood Reporter* that his malignant tumor on the left lung is "the type most receptive to treatment. . . . I've been through all the other tests and everything else is fine."

While he was undergoing treatment, a scandal magazine, the *Star*, printed a purported "confession," headlined, "My stormy marriage to Rita Hayworth was a tragic affair—confessed dying Dick Haymes." The article was simply a rehash of the old stories, but now that Dick was ill, the old stories began to reappear in the newspapers and magazines.

Sean was devastated by the news of his father's illness, on one occasion disappearing from his father's home for more than a day when Dick was in Cedars-Sinai Hospital, leading Wendy to notify the sheriff's office. When Sean first moved in with his father, Dick told Russ Jones that he was very concerned that he no longer had the vitality to do all the things with his son that he would like—"I feel so drained," he said. Russ promised that if anything ever happened to Dick, he would personally take Sean to the John Rossi Foundation.

One night, after having been diagnosed and starting treatment, Dick came into Russ's room and woke him up at 3 AM. It was highly unusual, and Dick apologized for waking up Russ, but asked if his friend would mind getting up and talking for a few minutes. Russ remembers, "We went into the living room, and he said, 'I'm not afraid anymore.'" He told Russ that he was unable to sleep, tossing and turning in bed, when suddenly he saw a woman dressed in white, and she came up next to him as he was lying in bed. He said that she gently took his hand and looked him straight in the eye and said, "It's OK; everything is going to be all right," and then disappeared. Russ thinks that he had some kind of spiritual encounter, for he was not prone to exaggeration; if anything, he underplayed everything. After that, Russ reports, he was at total peace with himself and completely lucid about events in the past and present.

Dick and his brother, Bob, had recently begun speaking after a hiatus of some years, and Marguerite phoned her son daily. Disc jockey William B. Williams of WNEW in New York City would telephone the hospital every day and report daily to his listeners on Dick's condition. Roger Dooner was genuinely touched when he received a telephone call from Dick, thanking him for all of the work he and others in the Dick Haymes Society had done for him over the years.

Russ went to the hospital every day along with Dick's daughter Nugent. Many of Dick's old friends and relatives phoned, wrote, and visited. His daughter Stephanie and his eldest son, Richard Jr., came to the hospital, as did Nora Eddington Haymes, who visited Dick accompanied by Al Lerner. Old friends Jack Carter, Virginia O'Brien, Helen O'Connell, and Ken Swoffard also visited. Pat Boone phoned and wrote and Dick was very touched by his attentions. Dick asked if Frank Sinatra had called—but Sinatra never phoned or sent a message. According to Dick's daughter, her father always believed that he and Sinatra were closer than they actually were. When Bob Hutton heard of his illness and telephoned from his home in the East, Dick cried throughout the call and told Bob that he did not want to die.

Yet during his illness and treatments, Dick was remarkably calm and appeared resigned to his death. He refused to continue his chemotherapy treatments because he knew that he would not have much longer to live, and he wanted to savor his last days. He felt he had little to live for, as his children were growing up, and Samantha had gone against him. One day, shortly before he died, Russ Jones helped Dick into a car to go to Pidge's home, where Nadine Marshall (Peter's ex-wife), Joanne Dru, and Nugent waited. Dick was very weak, and his body was cold. He wanted some scotch to warm him, and the alcohol affected him immediately. He and his family laughed as Russ carried him into the car, but he later called his daughter to apologize. He had not been drinking for some time before his illness and regretted having the drink that would be his last.

A few days later, Pidge went to visit her father in the hospital. After she returned home, Nugent phoned to tell her that her father was dying. An hour later, on March 28, 1980, he passed away, Nugent and Russ reporting that he died peacefully, finally released from the excruciating pain of his last days.

Richard Jr. went to the airport to meet Bob Haymes, whose plane arrived too late for him to see his brother before the end of his life. Pidge and Nugent planned the funeral, and Pidge requested that Wendy not attend. Samantha would not attend without her mother; when her father died she had clapped her hands: "The only thing I've ever regretted in my life," she says. "Now if I could take that back I would."

Turnley Walker, a writer and one of Dick's oldest friends from the 1940s, gave the eulogy at the funeral services attended by 150 people. Walker would later speak of his friend's gifts—he spoke French and Spanish fluently—his modesty, his loyalty to his friends, and at their last meeting, "weak as he was, he brought his hand to mine and gripped it with what must have been nearly the last of his strength. And the gentlemanly, sardonic, unsentimental warmth of affection were all there. Somehow intact. And the simple gallantry." As he requested, his ashes were scattered at sea by Nugent, Richard Jr., Sean, Stephanie, and Pidge.

Sean was perhaps the most affected by the death of his father. He had called Wendy when Dick went into the hospital and told her that he would return to her home, but Andy brought him back to Dick's place at the Marina. He stayed there alone, save for Russ Jones, who was at the hospital most of the time. Sean admits that he became unruly after his father died, and he was rebelling against his stepfather. Wendy decided to use a technique called "scared straight" to control Sean. She told him he would become a ward of the court and would go to a foster home for a year (she actually planned that he go for a week, but wanted to frighten him). He ran off the second day, and though alone, he felt that his father was looking after him. Russ took him to John Rossi's Youth Center, but Sean remembers that he had so much anger and was so hurt by his father's death that he contacted a friend with whom he had surfed and left with him for Miami Beach. In Miami he worked on a pool deck and then waited tables in the Florida Keys. Sean remembers that his father was "larger than life." He recalls their sailing together on Burl Ives's boat, their listening to classical music, and watching his father read. "I loved him," Sean says. He thinks that his mother saw only the dark side of his father, but he believes that she did love him. Sean would not return to California for four years, when he reconciled with his mother and Andy and moved into their home.

By September, Andy Maree had given Wendy a huge emerald engagement ring, and the couple announced their plans to wed. Wendy planned to write a book about Dick with Ray Strait, a biographer who had interviewed Dick some years earlier for a possible biography. She planned to call it "The Last Rogue." Wendy and Andy were happily married from December 1980 until her death in 2000 at the age of sixty-two.

Nugent was named executor of her father's will and learned quickly from Dick's attorney that there was no estate. Wendy, however, believed that there were hidden assets, so Nugent and Pidge agreed to let Wendy be the executor, and she would receive 50 percent of any assets and the remainder would be divided among the children. Wendy pursued past royalties and managed to find seventeen thousand dollars, which she split with all of Dick's children. During the years following his death, the children would receive small sums once or twice a year.

Tributes to Dick Haymes began almost immediately after his death. On the day that he died, Mel Tormé, appearing at Carnegie Hall, announced to the audience that the show that evening would consist only of ballads "because the world lost a great ballad singer today." In 1983, a special tribute to Dick was to be held in Hackensack, New Jersey. Among the "friends" scheduled to appear were Julius LaRosa, Helen Forrest, Fran Jeffries, Margaret Whiting, and special guest Vivian Blaine, along with Loonis McGlohan, the Song Spinners, and Dick's son "Skip" Haymes.

The Dick Haymes Society issued a memorial album, *The Last Goodbye*, and longtime admirer and critic Peter Reilly concluded his admiring review simply, "He'll be missed." In the years since his death, his memory has not faded among those who had appreciated his artistry, and new CDs with air checks of Dick's old radio shows receive praise from contemporary critics and listeners, both old and new. Aficionados of popular music and critics and viewers of films of the classic years still treasure Dick Haymes as one of the finest singers of his era and a memorable performer in some of the best musicals of the 1940s.

Epilogue

Dick Haymes was a complicated man; he could be both warm and affectionate and cool and self-absorbed. He could be a devoted friend and a loving father and husband. He could also be detached, distant, and unkind to his family when he was drinking. Yet each of his surviving wives, save Wendy, spoke of him fondly, and Joanne Dru would tell her daughter that she really regretted that she was quick to divorce her husband. She said that he could be abusive when drinking, and she was angered by the young women who pursued him. But he was, she said, truly a gentleman.

Dick Haymes, the star, would never again experience the adoration of the fans that had worshipped him during his golden years. He suffered from the malaise that often overtakes celebrities after the glow of youthful stardom has faded. As Leo Braudy, author of *The Frenzy of Renown*, an important examination of the phenomenon of fame, notes, "For performers so drawn to the terrifying edge of what it means to be visible, appreciation is vital, but none is ever enough. Any saving step between offstage and onstage has long since been obliterated, and their faces and their bodies [and their voices] are permanently in fief to their audiences."

Once one has reached the peak, nothing afterward can replace the moment when everything in life seems perfect, and there is no reason to think that it will not last forever. Perhaps he believed that because more than twenty years earlier he had been honored with two stars on the Hollywood Walk of Fame, his luster would never dim. Dick Haymes never really accepted the reality of time and age, and as he recognized, he remained in many ways the child who was always waiting to be rescued. Musician Bobby Scott, who accompanied him in his lowest period in the 1950s, wrote the finest, most acute and sensitive appreciation of Dick Haymes, his friend, a man who had struggled with personal demons and, in performing, had tried to bridge two dissimilar eras:

> Dick was victimized by too many forces, and by too many people for me to know where to put the blame for what happened to him. . . . His Hollywood years . . . were a time of power that he mishandled. I assume, as I fear I must, that he was his own worst enemy. Alas, self-destruction is compelling, even attractively intriguing, to all too many of us, and Dick had climbed to the pinnacle and then fell in phases. Miraculously, he would grab jutting crags with his fingertips, then fall again, only to take hold once more and steady himself at a still lower level, from which he could look up to where he had once been and feel the heart contract and burst. And he would have to try to remember at what level in his falling he had left what part of himself.
>
> He had his own sense of what was genteel behavior. And few people met his standard for it. The nemesis was crassness. His posture, then, was that of a qualified snob. I believe this snobbery to be part of some inner ideal of graceful living and a gentlemanly elegance of action. He therefore could be quite unforgiving of a *faux pas*. Someone with such criteria inevitably would have to hold many people in contempt. And he did. . . . That he had good reason to fear, I do not doubt. He had been promised the moon and now he was lucky to get bus fare. He could have handled it a lot better, but he didn't. This was the enigma of the man to me: this holding of failings to his breast simply because they were his failings. Somewhere in this there was more than a little of being *true to himself*. But at what cost?

Today, the artistry of Dick Haymes remains alive because of the heroic efforts of fans, both old and young. For a brief time, there seemed a chance that Dick Haymes would be introduced to a contemporary audience. After a TV miniseries on Frank Sinatra achieved high ratings in 1992, Robert Osborne in the *Hollywood Reporter* announced that there would be a miniseries on Dick Haymes: "If you don't know your show biz lore, Haymes was one of the really great band singers of the 1940s, *the* supreme singer as far as a lot of people were concerned; during that same decade he also had a brief run as an above-the-title movie star at 20th Century Fox." Osborne goes on to cite as the most interesting aspect of Haymes's life his many marriages, particularly the notorious years with Rita Hayworth. The producer was to be Gene Corman, and starring as Dick Haymes would be a young singer, George Bugatti. Nothing came of the venture.

Critic Will Friedwald, in a new discussion of the singing career of Dick Haymes, concludes, "His is one of the richest legacies in all of pop singing." Just how rich that legacy remains was illustrated in 2004, when Harry Connick Jr. appeared on the February 25 Craig Kilborn television show and the host related conversations he had had with his father about the best singers of his father's era. Kilborn's father selected Frank Sinatra, Nat King Cole, and Vic Damone. Connick replied immediately that he would have to add Dick Haymes to that list. Kilborn didn't seem to know who Haymes was, so Connick briefly informed him.

Dick Haymes remains a legend among connoisseurs of music, but like Bing Crosby and other singers of his generation (with the exception of Tony Bennett, who still performs with the newest stars of the contemporary era), there is little interest in the swing era. When Dick Haymes's name is mentioned, anyone who remembers him will invariably refer to his alcoholism and his cruelty to Rita Hayworth. I have tried to tell the whole story of Dick Haymes's life and career so that at last—more than twenty-five years after his death—he may receive the respect and admiration reserved for the finest artists of the twentieth century.

FILMOGRAPHY

Won Ton Ton, the Dog Who Saved Hollywood, 1976: Dir. Michael Winner; Prod. David V. Picker, Arnold Schulman, and Michael Winner; Paramount.

Cruisin' Down the River, 1953: Dir. Richard Quine; Prod. Jonie Taps; Columbia.

All Ashore, 1953: Dir. Richard Quine; Prod. Jonie Taps; Columbia.

St. Benny the Dip, 1951: Dir. Edgar G. Ulmer; Prod. Edward J. and Harry Lee Danziger; Danziger Brothers Production.

One Touch of Venus, 1948: Dir. William A. Seiter; Prod. Lester Cowan and William Seiter; Universal.

Up in Central Park, 1948: Dir. William A. Seiter; Prod. Karl Tunberg; Universal.

Carnival in Costa Rice, 1947: Dir. Gregory Ratoff; Prod. William A. Bacher; Twentieth Century–Fox.

The Shocking Miss Pilgrim, 1947: Dir. George Seaton; Prod. William Perlberg; Twentieth Century–Fox.

Do You Love Me? 1946: Dir. Gregory Ratoff; Prod. George Jessel; Exec. Prod.

Darryl F. Zanuck; Twentieth Century–Fox.

State Fair, 1945: Dir. Walter Lang; Prod. William Perlberg; Twentieth Century–Fox.

Billy Rose's Diamond Horseshoe, 1945: Dir. George Seaton; Prod. William Perlberg; Twentieth Century–Fox.

Irish Eyes Are Smiling, 1944: Dir. Gregory Ratoff; Prod. Damon Runyon; Twentieth Century–Fox.

Four Jills in a Jeep, 1944: Dir. William A. Seiter; Prod. Irving Starr; Twentieth Century–Fox.

DuBarry Was a Lady, 1943: Dir. Roy Del Ruth; Prod. Arthur Freed; Metro-Goldwyn-Mayer (uncredited backup singer, Tommy Dorsey Orchestra).

Dramatic School, 1938: Dir. Robert B. Sinclair; Prod. Mervyn LeRoy; Metro-Goldwyn-Mayer (uncredited).

Mutiny on the Bounty, 1935: Dir. Frank Lloyd; Prod. Albert Lewin and Irving Thalberg (uncredited); Metro-Goldwyn-Mayer (uncredited stunt man).

MAJOR TELEVISION APPEARANCES

Over Easy, with Hugh Downs; July, August 1979, PBS.
The Eddie Capra Mysteries, "Murder on the Flip Side," October 1978, NBC.
"Big Band Bash," with Helen Forrest; February 1978, PBS.
The Merv Griffin Show, "Salute to Harry James," with Helen Forrest; November 1977, syndicated.
Starsky and Hutch, "Long Walk Down a Short Dirt Road"; March 1977, CBS.
Marcus Welby, M.D.; 1977, ABC.
McMillan, "All Bets Off," with Rock Hudson; December 1976, NBC.
McCloud, "Sharks," with Dennis Weaver; February 1975, NBC.
Betrayal, with Amanda Blake; TV movie, December 1974, ABC.
Adam 12, "The Clinic on 18th Street," with Frank Sinatra Jr.; March 1974, NBC.
Hec Ramsey, "Scar Tissue," with Richard Boone; March 1974, NBC.
McMillan and Wife, "Free Fall to Terror," with Rock Hudson; NBC.
Tennessee Ernie Ford's "The Fabulous Fordies," with Maureen O'Hara, Betty Grable, and Frank Gorshin; February 1972, NBC.
The David Frost Show; October 1971, syndicated.
Alias Smith and Jones, "Smiler with a Gun"; October 1971, NBC.
The Tonight Show, with Johnny Carson; September 1971, NBC.
The Saint, "The Contract," with Roger Moore; May 1965, NBC, filmed in England.
The Ed Sullivan Show; March 1962, CBS.
Playboy Penthouse, with Fran Jeffries; 1961, syndicated.
The Tonight Show, with Jack Paar and Fran Jeffries; September 1960, NBC.
Playboy Penthouse, with Fran Jeffries; 1958, syndicated.
The Jackie Gleason Show, "America's Music Makers"; 1957, CBS.
The Walter Winchell Show; November 1956, NBC.
NBC Bandstand, featured as "Mr. Music" with Johnny Guarnieri Trio; September 24–28, October 1–5, and November 5–9, 1956.
Producer's Showcase, "The Lord Don't Play Favorites"; September 1956, NBC.
Stage Show, with Tommy and Jimmy Dorsey. February, May, July, August 1956, CBS.
The Ernie Kovacs Show; July 1956, NBC.

245

Screen Directors Playhouse, "Cry Justice"; February 1956, NBC.
Suspense, "Laugh It Off"; December 1953, CBS.
Lux Video Theater, "Song for a Banjo"; December 1952, CBS.
Ford Theater, "National Honeymoon"; October 1952, NBC.
Texaco Star Theater, with Milton Berle; May 1949 and November 1951, NBC.

Dick Haymes made nine appearances on television in England between 1963 and 1971. In total, he made ninety-eight appearances on television, beginning in 1943, when he performed on one of the early television broadcasts for the Dumont Network on station WABD in New York City.

SELECT DISCOGRAPHY

This list includes recordings that made the top thirty *Billboard* listings and other notable recordings.

Recordings with the Harry James Orchestra

"Lament to Love," August 1941, #10
"A Sinner Kissed an Angel," 1941, #19
"The Devil Sat Down and Cried," 1941, #23
"I'll Get By," 1944, #1 (recorded in 1941)

Recordings with the Benny Goodman Orchestra

"Idaho," 1942, #4
"Serenade in Blue," 1942, # 17

Independent Vocalist Recordings

"It Can't Be Wrong," 1943, #2, with the Song Spinners
"In My Arms,"1943, #7, with the Song Spinners
"You'll Never Know," 1943, #1, with the Song Spinners
"Wait for Me Mary," 1943, #17, with the Song Spinners
"I Never Mention Your Name," 1943, #14, with the Song Spinners
"I Heard You Cried Last Night," 1943, #19, with the Song Spinners
"Put Your Arms around Me, Honey," 1943, #5, with the Song Spinners

"For the First Time," 1943, #17, with the Song Spinners

"Long Ago and Far Away," 1944, #2, with Helen Forrest and the Camarata Orchestra

"How Blue the Night," 1944, #11, with the Emil Newman Orchestra

"How Many Times Do I Have to Tell You," 1944, #22, with the Emil Newman Orchestra

"Together," 1944, #3, with Helen Forrest and the Victor Young Orchestra

"It Had to Be You," 1944, #4, with Helen Forrest and the Victor Young Orchestra

"Janie," 1944, #22, with the Victor Young Orchestra

"Laura," 1945, #9, with the Victor Young Orchestra

"I Wish I Knew," 1945, #6, with the Victor Young Orchestra

"The More I See You," 1945, #7, with the Victor Young Orchestra

"I'll Buy That Dream," 1945, #2, with Helen Forrest and the Victor Young Orchestra

"Some Sunday Morning," 1945, #9, with Helen Forrest and the Victor Young Orchestra

"Till the End of Time," 1945, #3, with the Victor Young Orchestra

"Love Letters," 1945, #11, with the Victor Young Orchestra

"It Might as Well Be Spring," 1945, #5, with the Victor Young Orchestra

"That's for Me," 1945, #6, with the Victor Young Orchestra

"I'm Always Chasing Rainbows," 1946, #7, with Helen Forrest and the Earle Hagen Orchestra

"Slowly," 1946, #12, with the Victor Young Orchestra

"Oh! What It Seemed to Be," 1946, #4, with the Earle Hagen Orchestra

"In Love in Vain," 1946, #12, with Helen Forrest and the Earle Hagen Orchestra

"How Are Things in Glocca Morra," 1947, #9, with the Gordon Jenkins Orchestra

"Mamselle," 1947, #3, with the Gordon Jenkins Orchestra

"I Wish I Didn't Love You So," 1947, #9, with mixed quartet and rhythm accompaniment

"—And Mimi," 1947, #15, with the Gordon Jenkins Orchestra

"Little White Lies," 1948, #2, with the Gordon Jenkins Orchestra

"You Can't Be True, Dear," 1948, #9, with the Song Spinners

"Nature Boy," 1948, #11, with the Song Spinners

"It's Magic," 1948, #9, with the Gordon Jenkins Orchestra

"Every Day I Love You," 1948, #24, with the Vic Schoen Orchestra

"Bouquet of Roses," 1949, #22, with the Troubadours

"Room Full of Roses," 1949, #6, with rhythm accompaniment

"Maybe It's Because," 1949, #5, with the Gordon Jenkins Orchestra

"The Old Master Painter," 1949, #4, with Four Hits and a Miss

"Roses," 1950, # 28, with Four Hits and a Miss

"Count Every Star," 1950, #10, with Artie Shaw and his band

"Can Anyone Explain?" 1950, #23, with Four Hits and a Miss

"You're Just in Love," 1951, #30, with Ethel Merman and Gordon Jenkins' Orchestra

"And So to Sleep Again," 1951, #28, with Four Hits and a Miss

Other Notable Recordings

"How High the Moon," 1940, with the Harry James Orchestra
"Fools Rush In," 1940, with the Harry James Orchestra
"The Nearness of You," 1940, with the Harry James Orchestra
"Maybe," 1940, with the Harry James Orchestra
"Montivideo," 1941, with the Harry James Orchestra
"I Guess I'll Have to Dream the Rest," 1941, with the Harry James Orchestra
"Yes Indeed!" 1941, with Harry James Band, no strings
"You Don't Know What Love Is,"1941, with the Harry James Orchestra
"By the Old Corral," 1944, with the Ken Darby Singers and the Victor Young Orchestra
"If You Were the Only Girl in the World," 1944, with chorus and Camarata and his orchestra
"Where or When," 1945, with the Victor Young Orchestra
"How Deep Is the Ocean?" 1945, with the Lyn Murray Orchestra
"Come Rain or Come Shine," 1946, with the Victor Young Orchestra
"Aren't You Kind of Glad We Did?" 1946, with Judy Garland and the Gordon Jenkins Orchestra
"Stella by Starlight," 1946, with the Gordon Jenkins Orchestra
"Anything You Can Do," 1947, with Bing Crosby, the Andrews Sisters, and the Vic Schoen Orchestra

Dick Haymes with Ian Bernard and His Orchestra: Selected Recordings for Capitol Records, 1955–1956

"It Might as Well Be Spring"
"The More I See You"
"The Very Thought of You"
"You'll Never Know"
"If There Is Someone Lovelier Than You"
"How Deep Is the Ocean"
"The Nearness of You"
"Where or When"
"Little White Lies"
"Our Love Is Here to Stay"
"Love Walked In"
"Come Rain or Come Shine"
"If I Should Lose You"
"You Don't Know What Love Is"

"Imagination"
"Skylark"
"Isn't This a Lovely Day"
"What's New?"
"The Way You Look Tonight"
"Then I'll Be Tired of You"
"I Like the Likes of You"
"Moonlight Becomes You"
"Between the Devil and the Deep Blue Sea"
"When I Fall in Love"

Dick Haymes with Loonis McGlohan and His Group: Selections from the 1976 Recordings

"The Sounds around the House"
"Stella by Starlight"
"The Very Thought of You"
"Love Walked In"
"Someone to Watch over Me"
"Who Cares?"
"How Long Has This Been Going On?"
"I'll Get By"
"It Had to Be You"
"A Foggy Day"
"For You, For Me, For Evermore"

Selections from the 1978 Recording with Loonis McGlohan

"That's All"
"As Time Goes By"
"I'll Remember April"
"Emily"
"Last Night When We Were Young"
"I Love You, Samantha"
"Here's That Rainy Day"
"The Way We Were"
"There Will Never Be Another You"
"But Beautiful"

SOURCE NOTES

Epigraphs

Philip Roth, *The Human Stain* (New York: Random House [Vintage], 2001), 15.
Tony Bennett, in *Off the Record*, reprinted in *Perfectly Frank*, no. 303, April–May 2004.

Introduction

Many of the references throughout the book are from the *Dick Haymes Newsletter*, published by the Dick Haymes Society. The first fan club, dating from the 1940s, published the *Haymes Herald*, a small and enthusiastic fan magazine. But the *Dick Haymes Newsletter*, hereafter cited as *DHN*, which began publication in 1973 when the Dick Haymes Society was formed, reprints magazine and newspaper articles about Haymes, offers letters from individuals who knew him, and indicates sources for anyone interested in further research. Several of the articles that I will cite throughout this book were printed in the *Newsletter*. I shall indicate the original source, but if that is unavailable, I shall note the volume number of the *Dick Haymes Newsletter* where the original article was reprinted in that magazine. The many interviews I conducted throughout the past few years were essential to my research. The late Walter Boettger was conducting research for a biography of Haymes but died before completing it. His notebooks have been an invaluable resource for my work.

3	The scandal sheet *Star*: February 1980.
3	Even the obituaries were inaccurate: *New York Times*, March 30, 1980; *Billboard*, April 12, 1980; *Washington Post*, March 30, 1980; *Charlotte Observer*, April 1, 1980; *Time*, April 7, 1980; *Newsweek*, April 7, 1980.
3	Most painful in all the obituaries: interviews with Russ Jones and Joanna Haymes Campbell.
4	Critic Peter Reilly: *Stereo Review*, November 1978.

251

4	another critic, Brian Case: *Melody Maker*, March 1979.
4	Roy Carr, in a review: *Record Hunter*, 1980.
4	Doug Ramsey, another music reviewer: *Radio Free Jazz*, October 1979.
4	Peter Reilly again offered: *Stereo Review*, May 1979.
5	*Motion Picture*'s poll: *Motion Picture*, December 1946.
5–6	He was repeatedly asked: Ian Bernard, e-mail interview, August 9, 2003.
6	Sinatra never spoke: Sinatra radio interview from 1940s.
6	Margo Jefferson best described: "Sinatra, Not a Myth but a Man, and One among Many," Margo Jefferson, *New York Times*, June 1, 1998.
8	As Dave Gelly did: *London Observer*, April 6, 1980.
8	"They [his recordings] suggest a deep wistfulness": letter to author from Milton R. Stern, August 1, 2003.
8	Haymes's friend Turnley Walker: letter to Walter Boettger, *DHN (Dick Haymes Newsletter)* #40, 1997.
9	It has been difficult: Peter Elliott, e-mail interview with author, July 2003; author interview with Wendy Haymes Maree, August 1999; Dick Haymes, unpublished outline for autobiography.

Chapter One

For the background on the history of Argentina, I have relied upon two sources: James R. Scobie, *Buenos Aires: Plaza to Suburb, 1870–1910* (New York: Oxford, 1974); and David Rock, *Argentina, 1516-1987* (Berkeley: University of California Press, 1987). For the history of the Haymes family in Argentina, I am indebted to Bernardo Milhaus, who, via e-mail, has supplied me with important information about the Haymes family heritage. Walter Boettger's notebooks are filled with information that he culled from newspapers (brief articles from *Variety*) and family records in Argentina. The major source for the childhood of Dick and Bob Haymes is the unpublished biography of Dick Haymes by his brother, titled "Dick Haymes: Verse and Chorus." A member of the Dick Haymes Society provided me with this biography, consisting of one chapter. Every reasonable effort has been made to trace the owners of copyright materials in this book, but it has proven impossible. The author and publisher will be glad to receive information leading to more complete acknowledgment in subsequent printings of the book and in the meantime extend their apologies for any omissions. For the material on Bunny Berigan, I have relied on Robert Dupuis's biography.

10	"By the end of the first decade": Scobie, *Buenos Aires*, 11.
10	It was here that Richard Benjamin Haymes was born: Birth certificate #853, Argentine Republic, reprinted in *DHN* #41, 1997.

11   Duncan Stewart arrived: *La Nacion*, October 18, 1936, translated by
      Bernardo Milhaus, February 2000. Additional information supplied by
      Bernardo Milhaus, e-mail to author, February 16, 2000.

12   they were married: Marriage license #1127167, Argentine Republic,
      reprinted in *DHN* #41, 1997.

12   "My mother has that unique ability": incomplete autobiography by
      Dick Haymes, "I'll Get By."

13   "The boom ended abruptly": Rock, *Argentina*, 204.

13   In the early 1990s: Walter Boettger, "Searching for Dick Haymes, Part
      Two," *DHN* #41, 1997.

13   "He was a strange one": from W. Boettger's undated notes.

26   Almost fifty years later: Gene Lees, *Singers and the Song* (New York:
      Oxford, 1987), 133.

29   He had also worked briefly: *Silver Screen*, June 1944.

30   Their mother neither denied nor affirmed: Donald Spoto, *Dynasty: The
      Turbulent Saga of the Royal Family from Victoria to Diana* (New York; Simon
      and Schuster, 1995), 143–144.

31   But his management was careless: Robert Dupuis, *Bunny Berigan:
      Elusive Legend of Jazz* (Baton Rouge: Louisiana State University Press,
      1993), 261.

Chapter Two

For the history of the big band era and popular music of the 1940s, I have relied upon
Albert McCarthy, *Big Band Jazz* (New York: Putnam, 1974); George T. Simon, *Inside the
Big Bands* (New York: MacMillan, 1967) and *Sights and Sounds of the Swing Era* (New York:
Galahad Books, 1971); Donald Clarke, *The Rise and Fall of Popular Music* (New York:
Viking, 1995); Henry Pleasants, *The Great American Popular Singers* (New York: Simon &
Schuster, 1974); Will Friedwald, *Jazz Singing* (New York: Scribners, 1990); Barry Ulanov,
A History of Jazz in America (New York: Viking, 1957); Peter Levinson (*Trumpet Blues: The
Life of Harry James* (New York: Oxford, 1999); Helen Forrest with Bill Libby, *I Had the
Craziest Dream* (New York: Coward McCann & Geoghegan, 1982); and Candy Justice,
"The Big Bands," *Stereo Review*, March 1991. For the rankings of recordings by Dick
Haymes and other singers, Joel Whitburn's *Billboard Pop Hits: Singles and Albums,
1940–1954* (Menomonee Falls, WI: Record Research, 2002) is the primary source. For
background on the radio industry, see Gerald Nachman, *Raised on Radio* (New York:
Pantheon, 1998). Radio interviews were conducted on the Russell Davies Show, BBC,
October 2003, with segments from a Haymes interview in the late 1950s; the Brad
Phillips Show, "Battle Royal," New York; Dave Gelly's reappraisal of Haymes, BBC 2

Radio, March 22, 1988; Chris Ellis's show (rebroadcast), September 15, 1990; Alan Dell, BBC 2, "The Big Band Sound," a tribute to Dick Haymes on the occasion of his death, April 1980, with re-broadcast of March 17, 1969, interview.

34 "What was important was": Pleasants, *Great American Popular Singers*, 25.
34 "To him it was, or became, an instrument": E. J. Kahn, "Profile of Frank Sinatra," *New Yorker*, 1946, quoted in Pleasants, *Great American Popular Singers*, 187–188.
34 Gelly commented that Haymes's: BBC Radio 2, March 22, 1988.
34 "both swell fellows": New York *Daily News*, May 23, 1943.
36 "Crosby managed to sing": Nachman, *Raised on Radio*, 165.
38 Pianist Al Lerner, however: author interview with Al Lerner, August 21, 1999.
39 Reporter George Simon: Simon, *Inside the Big Bands*, 267.
40 Part of his problem, as Marshall notes: author interview with Peter Marshall, August 19, 1999.
40 In his reminiscence: Simon, *Inside the Big Band*, 267.
40 according to Dick's son: author interview with Richard Haymes Jr., September 27, 1999.
41 "I bowed so deeply": press release from Twentieth Century–Fox Studio, University of Southern California Archives, 1945.
42 "When I first joined Harry": interview in Fred Hall, *Dialogues in Swing* (Ventura, CA: Pathfinder Publishing, 1989), 24–25.
42 "It was a team effort": Hall, *Dialogues in Swing*, 25.
43 Lerner remembers one occasion: author interview, August 21, 1999.
43 Singer Helen Forrest recalled: Forrest, *I Had the Craziest Dream*, 119.
44 Dick met many women: Dick Haymes outline for autobiography, "I'll Get By," 1978.
44 Edythe did not pine: *Downbeat*, October 1, 1941.
44 "I can only tell you": Haymes, "I'll Get By."
45 Harry James, serving as best man: Suzanne Warner, "All about Haymes-James, Inc.," *Silver Screen*, November 1945.
45 She never forgot his generosity: Forrest, *I Had the Craziest Dream*, 112.
45 He "could outsing": quoted by Levinson, *Trumpet Blues*, 101.
46 Dick remembered that his biggest hit: Hall, *Dialogues in Swing*, 23.
47 "I, to this date, hate recording": Hall, *Dialogues in Swing*, 24.
48 "I think the draft board": Haymes, "I'll Get By."
48 "It was like being in captivity": Haymes, "I'll Get By."
48 As recently as September 2000: Tom Kuntz, "New York Mayor Wants It His Way, But Some Decry Sinatra Statue," *New York Times*, September 1, 2000.

50   "He didn't fire anybody": Forrest, *I Had the Craziest Dream*, 97.

50   Remarkably, Dick Haymes and Benny Goodman: Hall, *Dialogues in Swing*, 22.

51   and when he was introduced to audiences: original broadcast replayed on Jack Cullen radio interview with Haymes, Las Vegas, 1974; rebroadcast in 1980.

52   A special show, "Uncle Sam's Christmas Tree": script issued by D'Arcy Advertising Co., December 25, 1942.

53   He remembered, "We were working so hard": radio interview, "Be My Guest," with Alan Dell, BBC 2, March 17, 1969.

54   Years later, Dick told a friend: e-mail, Russ Jones to author, November 19, 2003.

56   Dick's two-week booking: review in *Variety*, May 26, 1943.

57   columnist Earl Wilson saluted: reported in *Motion Picture*, November 1944.

57   Word had spread of the plans: *Variety*, June 2, 1943.

58   "It did exactly the opposite": Hall, *Dialogues in Swing*, 28.

59   "For one thing, he exploited": Ulanov, *A History of Jazz in America*, 261.

59   Will Friedwald, reviewing: Friedwald, *Jazz Singing*, 194.

Chapter Three

For much of the material on Dick Haymes's life in the 1940s, I have relied upon material stored in the University of Southern California's Special Collections archives of Twentieth Century–Fox Studios. Biographies of stars were routinely issued and picked up by fan magazines that reprinted the studio's press releases almost verbatim. Fox issued biographies as press releases for Dick Haymes in 1943, 1944, and 1945. The fan magazines I have used in this chapter are *Photoplay*, February 1945 and June 1947; *Band Leaders*, September 1945; *Screen Album*, fall 1947; *Silver Screen*, June 1944; *Movieland*, June 1944; *Modern Screen*, September 1945; *Motion Picture*, November 1945; and *Calling All Girls*, April 1946. Newspapers articles concerning Dick Haymes's career appeared in the *Kansas City Star*, January 9, 1944; the *Knoxville Journal*, April 9, 1944; the *Milwaukee Journal*, January 2, 1944, and February 3, 1946; and the *Los Angeles Times*, April 25, 1945. Other newspapers are cited in the text and below. The radio interviews by Jack Cullen in 1974 and Alan Dell in 1969 provided many of Dick Haymes's comments about his career.

For material concerning Twentieth Century–Fox Studios, I have relied upon Aubrey Solomon, *Twentieth Century–Fox: A Corporate and Financial History* (Metuchen, NJ, and London, 1988); and Joel W. Finler, *The Hollywood Story* (New York: Crown, 1988). In addition to the *Dick Haymes Newsletter*, I have found the original fan newsletter, the *Haymes Herald* (1944–47) particularly helpful for background material on the mid-1940s.

61   "That first wild wind of success": F. Scott Fitzgerald, "Early Success," in *The Crack-Up*, ed. Edmund Wilson (New York: New Directions, 1945), 86.

61   He remembered years later: Hall, *Dialogues in Swing*, 27.

63   "There's a rush act": *Photoplay*, June 1947.

63   Joanne would remember: *Band Leader*, September 1945.

63   Richard Haymes Jr. remembers: author interview, September 27, 1999.

64   In the sheet music magazines: *Song Hits* (New York: Song Lyrics Inc.), December 1944; *Swing with Dick Haymes* (New York: Famous Music Corp.), 1943.

64   A fan magazine article: *Silver Screen*, June 1944.

64   Richard Haymes Jr. recalls: author interview, September 27, 1999.

64   Peter Marshall, Dick's brother-in-law: author interview, August 19, 1999.

65   Before he started work on his first film: radio transcriptions of *Here's to Romance*, July 1943–April 1944.

66   His next radio show: *DHM (Dick Haymes Newsletter)*, #36.

67   A music historian: Philip K. Eberly, *Music in the Air* (New York: Hastings House, 1982), 162.

67   Helen Forrest said: Forrest, *I Had the Craziest Dream*, 159–160.

67   Commenting on the popularity of the show: *Milwaukee Journal*, January 2, 1944.

67   "Just don't do it, Helen": Forrest, *I Had the Craziest Dream*, 171.

68   Gordon Jenkins remembered: Stan Britt's interview with Gordon Jenkins, *DHN*, #36.

68   Years later he would remember: Hall, *Dialogues in Swing*, 28.

69   Faye had been with the studio: Jane Lenz Elder, *Alice Faye: A Life beyond the Silver Screen* (Jackson: University Press of Mississippi, 2002), 163–165.

71   The studio did not foresee: *DHN*, #18.

72   The *New York Herald Tribune*: *Herald-Tribune, New York Times*, March 18, 1944.

79   The *Los Angeles Times*: April 29, 1945.

79–80   Reporter Diana Gibbings: "Regarding Mr. Haymes," *New York Times*, August 12, 1945.

80   At the end of a Chicago performance: *Chicago Sun-Times*, August 26, 1945.

81   "It's the way he looks at you": *Chicago Sunday Times*, August 26, 1945.

81   "For the past few weeks": letter to Virginia Haywood, January 1946.

81   A popular teenage fan magazine: *Calling All Girls*, April 1946.

81   *Variety* reported: quoted in *Haymes Herald*, October 1946.

82   He was quoted: *Los Angeles Daily News*, March 18, 1945.

82   "Marriage Is Worth Saving": *Motion Picture*, November 1945.

83   As Helen Forrest wrote: Forrest, *I Had the Craziest Dream*, 159–160.

83   A fan magazine story: *Modern Screen*, September 1945.

84   Forrest remembers: *I Had the Craziest Dream*, 159.

84   "average American": *Motion Picture*, November 1945.

86   Louanne Hogan remembers: from interview with Laura Wagner; e-mail to author, April 11, 2005.

87   In the same year, Alice Faye: Elder, *Alice Faye*, 175–192.

87   For Margaret, it was an important engagement: author interview with Margaret Whiting, January 18, 1999.

88   Dick wrote to his fans: letter to Virginia Haywood and Associates, July 1946.

88   Buddy Bregman, the record producer: author interview, July 16, 2001.

88   Peter, noting the expense: author interview with Peter Marshall, August 19, 1999,

89   Dick's son suspects: author interview, September 27, 1999.

89   His daughter Pidge: author interview with Joanna Haymes Campbell, August 18, 1999.

90   she would not go into details: telephone interview with Maureen O'Hara, December 13, 2002.

93   In 1945 she published a book: Marguerite Haymes, *The Haymes Way* (New York: Ergon Publishing Co., 1945).

93   Both sons felt: author interview with Wendy Haymes Maree, August 20, 1999, and conversations between Dick Haymes and Tee Dooley in 1978; author interview with Tee Dooley, January 7, 2000.

93–94   He reportedly studied: *Motion Picture*, December 1946.

94   "While we haven't crashed": *Photoplay*, June 1947.

94   But early success: F. Scott Fitzgerald, *Early Success* (New York: New Directions, 1937).

Chapter Four

For the history of Twentieth Century–Fox, I have relied upon Aubrey Solomon, *Twentieth Century–Fox*; and Joel Finler, *The Hollywood Story* (see references, chapter 3). For material on Nora Eddington Flynn Haymes, see her book, *Errol and Me* (New York: New American Library, 1960); Michael Freedland's *The Two Lives of Errol Flynn* (New York: William Morrow, 1979) and her interview with Walter Boettger, April 1996. The program for the presidential inaugural was issued on January 19, 1949. For the Academy Awards, see Mason Wiley and Damien Bona, *Inside Oscar* (New York: Ballantine, 1986). For Dick Haymes's recordings, I have used Charles Garrod and Denis Brown, *Dick Haymes: A*

Discography (Zephyrhills, FL: Joyce Record Club, 1990). For the Universal films, I used the Universal Archives at the University of Southern California Library. I have used the following fan magazines: *Silver Screen*, August 1946; *Movie Life Year Book*, 1947; *Movies*, "Haymes and Company," November 1947; *Sweet Sixteen*, "Young Man with a Voice," June 1947; *Radio and Television Mirror*, "He's My Boss, by Bob McCord," June 1948; *Movie Show*, "The Haymes Record," September 1948; *Motion Picture*, "Dream House for Sale," May 1948; *Radio Best*, "Who Put the Hex on Haymes?" June 1949; *Radio and Television Mirror*, "Now I Can Sing Again," by Dick Haymes, January 1950. For background material on director Edgar G. Ulmer, I have relied upon Andrew Britton, editor, *The Book of Film Noir* (New York: Continuum, 1983); John Belton, *Cinema Stylists* (Metuchen, NJ: Scarecrow Press, 1983); Todd McCarthy and Charles Flynn, editors, *Kings of the Bs* (New York: Dutton, 1975).

95	Forrest reports: Forrest, *I Had the Craziest Dream*, 150.
96	"I used to say": Forrest, *I Had the Craziest Dream*, 152–153.
96	the son of the owners: *Atlantic City*, "And the Bands Played On," May 1991.
98	A recent critic: Edward Joblonski, *Gershwin* (New York: Da Capo, 1998; originally published by Doubleday, 1988), 349.
100	Clearly this film: Edward Schallert, *Los Angeles Times*, March 27, 1947.
100	Because their measurements: *Movies*, November 1947.
101	Dick Haymes's public image: Twentieth Century–Fox press release, 1947.
101	Newspapers reported: *Los Angeles Times*, April 10, 1948.
101	A notice that he lost: *Los Angeles Times, Los Angeles Examiner*, April 26, 1948.
101	as was the settlement: *Los Angeles Examiner*, November 26, 1948.
102	"Haymes & Company": *Movies*, November 1947, and "He's My Boss," *Radio & Television Mirror*, June 1948.
102	*Variety* reported: *Variety*, October 3 and 19, 1948.
102	Haymes never loved the song: Hall, *Dialogues in Swing*, 33; Haymes, "I'll Get By."
102	Publicists, playing on the: press release, Universal Studios Archives, USC, April 1948.
103	The Sigmund Romberg: *DHN*, #42.
108	The story, as reported by: Louella O. Parsons, "Six Months to Year Parting Agreed On," *Los Angeles Examiner*, December 30, 1948.
108	Just a few months earlier: *Motion Picture*, "Don't Marry a Crooner," by Joanne Dru, July 1948.
109	The public statements: *Motion Picture*, May 1948.
109	It was just a series: Haymes, "I'll Get By."
109	Nora described Dick as: Nora Eddington Haymes, interview with Walter Boettger, *DHN*, #38, 1996.
110	Years later, Dick admitted: Haymes, "I'll Get By."

110   Nora would remember: Nora Eddington Flynn, interview with Walter
         Boettger, *DHN*, #38.

110–11   Years later, Dick Haymes: Haymes, "I'll Get By."

111   "My career had peaked": Haymes, "I'll Get By."

112   "Who Put the Hex on Haymes?": *Radio Best*, June 1940.

114   "Now I Can Sing Again": *Radio and Television Mirror*, January 1950.

115   He remembers his mother: author interview with Richard Haymes Jr.,
         July 11, 2000.

116   His sister believes: author interview, Joanna Haymes Campbell, August
         18, 1999.

116   His younger sister: author interview with Joanna Haymes Campbell,
         August 18, 1999.

117   *Variety* raved: *Variety*, October 4, 1949.

117   In an interview with radio host: *DHN*, #22.

117   In 1947 they had recorded: John Sforza, *Swing Out: The Andrews Sisters
         Story* (Lexington: University of Kentucky Press, 2000), 112–114.

120   In July 1951, he decided: *Variety*, July 5, 1951.

120   "little is required": *Variety*, July 5, 1951.

121   He read the script: Dick Haymes, notes for autobiography, courtesy of
         Wendy Haymes Maree, author interview.

121   "It's a far cry": Haymes, "I'll Get By."

124   He remembered that move as: Haymes, "I'll Get By."

125   "I am just about broke": Dick Haymes, notes for autobiography.

Chapter Five

I conducted much of the research for this chapter at the Academy of Motion Picture Arts and Sciences in Los Angeles, California. Their extensive microfiche files include newspapers that I have used for this chapter: from the *Los Angeles Times*, August 7, 1953; November 27, 1953; February 10, 1954; May 26, 1954; June 24, 1954; July 1, 1954; August 30, 1955; December 1,1955; from the *Los Angeles Daily News*, August 8, 1953; August 9, 1953; September 28, 1953; October 16, 1953 ("Dick Haymes actions will cost him fans," by Paul Price); March 24, 1954; May 26, 1954; June 24, 1954; July 1, 1954; from the *Los Angeles Herald and Express*, August 6, 1953; from the *Los Angeles Mirror*, August 19, 1953; August 25, 1953; September 24; from the *Hollywood Citizen-News*, October 6, 1953; February 22, 1954; March 24, 1954; May 12, 1954; June 24, 1954; June 28, 1954; November 5, 1954; from the *Los Angeles Examiner*, August 27, 1953; September 25, 1953; October 4, 1953; March 24, 1954; May 26, 1954; June 20, 1954 (Louella Parsons); June 24, 1954; April 12, 1955; June 1, 1955; December 30, 1955; from the *New York Sunday*

News, August 9, 1953 ("Just When Haymes Discovered Rita"); from the *New York Daily News*, November 4, 1953; from the *New York Post*, April 5, 1954 (Leonard Lyons); from *Variety*, August 25, 1953; November 4, 1953; May 26, 1954; August 24, 1955.

Fan magazines include *Quick*, November 25, 1953, "Rita's a Slave to Love, but Love Can Be So Fickle"; *Modern Screen*, October 1953, "Out of the Frying Pan," June 1955, "Rita and Dick: Things Are Looking Up," and October 1953, "My Side of the Story," by Dick Haymes; *People Today*, November 4, 1953, "First Photos of Dick and Rita at Home"; *Saga*, July 1954; *Motion Picture*, September 1954, Earl Wilson, "This We Swear"; *Movie Time*, February 1954, "The Truth about the Loves of Rita Hayworth"; *Movie Magazine*, December 1953, "Rita and Dick: Their Romance Will Last"; *Movie Stars Parade*, December 1955, "What Dick Did to Rita"; *Uncensored*, June 1964; *Whisper*, December 1958; *Suppressed*, July 1956.

Biographies of Rita Hayworth include James Hill, *Rita Hayworth: A Memoir* (New York: Simon and Schuster, 1983); John Kobal, *Rita Hayworth: The Time, The Place, and the Woman* (New York: W. W. Norton, 1977); Barbara Leaming, *If This Was Happiness: A Biography of Rita Hayworth* (New York: Viking, 1989); Joe Morella and Edward Z. Epstein, *Rita: The Life of Rita Hayworth* (New York: Delacorte Press, 1983).

126	Nora states: Nora Eddington Haymes, 173.
127	During the most difficult: Haymes, "I'll Get By."
127	Columbia producer Jonie Taps: Leaming, *If This Was Happiness*, 238. All of the quotations from Leaming may be found in pages 237–326.
127	Dick recalled: Haymes, "I'll Get By."
127	As columnist Earl Wilson: *Motion Picture*, September 1954.
127	As Dick said: Haymes, "I'll Get By."
130	Moreover, the McCarran-Walter Act: Alicia D. Campi, PhD, "The McCarran-Walter Act," Immigration Policy Center, published on the Internet, June 2004, www.ailf.org/ipc/mccarranwalterprint.asp.
131	A dramatic presentation: Smithsonian National Portrait Gallery, "Cultures in Motion, Rita Hayworth: Latin Love Goddess," October 15, 22, 29, 2001.
131	He quotes his source's judgment: Kobal, *Rita Hayworth*, 300.
132	"In some instances": Morella and Epstein, *Rita*, introductory paragraph, unpaged.
132	"Rita had this glazed unseeing look": James Hill, *Rita Hayworth*, 116.
133	Leaming does not use: Leaming, *If This Was Happiness*, 291.
133	Leaming describes Dick Haymes: Leaming, *If This Was Happiness*, 237, 241, 243, 254, 255, 292, 299, 304, 305, 306, 311.
133	She credits: Leaming, *If This Was Happiness*, 314.
134	In her dispute: Leaming, *If This Was Happiness*, 320.

134   "Willing, docile": "The Woman Who Never Was," *Adult Psychology*, December/January 1955.

136   "Haymes Arrested and Ordered Deported": August 7, 1953.

136   The *Los Angeles Times* reported: August 7, 1953.

137   By August 25, Senator McCarran: *Los Angeles Mirror*, August 25, 1953.

138   Rita announced to the press: *Los Angeles Examiner*, September 24, 1953.

139   "I was called an 'excludable'": *Modern Screen*, August 25, 1953.

140   Dick issued a statement: *Hollywood Citizen-News*, October 6, 1953.

141   Rita convened a news conference, unsourced news article, October 16, 1953 (from Margaret Herrick Library).

141   One columnist headlined: Paul Price, *Los Angeles Daily News*, October 16, 1953.

141   His lawyer, David Marcus: *New York News-Life*, November 4, 1953.

142   The article compares her own life: *Movie Time*, February 1954.

142   Another fan magazine found: "Rita and Dick: their romance will last," *Movie*, 1953

145   "[Haymes] wept": Leonard Lyons, *New York Post*, April 5, 1954.

146   Attorney David Marcus: unsourced, May 26, 1954 (Margaret Herrick Library).

146   An article headlined: *Los Angeles Examiner*, June 24, 1954.

148   A July 1954 magazine story: *Saga*, July 1954.

148   Columnist Earl Wilson: *Motion Picture*, September 1954.

149–51   Dick's son Skip: author interview with Richard Haymes Jr., July 11, 2000.

149–50   (His younger sister): author interview with Joanna (Pidge) Haymes Campbell, August 18, 1999.

151   A fan magazine: *Modern Screen*, June 1955.

152   As reported in: Louella Parsons, *Los Angeles Examiner*, June 20, 1954.

152   On May 31, 1955: *Los Angeles Examiner*, June 1, 1955.

152   Dick was speechless: *Modern Screen*, June 1955.

152   Yet Ian Bernard: author interview with Ian Bernard.

153   Rita was at ringside: *Variety*, August 24, 1955.

153   "We tried—but": Haymes, "I'll Get By."

153   Dick admitted years later: Dick Haymes publicity release biographical sketch, typed, ca. 1972.

153   He spoke openly: *Los Angeles Times*, August 30, 1955.

153–54   His son remembers his father: author interviews with Richard Haymes Jr., September 27, 1999, and August 11, 2000.

154   One headline from December: *Movie Stars Parade*, December 1955.

154   The most sensational magazines: *Suppressed*, July 1956; *Whisper*, December 1958; *Uncensored*, June 1964.

Chapter 6

Much of the material in this chapter is based upon interviews I conducted with the following: the late Cy Coleman, March 28, 2003; Al Lerner, August 21, 1999; Fran Jeffries, May 9, 2001; Richard Haymes Jr., July 11, 2000; Marion Evans, October 22, 2003; Ian Bernard, June 12, 2001; Helen Joanna Haymes Campbell, August 19, 1999; and Steve Blauner, July 14, 2000. The archives of the Museum of Television and Radio in New York City as well as several private collections have provided excellent source material, as has Dick Haymes's unfinished outline for his autobiography, "I'll Get By."

156	But Dick instead: author interview with Ian Bernard, June 12, 2001.
157	Reminiscing about: Jack Cullen radio interview, Las Vegas, 1974; repeated in 1978.
157	A few years earlier: "Dick Haymes refuses to sing 'current crud,'" by Mack McCormick, Chicago, 1952; syndicated, paper unknown, from collection of Harriet Wasser.
158	In an interview for *Downbeat*: Leonard Feather, "Haymes Has No Stars for Presley," January 1956.
158	Dick and Ian Bernard met: author interview with Ian Bernard, June 12, 2001.
159	Will Friedwald notes: Friedwald, *Jazz Singing*, 196.
159	Another critic felt: R. Coleman, *Melody Maker* (London), September 4, 1976.
159	Perhaps British radio host: Dave Gelly, BBC Radio 2, March 22, 1988.
159–60	We have seen: Alan Zeffertt, *Record Collector*, October 1971.
161	They opened at the Versailles: "Haymes proves he's still great," Gene Knight, *New York Journal-American*, December 13, 1956.
162	Cy Coleman liked Dick: author interview with Cy Coleman, March 28, 2003.
162	He recorded two songs in 1958: author interview with Marion Evans, October 22, 2003.
165	Al Lerner remembers: author interview with Al Lerner, August 21, 1999.
165	In February 1957: *Los Angeles Times*, *Los Angeles Examiner*, February 9, 1957.
166	Dick admitted years later: Haymes, "I'll Get By."
166	Dick was living: author interview with Richard Haymes Jr., July 11, 2000.
166	In 1955, Marguerite Haymes: *Los Angeles Times*, January 14, 1955.
168	One fan remembers: Jerry R. Browne, *DHN*, #24 (1987).

168	Another fan remembers: John G. Wira, *DHN*, #46 (2000).
169	Dick was booked: author interview with Fran Jeffries, May 9, 2001.
169	Fran says that: author interview, May 9, 2001.
170	A local reviewer: Neal Graham, February 19, 1959, unknown Los Angeles newspaper, collection of Ian Bernard.
170	After a lengthy: Robert Wahls, "Look Who's Back: Dick Haymes," *New York Sunday News*, August 28, 1960.
170	In *Cue* magazine: December 1960, *DHN*, #37 (1995).
170	Other critics: Gene Knight, "Haymes & Wife Click," *New York Journal American*, December 13, 1960; Ted Morello, "Haymes, Wife, at Waldorf," *New York World-Telegram & Sun*, December 13, 1960, in *DHN*, #37 (1995).
171	Dick's old friend: Earl Wilson, "Dick Haymes Hits the Comeback Trail, *Los Angeles Mirror*, August 5, 1960.
171	Flattering headlines: "The Return of Dick Haymes," *Modern Screen*, December 1961.
171	On March 18, 1960: Wahls, *New York Sunday News*, August 28, 1960.
172	After Darin concluded: author telephone interview with Steve Blauner, July 14, 2000.
173	On one of the latter shows, *Playboy Penthouse Show*, 1961 (syndicated).
174	Looking back at those years: author telephone interview with Fran Jeffries, May 9, 2001.
174	Richard Jr. remembers: author interview with Richard Haymes Jr.
175	She remembers: author telephone interview with Fran Jeffries.
176	As Dick recalls: Haymes, "I'll Get By."
177	In November 1962: *Hollywood Citizen-News*, December 18, 1962.

Chapter 7

Much of the material for this chapter has been supplied by British members of the Dick Haymes Society; the *Dick Haymes Newsletter*, which reprinted many reviews of performances in the United Kingdom; Clive Fuller's *Dick Haymes Companion* (self-published in United Kingdom, 2000); and British radio programs. My interviews with Wendy Haymes Maree, August 20, 1999; Romy (Rosemary Hutton) Starrett, November 6, 2000; Russ Jones, April 6, 2000; and Vern Howard (name has been altered for this book), October 2, 2004, have been very helpful in filling in details of the years abroad. Again, Haymes's outline for his autobiography, "I'll Get By," has provided useful information concerning this period of his life, as have the notes for an autobiography that Wendy Haymes Maree read aloud to me during our interview.

178   "I had run away": Haymes, "I'll Get By."
178   A show business agent: Michael Sullivan, *There's No People Like Show People* (London: Quadrant Books, 1982).
179   The appearance for Emery: *Radio Times*, October 1963; Haymes, "I'll Get By."
179   "It was getting": Haymes, "I'll Get By."
179   Ken Barnes interviewed: Ken Barnes, "A Talent in Limbo," in *Perfectly Frank*, 1963; reprinted in *DHN*, #43 (1998).
180   One exception was: Russell Davies, BBC Radio 2, December 1963, re-broadcast in 1974.
181   One reviewer praised: Peter Sykes, 1963, collection of Maurice Dunn.
181   Reviewer Bert Warner: "Dick Haymes at La Dolce Vita, Newcastle on Tyne," 1963, reprinted in *DHN*, #44 (1999).
181   Yet Skip E. Lowe: author telephone interview, January 25, 2001.
182   A friend and former business associate: author interview, Vern Howard, October 2, 2004.
182   Director Michael Winner: *News of the World*, United Kingdom interview, December 12, 1999.
183   Twenty years younger: author interview with Wendy Haymes Maree, August 20, 1999.
183   The club owner: *Sydney News, London Daily Mirror*, January 29, 1964.
184   "I fell in love": Haymes, "I'll Get By."
184   While shooting "The Contract": author telephone interview with Romy Starrett, November 6, 2000.
185   In January 1965: author telephone interview with Russ Jones, April 6, 2000.
185   "I had to stop": author interview with Wendy Haymes Maree, August 20, 1999.
185   "It can't be true": *London Evening Standard*, August 7, 1965.
185   I've lived there on and off": quoted in the *London Daily Express*, July 26, 1965.
185   His application: *London Daily Express*, December 16, 1965.
185   Wendy was now pregnant: Maurice Dunn, "Dick and Wendy: A Look Back," *DHN*, #47 (2000).
186   A British radio host: Chris Ellis, BBC Radio 2, 2002.
187   Romy remembers that: author telephone interview with Romy Starrett.
188   Although a reviewer: Alan Zeffertt, *Record Collector*, October 1971.
188   But there was little: Fuller, *Dick Haymes Companion*, 138.
188–89 In the *Gramophone*: *Gramophone*, April 1970.
189   The building: e-mail from "Stu2" to Clive Fuller, June 2, 2004.
189   Critic John Marley: *Brighton Evening Argos*, July 27, 1970.

189   When interviewed: Fuller, *Dick Haymes Companion*, 147, 151–152.

190   The critics were enthusiastic: Ken Barnes, *Brighton Evening Argos*, July 25, 1970; Laurie Henshaw, *Brighton Evening Argos*, July 23, 1970.

190   Bob Monkhouse: Fuller, *Dick Haymes Companion*, 159.

191   A few months earlier: Fuller, *Dick Haymes Companion*, 140.

191   A newspaper review: Barry Shinfield, "A Lot of Old (and new) Schmalz," late 1960s, source unknown, collection of Maurice Dunn.

191   Yet John Gibson: *Edinburgh News*, 1971, Fuller, *Dick Haymes Companion*, 163.

192   Wendy remembers: author interview with Wendy Haymes Maree, August 20, 1999.

192   He was very happy in Spain: Dick Haymes, letter to Peter Elliott, June 27, 1971.

192   In the second week of July: *Los Angeles Herald-Examiner*, July 14, 1971.

193   Dick was home again: Haymes, "I'll Get By"; "Return of Dick Haymes," *Los Angeles Times*, October 1, 1971.

Chapter 8

For the discussion of Dick Haymes's television appearances, I have relied upon archives of the Museum of Television and Radio in New York City and private collections.

Interviews that I conducted that are used in this chapter are with Joanna Haymes Campbell, August 18, 1999; Romy Hutton Starrett, November 6, 2000; Richard Haymes Jr., September 27, 1999 and July 11, 2000; Joy Holden, July 14, 2000; Alan Copeland, June 13, 2001; Tee Dooley, January 7, 2000; Loonis McGlohan, August 24, 2001. I have quoted extensively from Dick Haymes's private diaries, which he maintained from 1973 through early 1978. I have also read his unproduced screenplay, "Reprise."

194   Pidge had recently purchased: author interview with Joanna Haymes Campbell.

197   The reviews were: *Hollywood Reporter*, May 1, 1972; *Los Angeles Herald Examiner*, April 28, 1972; *Billboard*, April 1972 (reprinted in *DHN*, #29, 1989); *Daily Variety*, April 28, 1972; *Los Angeles Times*, April 22, 1972.

197   "It's like coming home": *Los Angeles Times*, April 22, 1972.

198   John Gibson, who had written: April 1972, *DHN*, #29.

198   Dick's older son: author interview with Richard Haymes Jr.

198   Dick had asked: author interview, Joanna Haymes Campbell.

198   Romy (Rosemary)Hutton Starrett: author telephone interview.

199   Alan Copeland: author interview.

199   He was again hailed: *New York Daily News*, May 25, 1972.

199	"Their career ran": *Variety*, April 28, 1972.
199	And columnist Earl Wilson: *New York Post*, May 23, 1972.
199	The influential musician: George Shearing, *Crescendo*, 1972.
200	"Bring back the '40s": Earl Wilson, *New York Post*, May 23, 1972.
200	Gene Lees, a writer: "The Last Comeback," in Lees, *Singers and the Song*, 1987.
201	"I must make every move count"; "That's the way it shall be"; "These people mean to be nice": all quotations from Dick Haymes personal diary (hereafter cited as DHD), January 1973.
202	Joe Delaney, a columnist: "Dick Haymes, the Guy Many Called 'The Best,'" *Las Vegas Sun*, September 2, 1973.
202	After the Sahara opening: *Las Vegas Sun*, September 6, 1973.
202	"the beginning of much television": all quotations from DHD, 1973.
203	He vowed: vows for 1974, DHD, December 1973.
204	"Somehow I must convince": DHD, January 1974.
205	But he rejected: DHD, March 1974.
205	"Got a lot of static": DHD, October 1974.
206	"It is mandatory": DHD, May 1974.
206	"She was a joy": DHD, June 1974.
206	"a right to ask for help": DHD, October 1974.
206	"I dismissed Alan": DHD, July 1974.
207	According to Copeland: author interview.
207	Joy Holden: author telephone interview.
207	"I'm so sick and tired": DHD, October 1974.
207	Local singer Andy Roberts: "Personal View," *DHN*, #26, 1988.
208	"Saw the Sinatra Special": DHD, October 1974.
208	Bert Schneider, producer: Mason Wiley and Damien Bona, *Inside Oscar*, 1986.
208	"I saw Sinatra on the Awards": DHD, April, 1975.
208	The *Los Angeles Herald-Examiner*: October 8, 1974.
209	"Wendy must get over": DHD, October 1974.
209	"I must help"; "best Christmas": DHD, December 1974.
210–11	In an interview: *DHN*, #11, 1975–1976.
210	*Modern Screen* sent: "Catching up with Dick Haymes," April 1975.
211	"I am a super-star": frequent diary entry, DHD 1974, 1975.
212	"in the nick of time"; "love and romance": DHD, June 1975.
212	"Tomorrow I shall find": DHD, August 1975.
212	In late September: *New York Daily News*, October 2, 1976; Earl Wilson, *New York Post*, October 1, 1975; *Variety*, September 17, 1975, and October 15, 1975.

213   Cary Grant "graciously"; "When I am solvent"; "I don't like what I'm doing": DHD, October 1975.

213   His saddest thoughts: DHD, November 1975.

213   He thought Maree; "I now realize"; "How can I remain angry?": DHD, January 1976.

214   Radin may be remembered: Steve Wick, *Bad Company: Drugs, Hollywood, and the Cotton Club Murder* (New York: Harcourt Brace Jovanovich, 1990).

215   Dick's luck would change: Internet site, www.schirmer.com.

215   Dick sang popular ballads: *DHN*, #11, broadcast, "American Popular Song," January 16, 1977.

216   McGlohan had asked Dick: author telephone interview with Loonis McGlohan.

216   He was interviewed by: Tee Dooley, "An Interview with Dick," *DHN*, #11; author telephone interview with Tee Dooley.

217   "I would like to 'like me' again": DHD, January 1977.

217   "Oxnard? We shall see": DHD, January 1977.

218   "she deserves it": DHD, late January and early February 1977.

218   "day of sobriety"; "I am a bit sad": DHD, April 1977.

218   Again, Wendy sold: *The Islander* 8, no. 9, September 1977.

220   "Yeah. He'll be around": unpublished script, *Reprise*, registered with Writer's Guild of American, August 5, 1977.

220   "I have owed": DHD, September 1977.

221   "I should become very much in demand again": DHD, October 1977.

221   "I am living day to day": all quotations from DHD, November 1977.

Chapter 9

For this chapter, I have relied upon interviews with Sean Haymes, March 17, 2003; Samantha Haymes Maree Shiner, August 23, 1999; Russ Jones, April 6, 2003, many e-mails; and several interviews previously cited: Joanna Haymes Campbell, Tee Dooley, Loonis McGlohan, and Wendy Haymes Maree. I have also used Dick Haymes's diaries, which continued through early 1978.

224   "Many think": *Public Broadcasting System*, ca. 1985, syndicated.

225   Helen Forrest remembered: Forrest, *I Had the Craziest Dream*, 162.

225   "What is it?": DHD, February 1978.

225   Dooley remembers: author telephone interview.

226   "As this is my brother's song": author interview, Loonis McGlohan, August 24, 2000.

226   Loonis McGlohan remembers: author telephone interview.

227   Dick sang so brilliantly: *DHN*, #18, 1983.

228   According to Russ Jones: author telephone interview.

228   But Wendy was worried: author interview.

228   Their daughter, Samantha: author interview with Samantha Haymes Maree Shiner.

228   Sean, however: author telephone interview.

229   "Go live with your father": author interview, Joanna Haymes Campbell, August 18, 1999.

229   Clearly, Dick: author telephone interview with Russ Jones.

229   When the London *Daily Express*: September 27, 1979.

229   Dick was feeling upbeat: Peter Reilly, *Stereo Review*, December 1978.

230   He appeared with Helen Forrest: Richard Houdek, *Los Angeles Times*, January 20, 1979.

230   At a party: author telephone interview with Russ Jones; Jess Stearn, *Soul Mates* (New York: Bantam, 1984), chapter 12, "A Psychologist Ponders a Soulmate," 160–170.

230   Although he was not touring: Peter Reilly, *Stereo Review*, April 1979.

231   In his letter: Dick Haymes, letter to Roger Dooner, April 12, 1979.

231   In Canada: *St. Catherine's Standard*, February 16, 1980; Doug Ramsay, *Radio Free Jazz*, October 1979; Ken Barnes, letter to Dick Haymes Society, March 11, 1979.

232   Singer Garry Stevens: author interview with Gregory Moore, November 20, 2004.

232   For years, Don Rickles: on *The Tonight Show with Johnny Carson*, where Rickles appeared more than thirty times from 1970 to 1984

232   Some years later: letter from Harriet Wasser to the editor, *Billboard*, March 19, 1983.

232   In July, Dick was invited: *PBS*, July 1979.

233   Tee Dooley sent: letters sent by Dooley and Roger Dooner, with replies received from Jean Ferrari, for Hugh Downs; Charles Champlin; Arthur Mathonet, for Theatre Ancienne Belgique; Dave Dexter, for *Billboard*; Ed Walker, WAMU-FM; Irv Kratka, MMO Music Group.

234   Leo Seligson of *Newsday*: *Newsday*, September 19, 1979.

234   Bob Sixsmith: letter to Dick Haymes Society, March 30, 1980, in *DHN*, #16 (1978–1979).

234   He called his daughter: author interview, Joanna Haymes Campbell, August 18, 1999.

234–35 He told the *Hollywood Reporter*: *Hollywood Reporter*, October 8, 1979.

235   While he was undergoing: *Star*, 1980; *Star*, January 15, 1980; *San Francisco Examiner*, December 25, 1979.

235   Sean was devastated: *Minneapolis Tribune*, January 26, 1980.
235   "We went into": author interview, Russ Jones, April 6, 2003.
237   "The only thing": author interview, Samantha Haymes Maree Shiner, August 23, 1999.
237   Turnley Walker: Dick Haymes Memorial tribute, Ballad Records, 1982.
237   She told him: author interview, Sean Haymes, March 17, 2003.
238   By September: *Los Angeles Herald-Examiner*, September 19, 1980.
238   Mel Tormé: Bob Sixsmith, *DHN*, #16.
238   The Dick Haymes Society: Peter Reilly, *Stereo Review*, April 1983.

Epilogue

239   She said that he could: author interview, Joanna Haymes Campbell, August 18, 1999.
239   As Leo Braudy: Braudy, *The Frenzy of Renown* (New York: Oxford, 1986), 581.
239–40 Perhaps he believed: See Samantha Hart, *The Hollywood Walk of Fame* (Glendale, CA: CP Graphics, 2000). Dick Haymes's stars are located at 6100 Hollywood Boulevard, just west of Gower St., south side of boulevard (radio award), and at 1724 Vine St., one-half block north of the famous intersection of Hollywood and Vine, on the east side of the street (for recording career).
240   Musician Bobby Scott: "The Dick Haymes Enigma," *Gene Lees Newsletter*, August 1984.
241   After a TV miniseries: Robert Osborne, *Hollywood Reporter*, November 17, 1992.
241   Critic Will Friedwald: Will Friedwald, essay on Dick Haymes in the biographical *Dictionary of Jazz and Pop Singers*, by Will Friedwald (New York: Pantheon, forthcoming).

INDEX